Private Equity and Venture Capital in Europe
Markets, Techniques, and Deals

Stefano Caselli

AMSTERDAM • BOSTON • HEIDELBERG • LONDON
NEW YORK • OXFORD • PARIS • SAN DIEGO
SAN FRANCISCO • SINGAPORE • SYDNEY • TOKYO

Academic Press is an imprint of Elsevier

Academic Press is an imprint of Elsevier
30 Corporate Drive, Suite 400, Burlington, MA 01803, USA
Elsevier, The Boulevard, Langford Lane, Kidlington, Oxford, OX5 1GB, UK

Notices

Knowledge and best practice in this field are constantly changing. As new research and experience
broaden our understanding, changes in research methods, professional practices, or medical treatment may become necessary.

Practitioners and researchers must always rely on their own experience and knowledge in evaluating and using any information, methods, compounds, or experiments described herein. In using
such information or methods they should be mindful of their own safety and the safety of others,
including parties for whom they have a professional responsibility.

To the fullest extent of the law, neither the Publisher nor the authors, contributors, or editors,
assume any liability for any injury and/or damage to persons or property as a matter of products
liability, negligence or otherwise, or from any use or operation of any methods, products, instruc-
tions, or ideas contained in the material herein.

Library of Congress Cataloging-in-Publication Data
Caselli, Stefano, 1969-
 Private equity and venture capital in Europe : markets, techniques, and deals/Stefano Caselli.
  p. cm.
 Includes bibliographical references and index.
 ISBN 978-0-12-375026-6 (hardcover : alk. paper) 1. Venture capital-Europe. 2. Private equity-
Europe. 3. Business enterprises-Europe-Finance. 4. Investments-Law and legislation-Europe. I. Title.
 HG5428.C37 2010
 332'.04154094-dc22

                                              2009037952

British Library Cataloguing-in-Publication Data
A catalogue record for this book is available from the British Library.

ISBN: 978-0-12-375026-6

For information on all Academic Press publications
visit our Web site at www.elsevierdirect.com

Printed in the United Kingdom
09 10   9 8 7 6 5 4 3 2 1

To Elisa and Lorenzo

Contents

PART 1   GENERAL FRAMEWORK

PART 2 THE PROCESS AND THE MANAGEMENT TO INVEST

Foreword

The private equity industry, dominated since 1988 by Kolhberg Kravis Roberts & Co., architects of the famed $30 billion LBO of RJR Nabisco in 1988, stood in awe in June 2007 after the initial public offering of The Blackstone Group, a diversified alternative asset investment manager with $88 billion of assets under management was successfully launched and traded to a premium. The offering, which included a non-voting $3 billion investment by the State Investment Company of China, was priced at $31 per share, and opened for trading at $36.45 per share just two days after two Bear Stearns hedge funds collapsed, ushering in the beginning of the 2007–2008 mortgage securities crisis. The offering valued Blackstone at about $38 billion, and revealed that CEO Steve Schwartzman would take out $677 million in cash while retaining a 24% interest in the firm, valued at $10 billion. His co-founding partner, Peter Peterson, 80, would withdraw $1.9 billion and retain a 4% interest valued at $1.6 billion.

No wonder private equity had been the hottest thing in the market for the past three years!

Peterson and Schwartzman founded Blackstone in 1985, soon after Peterson retired from Lehman Brothers, which he had headed since 1973. Peterson, a former CEO of Bausch and Lomb, an industrial company, and Secretary of Commerce in the Nixon administration, was able to negotiate an investment by Lehman in a new firm he planned to form with an initial investment of $400,000. He invited Schwartzman, then a 38-year-old merger specialist, to join him, and the two set out to see what they could do. Peterson was very well liked by his many friends and clients among corporate CEOs, and he attracted merger and other advisory business, which Schwartzman was good at executing. But they looked around after a while, especially at KKR, and decided to shift their focus from corporate advisory work to investing money on behalf of institutional clients in LBOs and real estate deals. In 1987 (more than ten years after KKR) they began to raise their first investment funds, which required a 2% management fee and a 20% share of profits. Their investors included university and other endowments and a few pension funds. In the 20 years since it was founded, Blackstone's funds have taken control of 112 companies with a combined market value of $200 billion, and provided returns on investment 10 to 20% higher than the S&P500 stock market index. Earlier in the year, it had completed the purchase of Equity Office Properties for $39 billion — the largest private equity buyout ever (at least for a few months), topping the RJR Nabisco record. By the end of 2007, Blackstone managed over $100 billion of real estate, corporate private equity, and hedge funds. Revenues for 2007 were $3.1 billion and net income (after many adjustments to convert from a private partnership to a public limited partnership that distributes the bulk of its income directly to its investors) was $1.6 billion, down from a record income in 2006 of $2.3 billion. Peterson and Schwartzman, in modeling themselves after KKR, twenty years later, had passed it by.

"We raise money to provide alternative asset opportunities for institutions that know us," they might have said.

> *"We charge hedge fund fees and use the money we raise, plus a lot of leverage from banks and the junk bond market, to acquire companies we can improve and re-sell. We hire the industrial management skills we need, use our many connections to build a deal flow, and sit back and watch the money flow in, which is then taxed predominantly at capital gains rates. We keep the game going by selling new funds every couple of years, hopefully in ever-larger amounts. We avoid investing much of our own money in the funds, and therefore take much less risk than our investors. We also avoid hostile deals, conflicts of interest, and areas of heavy business regulation, which further lowers risks, and can stick to the morally defensible 'high road' because the nature of the business makes it relatively easy to do so. We can do all this with only a small staff of experienced professionals for whom we provide a friendly, supportive environment to work in. We don't need to retain a lot of capital in our management company, or borrow money or subject ourselves to trading risks. Ours is a high margin business that is very different from cut-throat investment banking, competing for business with endlessly demanding clients against powerful competitors with huge balance sheets, or, as traders, subjecting ourselves to a lot of market and other risks."*

No wonder so many stars from Wall Street and the City of London had decided to leave the investment banks that had recruited, trained, and nurtured them — the grass in private equity land had never appeared to be so much greener.

Blackstone's post-IPO share price valued the firm at about 10 times book value, and 24 times earnings, as compared to an average of about 1.5 to 2.5 times book and 8 or 9 times earnings for the best of the investment banks. The IPO was a breakthrough for the secretive private equity industry that had prized its ability to avoid regulation and public scrutiny. The high valuations provided by the Blackstone IPO would surely attract others among the leading figures of this powerful, fascinating but shadowy industry. Everyone would want to be public now.

In fact, some other fund management companies had already gone public by the time the Blackstone deal came along. KKR had sold shares in a specialty finance company, KKR Financial Holdings in London in June 2005, and followed up with an IPO of KKK Private Equity Investors on the Amsterdam market a year later. These funds were designed to allow small investors to invest in KKR's deals alongside the big guys and were sold in Europe where they didn't have to be registered with the SEC, which took a dim view of complex LBO funds luring unsophisticated investors into risky investments. Neither of these companies fared well in the markets, though, and KKR had to inject additional capital into Financial Holdings, which had been hurt by the mortgage crisis. There were also some hedge fund managers — Off-Ziff Capital Management, Fortress Investment Management, and GLG Partners — that had established public trading markets in their firms. In July 2007, just after the Blackstone IPO, KKR announced it too was going to sell $1.25 billion in shares in an IPO scheduled for the fall, all the money was retained in the firm and none of the firm's founders were selling any of their shares. The initiative would signify a major shift in strategy for the firm, which now saw itself branching out into a more comprehensive, multi-platform financial firm like Blackstone.

Blackstone's IPO, however, came at the same time as the market meltdown that began in the summer of 2007 and lasted for nearly two years. Blackstone had no exposure to the mortgage-backed securities business, and its exposure to real estate was limited to commercial real estate, which did not suffer too badly initially in the residential sector. Its principal exposure, of course, was to private equity investments, most of which were fully financed. Some deals in process were cancelled or renegotiated without any harm to Blackstone. The problems lay in the virtual halting of all new deals (the banks, suffering as they were from major write-offs did not want to make any new leveraged loans, which were also falling sharply in value), and the need to apply fair value accounting to the positions they did have. Soon after the IPO, however, the share price began to drop, and continued to do so for most of the rest of the year and the next, reaching a low of $3.55 per share in February 2009, a 91% decline from its high of $38.

For the year 2008, Blackstone announced a net loss of $1.16 billion, as compared to a profit of $1.62 billion for 2007 (almost all of which had been earned in the first half). The loss was attributable to restating the value of investment positions held and reduction in the amount of performance fees due on them. "We hold our assets for the long term," said Tony James, President and Chief Operating Officer, "and expect their value will rise as we come out of the cycle."

Building the cycle

The cycle Tony James was referring to was the third one since LBOs became active in capital markets in the mid-1980s. The first one ended in 1990 when the junk bond market collapsed. There was an active, but smaller scale LBO business from 1993–2000 that was halted by the collapse of the technology and telecommunications sectors and the record levels of bankruptcies that ensued.

In 2003 the third cycle began and peaked in mid-2007, just as the Blackstone deal was brought to market, when private equity fundraising reached the $250 billion per year record level it had achieved in 2000 and then slightly exceeded it. During the four and a half years of this cycle, one now that comprised as much activity in Europe as in the United States, over a trillion dollars was raised for private equity investments. During the first half of 2007, nearly one out of four US and European acquisitions was in the form of an LBO, including a $45 billion transaction for the Texas public utility, TXU, arranged by KKR and Texas Pacific Group, and later a record-smashing $52 billion deal for the Canadian phone giant, BCE led by Providence Equity Partners. There was also a $100 billion buyout of the ABN Amro Bank by a consortium of European banks intending to break it up that, though technically not a private equity transactions, was considered by many European observers to be one and the same.

Most of the funds raised for private equity investments end up financing the equity component of LBO acquisitions, which are supplemented by substantial amounts of debt financing provided by banks or subordinated lenders. Private equity funds also exist to provide venture capital, mezzanine debt, financing for distressed company work-outs or turnarounds, and to fund portfolios of private equity investments of various types acquired in the secondary market from original investors wanting to sell their positions before the termination of their funds. They also exist to finance real estate investments of various kinds. All of these different forms of private equity investments now operate globally — in Europe, Japan, and in many emerging market countries.

During the most recent cycle, activity was accelerated by low interest rates and extremely easy borrowing conditions. Whereas the buyout firms have argued that their investment activity improves companies, creates growth and jobs, and meaningfully contributes to the economy, and academic studies support this claim, their critics say that the success of the LBO firms is due to the use of leverage, and because of the scale of the industry now, these firms subjected the economy to serious credit and liquidity risks. After 2003, LBOs of large, worn-out, difficult to improve companies (like Burger King, Hertz, and K-mart) occurred with little prospect for intrinsic value enhancement. But because of the ability to borrow cheap money, and to borrow more later to pay special dividends, the LBO operators could make a good and quick return.

Leverage ratios of buyout companies increased after 2003, and credit quality standards deteriorated to what came to be known as *covenant light* loans that required hardly any of the restrictive covenants that are usually demanded by lenders to keep the companies under financial control, because the loans were going to be repackaged into collateralized loan obligations (CLOs) and sold as asset-backed securities, in the same manner as mortgage-backed securities were then being created and sold. Banks making these kinds of corporate loans were also eager to get themselves into the group of investment banks advising the private equity firms on their deals so they could share in the fees and the credit to be reflected in league tables. These banks, especially Citigroup and JP Morgan Chase, became so competitive with their credit facilities that the investment banks were forced to meet them by offering credit facilities of their own. By the spring of 2007, with the market roaring along, the advantages in negotiating financing were all with the LBO fund managers.

But all of this changed suddenly as the crisis in mortgage-backed securities widened and spread from a few hedge funds to infect major banks. After the collapse of two Bear Stearns hedge funds in June of 2007, despite the positive momentum of the Blackstone IPO, the market for LBOs came to a halt. By August 2007, the mortgaged-backed securities market was nearly in free fall, and had affected the market for collateralized debt securities, into which many LBO loans had been sold. Banks were unwilling to lend for new deals and were struggling to meet their commitments for deals arranged a few months earlier at very generous terms. The problem only worsened as the banks began to report huge losses in the third and fourth quarters of 2008.

Without access to the debt market and the high levels of leverage the LBOs require, the industry was forced to look to other investment possibilities. Texas Pacific organized a $7 billion investment in Washington Mutual, only to see the whole thing lost as the bank had to be taken over by its regulators a few months later. Some, like Goldman Sachs, took over the portfolios held by others, especially ailing banks such as Wachovia that were forced to undergo top to bottom restructuring as part of a merger arrangement. Investors led by Harvard University said they might increase sales of their private equity positions in the secondary market to more than $100 billion in 2009. Some private equity managers like Black Rock prospered by acquiring distressed portfolios of mortgage securities from others. Some others intended to use their capital like hedge funds to arbitrage the low prices of mortgage-backed securities against their supposedly higher intrinsic value.

The entire industry felt the pain of the market meltdown. Their funds declined by 30 to 50%. They received no performance fees, and some were required to return fees earned in earlier periods. There were very few new deals on which fees might be earned, no existing deals ready to be refloated to the market could be sold in the non-existent IPO market. And, several deals that had been agreed upon, but not yet closed, faced serious financing risk if the banks that were committed decided to pull out or wanted to renegotiate the terms. Many highly leveraged companies previously acquired through LBOs would find the global recession too difficult for them and be forced into bankruptcy. The private equity industry had never experienced such a storm of difficulty and hostile markets before. All private equity firms suffered large losses. KKR abandoned its plans for a public offering. Several large investors threatened to avoid future capital calls by assembling a majority of fund investors to vote to reduce the principal amount of the funds. New funding was extremely difficult, although Carlyle managed to raise some additional equity.

Not all was entirely gloomy, however. Most private equity finds were of a ten-year duration, with several years more to go before having to wind up. As markets recover, some of the write downs will be reversed. Many private equity managers were also pointing out that they would be able to take advantage of the market declines by acquiring new investments at knock-down prices, often low enough to enable them to complete the deals with little if any leverage. As the recession entered its second year, a backlog of uncompleted restructurings in Europe, Asia, and America were just waiting to be done when they could be again. And, investors withdrawing their capital from private equity were not finding any other markets likely to provide healthy equity returns. They might as well stay where they were.

The industry will recover, and, indeed, return to the markets under more conservative, sensible terms and conditions. When it does it will find this detailed and wide ranging book by Stefano Caselli, who teaches finance and private equity at Bocconi University in Milan and consults widely throughout Europe, to be a useful handbook to guide investors and corporate practitioners, large and small, through the processes of arranging finance for private equity transactions. Students, too, will find this exacting description of all of the steps and practices involved in completing successful deals to be of great value.

There are still risks of the sort that Blackstone experienced after going public, but those risks are atypical, reflecting a sudden halt to new deals and an abrupt devaluation of existing holdings. Blackstone and KKR both experienced similar erosion to their stock prices as did the average large investment bank from 2007 to 2008. Over a longer term, private equity activity may prove to be less risky and worthy of higher price-to-book and price-earnings ratios than the traditional form of investment banking, in which current income from fees and proprietary trading is entirely dependent on current market conditions. But that may take some time to happen while the memory of the sharp write-offs of values in their investment portfolios caused by the 2007–2008 market conditions still lingers.

Roy C. Smith
Kenneth Langone
Professor of Entrepreneurship and Finance
NYU Stern School of Business
New York, March 2009

Preface

About the Book

I started studying and writing about corporate banking and the issue of financing companies in 1994. In those days the European Banking System was coming out from a big turnaround involving a unique legal framework based on the concept of the Universal Bank and its governance. The focus of the banking system (as well as researchers, consultants, and practitioners) was devoted to analyzing the different financing companies moving from a vision mostly bank-based to financial markets as a complementary/competitive source of funding for big companies and SMEs. With the exception of the UK, where the tradition of merchant banking was quite deep and old, the private equity (and the specific cluster of venture capital) was quite new and innovative in the rest of Europe. Because of the strong relationship between the European banking system and European companies, private equity started to be one of the tools used in old and new finance the companies. This was (and this is) a fundamental difference between the concept of private equity in its mother country (i.e., the United States) and the EU.

Private equity is an extraordinary source of creating new ventures and stimulating research projects with a seed investor approach, but it is also a very powerful instrument with which to gain leverage value and multiply company size, even with a pure speculative approach. This showed its negative side during the big financial turmoil in 2001–2002 and, especially, in 2007–2009. Multiples, debt, and a majority shareholding strategy are the common roots of a private equity system that works along with the financial system as a whole, playing a relevant (even leading) role in economic development.

Private equity is a part of the financial system and, for this reason, is supervised in many European countries. Private equity is seen and used mostly as a tool to integrate the debt and to finance companies who want to expand and are in the mature stages to launch acquisitions or run new investments. Big buyouts, pushed in many cases by privatization, are managed by investment banks and M&A boutiques, and rarely by private equity firms. Research projects and new ventures are not a typical target for private equity firms, but they survived because of State intervention (declining from the early 1990s because of deficit constraints) and the use of private money coming from families of entrepreneurs and high net worth individuals.

Even in the new financial environment of 2008–2009, American and European private equity perspectives remain disparate because of different traditions and different legal and fiscal frameworks. Things are changing toward a new era of similar concepts and drivers between finance companies. The lesson of past crises is evident and relevant: the traditional blend of using multiples and leverage with a majority stake has ended and the right (and wise) use of money is, and will be, predominant. But an approach based only on a minority stake and a conservative use of money as a pure substitute of debt is not enough. Because of this, there is a need for private equity to play a prominent role as a competitor–partner of debt financing, with a clear focus on creating value through company growth and to give and share added value by transferring industrial and competitive knowledge.

It has been 15 years since I first worked with corporate banking and at that time private equity in Europe was for pioneers and quite distant from European culture, and meant to be studied in a laboratory with a pure theoretical mindset. Today, private equity stays in the debate not simply as a "tool" but as a way to develop companies and interact with the banking system to finance them, to promote knowledge, and to improve governance. These reasons, linked to my personal experience as a researcher, teacher, manager of executive education, and consultant drove me to write a book covering all topics relevant to understanding, applying, and managing private equity in the European market. I took on this very ambitious project not to promote conflict between an "American" and a "European" view of private equity, but only to contribute and identify the very different approaches to the same job. My personal story was a continuous work researching different sides, teaching both pre-experience and executive classes, and consulting and advising companies and financial institutions. It is my desire to give a very large audience a book that is useful for undergraduate and mostly graduate students attempting to understand the world of private equity with a very broad approach; executives and practitioners working both in the banking and private equity sectors to improve their technical skills along a wide spectrum of topics; MBA and Masters students desiring to understand the issues and links between entrepreneurship and management of companies with the difficult job of raising money from the banking system; and entrepreneurs willing to share their projects, their futures, and capital with a financial partner.

To give an exhaustive picture of private equity, this book is divided into three parts: General Framework, The Process and the Management to Invest, and Valuation and the "Art of Deal Making." Part One is devoted to building the pillars of knowledge through the analysis of private equity fundamentals (Chapter 1), the definition and understanding of the very different clusters that represent the private equity market throughout the world (Chapter 2), the understanding of the theoretical framework built by researchers (Chapter 3), the design of the legal framework in Europe (Chapter 4), the design of the legal framework in the United States and the UK (Chapter 5), and analysis of the relevant mechanism involving taxation issues (Chapter 6). The general aim of Part One is not to simply cover the traditional topics such as venture capital, expansion financing, turnaround financing, distressed financing, etc., common in many handbooks, but to analyze the legal entities investors can use both in the European, American, and British context. Knowledge of the fiscal framework gives an additional advantage when combining legal issues and strategic choices with the understanding of a relevant driver of costs and revenues into legal entities.

Part Two analyzes the entire management cycle in a private equity world, crossing the whole spectrum of tools a private equity manager has to master within a private equity firm. Chapter 7 illustrates the map of the different life cycle phases involving relevant decisions, moving beyond fundraising, investing, managing, and monitoring, and the exit phase. Chapters 8 to 11 cover indepth the details and techniques for every phase. Fundraising is the main topic of Chapter 8, which demonstrates the actions of private equity firms relating to the creation of the business ideas to the negotiation with potential investors to obtaining the necessary commitments. In Chapter 9, through the perspective of company valuation (which is preliminary to investment decisions), the decision to invest as well as the corporate governance design issues to negotiate with the venture-backed company are explained. Managing and monitoring are the issues for Chapter 10 with the focus on formal and informal rules necessary to ensure peaceful dealings with the private equity investor by avoiding divergence of opinion and conflicts. Lastly, exiting is the topic of Chapter 11 where the pros and cons of the different exit strategies for private equity investors — IPO, buy back, sale to another private equity investor, trade sale, and the write-off — are analyzed.

Part Three faces the issue of creating and managing private equity deals into the different clusters (as seen in Chapter 2) and using different exit strategies. Real, detailed examples and cases are inserted in the appendices of many chapters to highlight and strengthen the techniques and patterns explained in the text. Part Three is focused on private equity deals with the last part divided into three different logical areas. First, Chapters 12 and 13 deal with the issue of company valuation starting from a general summary of the different techniques and moving to a very analytical application to private equity situations. Later, Chapters 14 to 18 cover every type of deal made with private equity. Chapter 14 reviews the topic of seed and start-up financing; Chapter 15 expands on growth financing (i.e., both early stage and expansion); Chapter 16 manages the topic of buyouts, which represents about half of the market in the world; Chapter 17 analyzes the deal of turnaround and distressed financing; and Chapter 18 illustrates successful deal exiting represented by the IPO. Lastly, Chapter 19 explains the competitive strategy of private equity firms and creates a (visionary) futuristic picture of its destiny. In this sense, Chapter 19 is written to stimulate a debate about the role private equity plays in the future of the economic system. But this is a new gamble, and for the next 15 years we can analyze and build successful relationships between companies and the future financial system.

Acknowledgments

To write a book is like a very long journey where you meet and discover new and old people, important travel mates, unknown places, and come across minor details that inspire you to finish. Everyone you meet contributes, sometimes importantly, sometimes incredibly, to the journey. And now as I'm writing the last pages of this book, I owe a debt of gratitude to the many friends, colleagues from academia, and practitioners I met during my journey through the private equity system in Europe and with whom I shared many days, sometimes years, together.

Particularly, I would like to thank my many colleagues. Pierluigi Fabrizi, Giancarlo Forestieri, Paolo Mottura, and Roberto Ruozi, who supported me in the beginning of my research and teaching activity in Bocconi University and who gave me tools, knowledge, and patterns to understand the financial system I will never forget. Stefano Gatti, with whom I shared a lot of research projects on the topics of corporate banking and corporate finance both at a domestic and international level. Luisa Alemany, Emilia Garcia Appendini, Marina Brogi, Vincenzo Capizzi, Francesco Corielli, Alberto Dellacqua, Alberta Di Giuli, Renato Giovannini, Jiri Hnlica, Filippo Ippolito, Stefano Monferrà, Paola Musile Tanzi, Jose Marti Pellon, Francesco Perrini, Maria Rosa Scarlata, Andrea Sironi, Janos Szas, and Markus Venzin, for their support reading chapters of the book, for helping with research projects and executive education projects based on private equity and the corporate finance sector, and for suggestions while working at the Bocconi University and in SDA Bocconi School of Management. John Doukas, whose energy and proactive approach promoting the activity of European Financial Management Association was relevant to my research and the very friendly and enthusiastic discussions we had about research projects. Roy Smith, who didn't simply write the foreword of this book — which is a great honor for me — but also supported me in the design of the Masters of Science Private Equity course at Bocconi University and the Private Equity Executive course at SDA Bocconi School of Management whose content and readings strongly contributed to making this book rigorous and relevant for practice. The Newfin, the pioneer Research Centre of Bocconi University managed by Paolo Mottura and Francesco Saita, and Carefin, the new Research Centre of Bocconi University managed by Andrea Resti, who both encouraged and sponsored many of my private equity research projects.

But a very special thanks is dedicated to four people I will never forget who represent my academic and personal life: Adalberto Alberici, formally my thesis advisor, but also the mentor every young researcher should have the luck to meet; Guido Corbetta, whose great encouragement and long discussions about family firms, private equity, and company development represent a permanent support and stimulus to improve my research and the quality of my analysis; Giacomo De Laurentis, who really introduced me to the world of corporate banking and with whom I shared many challenging activities both in designing executive programs and running research projects in the field of corporate banking; Gino Gandolfi, a terrific and unique friend with whom I started my academic career and who will always represent an irreplaceable reference point, both in good and in bad times.

I am also grateful to many people out of academia who gave me the chance to deepen my view of the private equity world: the Board and the team of MPS Venture, the largest Italian private equity firm, where I have served as independent director since 2002, with specific regard to Saverio Carpinelli, Gabriele Cappellini, Roberto Magnoni, Marco Canale, and Paola Borracchini; the members of the independent governing body of PEREP Analytic (I joined in 2008) within the European Private Equity and Venture Capital Association (EVCA), with special regard to Mario Levis and Philippe Desbrières who both supported the project with very helpful comments and suggestions and to the very energetic environment of EVCA itself; and the CEMS network and its Interfaculty Group of Entrepreneurial Finance, where I was able to meet colleagues from 17 schools in Europe and to interact with them and receive suggestions and comments about my research activity on private equity. I was also helped and supported by the exceptional work of Sara Caratti and Fabio Sattin, Founder and CEO of Private Equity Partner and past president of EVCA, a "master" of private equity whose suggestions and creative visions helped me identify new ways to scan the future of the market. My students joining the Private Equity course in Bocconi University and the Private Equity Executive courses in SDA Bocconi School of Management were great contributors: these very large audiences coming from many countries, year after year, have represented the most challenging and severe trial for my hypotheses, cases, and readings. This book greatly benefits from these experiences, because nothing is more enriching than a group of students continuously working on a complicated topic.

This book also benefited from the very useful and relevant suggestions of the panel of five anonymous referees coming from Europe and the United States and from the competence, enthusiasm, and energy of Karen Maloney from Elsevier who supported the project from the very beginning, providing me with truly precious advice to improve the final result. A very special thanks for the careful and precious work of Marcella Tagni, mentioned later as a contributor, whose energy, rigorous method, and creativity helped to determine the final outcome.

But the most important "thank you" of this very long list is for my family: Anna, my wife, and Elisa and Lorenzo, our sons. What I feel for them cannot be written in a book, it is for me to hold inside. But I am sure, without their silent and patient support, this book and all I have done would never have been realized.

About the Contributor

Marcella Tagni is the Key Account Manager for Executive Education Custom Programs for Banks and Financial Institutions at SDA Bocconi School of Management. She holds a Master's of Science in Management from Bocconi with honors from the University in Milan as well as a Bachelors Degree in Politics and International Relationship with honors including course studies in Economics at "Università Statale" in Milan. Before her graduate studies, she worked for seven years in the finance department of a private trade company.

About the Author

Stefano Caselli is a Full Professor of Banking and Finance at Bocconi University where he is Director of the Masters of International Management for CEMS. He is the Head of Executive Education Custom Programs, Banks and Financial Institutions Division at SDA Bocconi School of Management. He specializes in corporate finance with specific attention to private equity and venture capital, SMEs and family firm financing, and corporate banking. He is the author of several books and publications on these topics and serves as a strategic consultant to many financial institutions and corporations.

General Framework

The fundamentals of private equity and venture capital

This chapter presents the fundamentals of private equity and venture capital. The first section covers private equity and venture capital, underlining important differences between American and European approaches to funding start-ups and the typical characteristics of the business. The second section explains how private equity finance is different from corporate finance, emphasizing the distinguishing elements. The third section analyzes private equity and venture capital from the entrepreneur's perspective, while the last section discusses the views of all types of potential investors.

1.1 DEFINITION OF PRIVATE EQUITY AND VENTURE CAPITAL

There is evidence that investing in the equity of companies started during the Roman Empire. However, the first suggestion of a whole structured organization that funded firms to improve and make their development easier was found during the fifteenth century, when British institutions launched projects dedicated to the increase and expansion of trade to and from their colonies.

Modern private equity and venture capital have been around since the 1940s when it started to be useful and essential for financial markets and a firm's development. Financing firms by private equity and venture capital has become increasingly more important, both strategically and financially.

Because this type of business has been around so long, together with differences between firms and financial markets, one worldwide definition and classification for private equity and/or venture capital does not exist. However, it is clear that a broad definition does exist: private equity is not public equity because it includes the investments realized from the stock market.

In the third part of this book, various definitions are formulated based on the operation, the stage of the firm's life cycle, the operator's approach, and the type of support.

Institutionally, private equity is the provision of capital and management expertise given to companies to create value and, consequently, generate big capital gains after the deal. Usually, the holding period of these investments is defined as medium or long.

This definition, even if very broad, cannot be applied to the real world, because operators' national associations (i.e., NVCA, EVCA, BVCA, AIFI), or central banks interpret the definition according to the countries in which they operate. For this reason, many definitions still exist. According to the American version, venture capital is a cluster of private equity dedicated to finance new ventures. Therefore, venture capitalists fund firms during their initial phases or look for sources to expand and develop the activity of the firm, whereas private equity operators fund firms at the end of their first/fast growth process.

The European definition proposes that private equity and venture capital are two separate clusters based on the life cycle of the firm. Venture capitalists provide the funding for start-up businesses and early stage companies, whereas private equity operators are involved in deals with older firms. Different from the American definition, the European definition does not consider the expansion phase (the phase after the beginning and the start-up) as a part of venture capital, but more of an autonomous subcategory.

Although there are differences in definition, private equity and venture capital create a strict relationship between the investor and the entrepreneur. This is a unique characteristic not found in any other financial institution. This is attributed to the typical characteristics of private equity and venture capital financing schemes:

Modification of shareholder composition
Knowledge and non-financial support
Predefined time horizon of the investment

Private equity and venture capital investment are used to invest in equity; for this reason, operators specializing in these kinds of deals may decide on the firm's strategy and day-by-day management. This participation, or the admission of a new subject among the original shareholders, generates a metamorphosis in the decision process. Additionally, a modification in the stability and symmetry of the organization and its consequences among original shareholders may be noted.

The operation of private equity and venture capital is not limited to simple money provision; the financial support comes from managerial activity consisting of a series of advisory services and full-time assistance for firm development. For young firms or a new business idea, cooperation with financiers is very important, because reputation, know-how, networking, relationships, competencies, and skills are the non-financial resources provided by private equity and venture capital operators. Although difficult to measure, these resources are the real reason for the deal and important for firm growth.

Private equity and venture capital agreements always define length and exit conditions for financial institutions. Even though funding institutions are active shareholders and engaged in company management, they are not interested in taking total control or transforming their temporary participation into long-term involvement. Venture capitalists and private equity operators, sooner or later, sell their position; this is the most important reason for defining this type of investment as "financial" and not "industrial." The presence of a predefined time horizon for the investment makes private equity and venture capital useful for firms wanting quick development, managerial change, financial stability, etc.

1.2 MAIN DIFFERENCES BETWEEN CORPORATE FINANCE AND ENTREPRENEURIAL FINANCE

What is the difference between corporate finance and private equity finance (or entrepreneurial finance)? This is a very interesting question and the answer is not as easy as it may seem. The question can be answered in two different ways: institutionally and environmentally (see Figure 1.1).

Corporate finance, which is the most traditional way to fund firms, is more standardized, less flexible, and focused on debt. Expected returns are lower and linked to the costs that financial institutions incur while collecting money from savers. The reference point for the valuation (i.e., costs, feasibility, etc.) is the whole company, independent of funded sources. Another interesting point is the financial institution's unwillingness to participate in the firm's decision framework.

Private equity finance is very flexible and the expected returns are higher (non-financial resources must be paid) than corporate finance. It is characterized by a medium to long time horizon, higher options available for the financial institution's exit strategy, and by its high profile in the decision process. The focus of private equity finance is the potential growth path of a company.

	Corporate finance	Private equity finance
Participation	Focus on debt	Focus on equity
Reference point for the valuation	The whole company	Potential growth
Collateral	Usually real estate	No guarantees or agreement between company and financier
Target return	Spread over the financial costs of funds collections	High or very high, consisting of capital gain realized at exit moment
Exit	Repayment	Different options: - IPO - Buy back - Trade sale - Write-off
Time horizon	Variable	From medium to long, 5/7 years
Financial institution participation	NO	For the whole length of the deal
Flexibility	Usually low	Very high

FIGURE 1.1

Corporate finance versus private equity finance.

The institutional approach, even though it is able to distinguish between corporate and entrepreneurial finance, does not consider the environment companies face when they contemplate private equity as a financing option. The environmental approach does consider the environment and the situation faced by entrepreneurs during the financial selection process. Some aspects of the environmental approach are the same as the institutional approach, whereas some aspects better explain the consequences of entrepreneurial finance.

The elements in the following list distinguish private equity finance from corporate finance using the environmental approach.

Interdependence between investment and financing decision
Managerial involvement of outside investors
Information problem and contract design
Value to entrepreneur
Legal and fiscal ad hoc rules

With the institutional approach, private equity financing does not fund the whole company. In this scheme of financial and non-financial support, a specific project the entrepreneur needs to finance is targeted. Because of this, a strong and effective interdependence between the firm's investment and financing must exist and must continue during the entire length of the deal.

Private equity operators and venture capitalists provide financial and non-financial sources. This generates the involvement of third parties (external investors) in the decision process and/or company management. It must be emphasized that only in private equity finance is there a decisive participation in the firm's administration.

The third issue seen in the environmental approach is that private equity operators support firms on risky projects. This increases conventional information problems occurring in all firm financing schemes. These problems lead to a lack of standardized agreements, so a special settlement is signed for every funded project.

The strong interdependence among companies and financial institutions generates problems in wealth and value distribution too. As private equity financiers became shareholders, a strong co-participation between the entrepreneur's desires and the financial institution's purposes exists. Private equity financiers support firms with their skills, competencies, know-how, etc. Because this creates value for funded firms, the investor allows the entrepreneur to take value from the funded idea. In most cases, without private equity or venture capitalists, firms would not be able to develop projects.

The special legal and fiscal framework for the investor and/or vehicle used to realize the deal is the last factor that sets private equity finance apart from venture capital. It will be shown throughout the following chapters that the private equity industry, because it simultaneously acts as entrepreneur/shareholder and financier, needs special treatment regarding taxes and legal frameworks to develop and carry out investments.

In the private equity business, relationships between entrepreneur, shareholders, and external investors are intertwined. In large deals within large corporations there is a clear convergence between the entrepreneur (and many times, his family) and the shareholders. This modifies the traditional perspective of corporate finance in which shareholders and managers are two separate blocks with different goals and tasks.

This is particularly true for venture capital. The smaller the firm or the earlier the life cycle, the more likely the entrepreneur is the shareholder and the manager. This makes it easier for the deal to be realized, developed, and carried out.

1.3 THE MAP OF EQUITY INVESTMENT: AN ENTREPRENEUR'S PERSPECTIVE

Development of the private equity and venture capital industry starts when the entrepreneur realizes he needs to be funded by external investors to support the expansion or the transformation of his firm. Therefore, equity investment provides a firm's specific financial needs or the finances to create a firm.

Firms need funding during sales development, which occurs during different stages for each firm. The drivers that measure the firm's need for funding are investment, profitability, cash flow, and sales growth. These four variables are strictly linked together, and should be evaluated from a long-term perspective. These four variables/drivers represent the stage the firm is in, which helps financiers define their strategy.

Analyzing the four drivers, typical stages of the firm used to classify financial needs can be identified. There are six different stages:

1. Development
2. Start up
3. Early growth
4. Rapid growth
5. Mature age
6. Crisis and/or decline

These stages impact the four drivers — investment, profitability, cash flow, and sales growth — used when analyzing financial needs and equity capital demand of a firm as seen in Figure 1.2.

During the first stage, the entrepreneur has to cope with development, the length of which depends on the business features and the entrepreneur's commitment. The objective is to define the most convenient structure for the project's progress. In this phase, sales do not exist and profitability and cash flow are negative due to the presence of compulsory investments such as the completion of information memorandum, costs for legal and fiscal advisory, engineering development, etc.

The start-up stage consists of company creation and launch of firm activity. During this period, sales start, but the trend is not solid enough to support costs incurred by sizeable and substantial investments related to the acquisition of productive factors. Consequently, cash flows and profitability are strongly negative.

The next stage, early growth, occurs just after start up. Investments have been made and the firm's current needs are related to inventory, rather than working capital; the revenues realized by the company are increasing. There is a rise in profitability and cash flow, even though they remain negative. However, the whole trend is positive and stable and the negative value is slowly becoming greater than zero.

	Investment	Profitability	Cash flow	Sales growth
Development	Focused on the acquisitions of productive factors	Negative	Negative	Not available
Start up	Focused on the acquisitions of productive factors	Strongly negative	Strongly negative	Starting
Early growth	Limited to the inventory financing	Negative but reducing	Negative but reducing	Positive and increasing
Rapid growth	Limited to the inventory financing	Positive and increasing	Positive and increasing	Positive but decreasing
Mature age	Focused on the inventory or on the replacement	End of increasing	End of increasing	Getting to zero
Crisis or decline	Not possible to be identified	Falling down	Falling down	Negative

FIGURE 1.2

The characteristics of the four drivers in a firm's six different stages.

The next stage is rapid growth. The investments needed are the same as the early growth stage. In this period, sales are increasing but the growth trend is negative and cash flow and profitability are positive and increasing.

After the rapid growth stage, there is a period of maturity and firms enter the mature age phase. The sales growth tends to zero while profitability and cash flows level off. During this phase, investments are not just related to inventory and/or working capital but the replacement of ineffective or unused assets also must be taken into account. The last of the six stages is the crisis or decline phase. During this period, sales, profitability, and cash flow fall and the firm is unable to decide what investments should be completed to overturn the decline.

These stages create a demand for financial resources measured by the net cash flow produced by the firm. Demand for financial resources is satisfied by different players with different tools ranging from debt capital to equity capital.

1.4 THE MAP OF EQUITY INVESTMENT: AN INVESTOR'S PERSPECTIVE

Private equity operators and venture capitalists are just a sample of the groups in the financial system. They represent one of the various options that entrepreneurs consider to finance their business. At the same time, entrepreneurs must think about profitability, investment needs, sales growth, and cash flow to find the right counterparty.

Many potential investors are considered from both a debt and an equity perspective:

Founder and family
Other partners
Business Angels
Private equity operators and venture capitalists
Banks
Trade credit operators
Financial markets

For equity investors it is critical to answer these questions:

1. What is the financial need?
2. What part can be satisfied through equity capital?
3. How long before the firm is able to repay the equity investor?

The first question determines the size of resources required by the firm and the amount of resources that the financial institutions have to satisfy this need. The greater the amount the firm requires, the greater the size, reputation, and skills of the counterparty. The second question ascertains what sort of financial resources the firm needs; for example, venture capitalists and private equity operators tend to participate with equity, whereas banks are focused on debt. At the same time, the founder and the family equity investment in the firm or trade credit institutions only propose debt. The third question defines the time horizon and the capability of investors to wait and remain confident in their deals.

The answers to these questions help to define profiles of investors with different levels of risk tolerance, chances to invest in equity, and the ability to support a shorter or longer payback period. The different profiles are related to different risk–return combinations and time horizons (Figure 1.3).

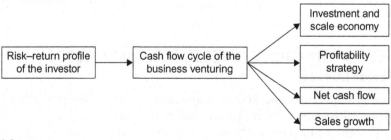

FIGURE 1.3

The relationship between risk–return profile and characteristics of the investment.

The risk–return profile of the investors is strictly connected to the cash flow produced: the smaller the amount of sources generated by management, the greater the risk, and the greater the need for equity and the risk-taking profile of the investor.

If firm-developing phases and types of investors are considered simultaneously, the different risk–return profiles like the ideal or potential size of investors create an interesting scheme of equity capital investment availability.

Figure 1.4 illustrates the potential role of private equity and venture capital as the only financial institutions who can support firms during all stages. In some stages the amount of assistance can be very large (i.e., start-up or growth phases), while in other stages, such as the development phase or during the decline, the assistance may lessen. At the same time, it must be emphasized that private equity and venture capital are not the only financial institutions available for entrepreneurs. Founder and family members are important during the most risky and less stable phases such as development and start up. At the same time, financial markets may be considered concrete options only during the more stable mature age.

According to Figure 1.4, the banking system is a suitable counterpart for fully developed firms who have already gone through development and start up.

Investor types / Firm stages	Founder & Family	Other Partners	Business Angels	Private Equity	Banks	Trade Credit	Financial Market
Development	■ Black	░ Gray	░ Gray				
Start Up	■ Black	■ Black	■ Black	■ Black			
Early Growth				░ Gray	■ Black		
Rapid Growth				░ Gray	░ Gray		
Mature Age				░ Gray	░ Gray		░ Gray
Crisis or Decline	░ Gray	░ Gray		■ Black	■ Black		

FIGURE 1.4

The different types of investors during the different stages.

Banks are more useful during the rapid growth and the mature age periods. Similar conclusions may be reached for trade credit, which is most appropriate for firms in the rapid growth phase. Finally, there are Business Angels whose commitment can be compared to founders or family members, rather than "industrial" partners who help the entrepreneur develop the initial idea. Every kind of investor can help develop firms in any phase and entrepreneurs can find suitable investors to satisfy their financial needs.

1.5 THE PRIVATE EQUITY MARKET IN EUROPE

In the 2007 Annual Survey conducted by the European Private Equity and Venture Capital Association (EVCA) based on activity realized in Europe, private equity investment reached a record level of €73,8 billion, representing a 3,7% increase compared to the €71,6 billion invested in 2006. It is also important to analyze data from private equity investment, fundraising, and divestment activity to present an overview of the European private equity market.

1.5.1 Investment activity during 2007

Considering the investment analysis:

- The number of investments has decreased by 21,8% with 8,411 deals executed in 2007 (10,760 deals in 2006); 43,8% of these operations were executed as first-time investments and 50% were follow-on financing. Considering the amount of funds involved, the picture was exactly the opposite — 58,5% focused on first-time investments and 35,9% on follow-on financing.

- The average financing per company was €13 million in 2007 representing a huge increase compared with €9,4 million in 2006.

- Of the investments, 79% (€58,3 billion) were buyouts.

- Seed investments maintained the same level as 2006 with €184,7 million.

- Start-up investments were reduced by more than 50%, reaching €2,5 billion in 2007; considering the number of start-ups, this represents 30,6% of the total number of deals with 2,576 deals in 2007.

- The largest cluster of operations in 2007 was the expansion stage with 34,1% of the total number of deals closed, representing 12,7% of the total amount invested (€9,4 billion).

- The first three industry sectors targeted for private equity activity were business and industrial products (€10,3 billion, 14%), the consumer goods and retail (€9,5 billion, 12,9%), and communications (€9 billion, 12,2%).

Focusing our attention on the country in which the operations have taken place:

Of €74,4 billion, 95,1% concentrated on European companies, similar to 2006 (95,2%).

The most attractive countries in terms of investments were the UK (26,7%), France (15,1%), Germany (13,5%), the Netherlands (7,3%), and Spain (5,4%).

The figures regarding buyouts and venture capital investments show:

Total amount of buyouts realized equals €56,8 billion (78,8% of the total) and venture capital deals amounted to €12,3 billion.

Small buyouts realized were 6,7% of the total number of deals, with a total value of €5,5 billion and an average deal size of €4,1 million.

Mid-market deals have attracted the highest amount with €24,6 billion (43,2% of the total) in 546 deals.

Mega buyouts reached a total value of €12,4 billion; 28 deals with an average deal size of €441 million.

Finally, considering the investment distribution through the different sectors, the distribution of venture capital and buyout investments is very different.

The main sectors financed in the venture capital businesses were life sciences, computer and consumer electronics, and communications representing 47,9% of all venture capital investments and 58% of the deals.

The main sectors financed in buyout businesses were business and industrial products and services and consumer goods and retail, representing 41,9% of the total amount and 47,6% of the total number of deals.

1.5.2 Fundraising activity during 2007

Analysis of fundraising activity, which consists of the valuation of funds raised by European private equity and venture capital companies, shows the following results:

Total collected funds amounted to €79 billion with a 30% decrease when compared to €112,3 billion from the year before.

Expected allocation of funds to buyouts was 76% or €60 billion.

Fundraising for high-tech investments, mainly early stage and expansion, has increased to €7,3 billion from €5 billion in 2006.

Fundraising expected to be invested in venture capital decreased from €17,5 billion in 2006 to €10,3 billion.

Considering the countries in which the private equity groups are based, the groups from the UK contributed the largest amount of funds raising €41,4 billion, 52,4% of the total; French operators have raised €6,6 billion, 8,3% of the total; and German groups have collected €5,7 billion, 7,2% of the total.

The largest single source of capital was pension funds with €13,9 billion raised, 18% of total funds. This represents a huge drop from 2006 (€29,2 billion). The second largest contributors were banks with €9,1 billion or 11.8%; a considerable decrease from 2006. Finally, proceeds for funds were the third largest contributors raising €8,7 billion or 11,2%.

Moreover, 93,4% of the funds raised were supplied by independent sources, 4,4% by captive companies, and capital gains raised the remaining 2,2%.

1.5.3 Divestment activity during 2007

If we analyze the divestment activity of 2007 classified by country:

The highest amount divested, €12 billion (44,4% of the total European amount), is realized by the UK groups with 1,079 operations.

French private equity operators divested €3,5 billion (12,9% of the total).

German private equity houses represent 10,7% of the total with €2,9 billion.

In 2007, 2,726 companies were divested and 4,448 were divested in 2006. If the exit strategies were analyzed:

The sale to another private equity house was the largest exit, amounting to €8,2 billion (30,4%), 412 divestments.

Trade sales were the second largest category increasing slightly to €7,6 billion in 2007 from €7,5 billion in 2006.

Divestments by public offering (IPO and sale of quoted equity) represented half of the 2006 figures at €2,6 billion.

Write-offs were €0,5 billion in 2007, continuing a decreasing trend from last year and representing only 1,8% of the total amount divested.

The analysis per firms divested shows that

Out of the 26,3% of the total European amount divested, €7 billion is represented by the British private-equity-backed companies.

German companies divested were 18,7% of the total (€5 billion).

French firms divested were 15% of the total (€4 billion).

Clusters of investment within private equity

This chapter explains the different clusters of investment private equity operators and venture capitalists put in place to meet a firm's needs. The first section illustrates two approaches explaining the relationship between investment and activity implemented by investors: traditional and firm-based. It concludes by explaining why investors choose the first approach. The second section identifies the most important features of every cluster of investments: definition, risk–return profile, critical issues, and managerial involvement. The last six sections analyze different investment typologies.

2.1 PRELIMINARY FOCUS ON THE DIFFERENT CLUSTERS OF INVESTMENT

Different clusters of equity investment define the activity of the investor. There are two approaches implemented by investors explaining the relationship between investment and activity: traditional and firm-based (or modern approach). The traditional approach is based on the relationship between the firm's development and its financial needs. The firm-based approach, on the other hand, is a relatively new method of analysis. It evolved because of competition and great difficulty matching a firm's needs with the activities of the private equity investor.

According to the traditional approach, the stages of equity investment are

Seed financing (development)
Start-up financing (start up)

Early stage financing (early growth)
Expansion financing (rapid growth)
Replacement financing (mature age)
Vulture financing (crisis and/or decline)

A very close relationship exists between each stage and financial need. For example, during the development phase, the firm needs to fund the business idea, while during the start-up phase, the financial resources fund operations.

The traditional approach is based on the firm's life cycle and the private equity investor. The modern approach identifies three different investment categories based on private equity operator actions and involvement of the financial institutions:

1. Creation financing
2. Expansion financing
3. Change financing

Creation financing supports a new economic venture from the original idea. The need for private equity finance emerges when an entrepreneur looks for support when developing a new product or service or renewing an existing production process. Usually, entrepreneurs approach financial sources to make the development faster and non-financial sources to define the competitive environment. According to the definition presented in Section 1.1 of Chapter 1, creation financing includes all venture capital deals.

Expansion financing includes all deals related to problems with growth and the increasing size of a firm. Firms follow three different paths to this growth:

In-house growth path — Projects originate by sales development plans, rather than production capacity expansion. The support of private equity operators is primarily focused on financial sources, because firms have already developed their sales plans.

External growth paths — Projects are linked to M&A deals. Private equity operators find their ideal partners or the best target company. International or supranational expertise represents a competitive advantage for financial institutions looking to operate in this business.

Vertical or horizontal integration path — Projects create a holding that includes operative and complementary firms with similar supplied business areas, technologies, customers, etc. Private equity operators develop the holding's strategic issues, rather than the funding of the structure design (cluster venture).

Change financing funds operations that change a firm's shareholder composition.

Different from expansion financing, the most modern approach is based on the needs of the firm satisfied by private equity operators or venture capitalists. Because there is no clear relationship between financial need, stage of the firm, and type of financial institution, this approach relies on private equity operators.

The traditional approach creates a link between stage, financial needs, financial institution, and activities implemented during the investment phase, whereas the most modern approach proposes an easier way — focusing attention on the firm's needs and activities.

The modern approach is not innovative, but it is a newer, easier, and more firm-oriented way to use private equity finance. Theoretically, the traditional approach is more precise. Moreover, the traditional approach better illustrates the investor's role and activities implemented to satisfy the needs of the entrepreneurs. In the following sections these two approaches are presented in more detail.

2.2 THE MAIN ISSUES OF INVESTMENT CLUSTERS

Different clusters of equity investment have specific features that contribute to investor activity. Every cluster is classified by

Definition
Risk–return profile
Critical issues
Managerial involvement within business venturing

Every stage is characterized by a risk–return profile related to the four drivers presented in Chapter 1: investment, profitability, cash flow, and sales growth. Every firm stage has risk measured as total or partial loss of invested sources, delays in project implementation, lower profits, etc., and an expected return usually measured as the internal rate of return (IRR).

The first term, definition, describes the agreement between entrepreneur and financial institutions. It explains the financing rationale and, indirectly, the firm's needs including why the firm is looking for money and how that money is used. There are critical issues to manage at every stage in a firm's growth. The most critical is deciding which firms wait for private equity finance, and which financial institutions meet the requirements of each firm.

The last term in the list, managerial involvement, identifies the financial institution's contribution to the growth of the firm and analyzes the decision process, rather than the percentage of shares owned. Therefore, in private equity finance, very low/high level managerial involvement is not related to the number of held shares.

2.2.1 Seed financing

Seed financing is necessary for the development of a new firm. Development specifies the business idea or the development plan of a product not yet created. During this type of financing, funded firms do not have an actual product to sell and are unable to earn revenue. This is also called first round or initial financing.

The purpose of seed financing is to transform R&D projects into successful business companies or start-ups. Therefore, seed financing funded by financial institutions is used to create new ventures. The risk–return profile is very difficult to define, because risk is very high, while expected returns are impossible to calculate due to the uncertainty of R&D results and the difficulties with transforming R&D into business.

Equity-based financing is preferred to alternative debt-based instruments that are more expensive and rely on collateral, which entrepreneurs cannot provide. Entrepreneurs should also realize seed financing might be divided into pre-seed and seed capital finance. Pre-seed or "proof of concept" finance is generally provided from public sources and relates to basic research, while seed capital can be readily applied.

Seed financing investors do not ask financiers to be firm managers because the firm has just been created. However, the role played by investors is not passive. They support research activities, translate the business idea into a patent and production process, build the company team, and manage any sudden death risk. The most important elements financiers provide are the business plan preparation, analysis, and validation (see Figure 2.1).

Because of the high risks, both public and private investors offer seed financing. There is no clear distinction between them, but the private sector provides the expertise required for efficient and effective management, even if the funding is (partly) provided by public authorities. Public authorities have a clear leadership role in development decisions, i.e., deciding how to allocate public funding used to address shortcomings in seed capital provision and to develop the market.

2.2.2 Start-up financing

Seed financing transforms R&D into a business idea, and start-up financing converts the business idea into a real operating company. For entrepreneurs, start-up financing is used to set up projects and launch production. The funded sources are used to buy equipment, inventory, plants, and anything else useful to move the business idea to operations.

Start-up financing is a gamble for the financier. Although the investors think the business idea is worthwhile, they do not know if the market will support

Seed financing	
Definition	Financing of a business idea or of a research activity in order to produce a business idea; money is not used to create the new venture.
Risk–return profile	Money is used to finance research. Risk is very high because of the uncertainty of the research activity and of the development of the business. The calculation of the expected IRR is very difficult.
Critical issues to manage	To give strong support to research; To translate the business idea into a patenting process; To build the team; To support research; To manage sudden death risk.
Managerial involvement	Very limited.

FIGURE 2.1

Seed financing.

the idea transforming it into a profitable business. The risk–return profile of investors assumes high returns, measured as expected IRR, and high risks with possible delays in or the default of the project.

During seed financing, financiers are expected to be experienced in technical and engineering fields. In start-up financing, because the R&D stage has already been completed, financiers are expected to support the business plan, have an in-depth understanding of its nature and its assumptions, value the management team, and define the strategy used to implement proposals.

For this reason, private equity operators or venture capitalists are very involved in a firm's management and own a large number of shares. Their shares may be the majority of shares issued or make the financial operators the biggest shareholders (see Figure 2.2).

2.2.3 **Early stage financing**

Early stage financing is essential when moving from the start-up to the real business life cycle. In this phase, sales and firm growth begin. The objective of early stage financing is to create a stable and permanent organization.

During this phase, all problems related to project, design, test, and launch have been resolved. Financial resources are used to fund a little developed company that needs equity to further its growth. For financiers, this is the stage where financing really begins.

Start up financing	
Definition	Financing of the start up of a new venture that moves from the idea to the operations. Money are used to buy all what is necessary to start (equipment, inventory, building, etc...).
Risk–return profile	Money is used to finance a firm.
	Risk is very high because of the uncertain of the future development of the business.
	It is possible to calculate the expected IRR even if the maturity of the investment can be very long.
Critical issues to manage	To give strong support to the business plan; To offer capability in deeply understanding the nature and the assumptions of the business plan; To realize strong valuation of the team.
Managerial involvement	Very strong and related to all activities which are necessary to produce the business plan. The percentage of shares could be also very high.

FIGURE 2.2

Start-up financing.

The risk–return profile at this stage is similar to earlier phases: there is more uncertainty within the market rather than technical items or feasibility questions. Because of this, financing during this phase is opened to investors new to the sector or the market.

The expected IRR and the linked risk are high, because investments are already made and there is no certainty about sales development. In this phase financial institutions are asked to revise and strengthen the business plan. Private equity operators or venture capitalists are very involved in management and own a large numbers of shares. Realized and required activities range from assistance to strategic decisions to business plan certification to marketing and financial advice (see Figure 2.3).

2.2.4 Expansion financing

Expansion financing is for companies that need or want to expand their business activity. If the market conditions are right, it can be a great move; some businesses find they need expansion financing when fast business growth is possible.

Equity or debts are provided to support growing debt and inventories. The company is growing but may not be showing a profit at this stage. Funds may be provided for the major expansion of a company that has increasing sales volume

Early stage financing	
Definition	Financing of the phase of growth of a venture baked company that moves from the start up to sales. Money is used to buy inventory and to sustain the gap existing between cash flow and money needed.
Risk–return profile	Money is used to finance the first steps of a "baby firm." Risk is very high because of the uncertainty of the future of the development of the business. It is possible to calculate the expected IRR and revised properly the previous business plan.
Critical issues to manage	To give strong support to the first steps of the firm (mentoring, advisory); To offer capability in verifying if the nature and the assumptions of the business plan are realistic; To give strong assistance in strategic decision processes.
Managerial involvement	Very strong and related to all activities which are necessary to avoid mistakes. The percentage of shares could be also very high.

FIGURE 2.3

Early stage financing.

and is breaking even or has achieved initial profitability. They are utilized for further plant expansion, marketing, and working capital or for development of an improved product, a newer technology, or an expanded product line.

The risk in expansion financing is moderate and depends on the sector. Money is used to finance sales growth or to improve projects in known fields so there is no risk due to uncertainty. Returns should be lower at this stage.

Although firms are already operating, financial institutions also play a fundamental role during this phase. At this point they are asked to develop effective growth plans. Because of the size of a firm and the financier's need to diversify his portfolio, the percentage of shares held by private equity operators or venture capitalists during this phase is low. Expansion financing projects do not require specific technical skills or industrial abilities, so these deals may be funded by a very large number of financiers (see Figure 2.4).

2.2.5 **Replacement financing**

After the growth (rapid and slow) phase, firms become more stable and enter the mature age. Although profitability and cash flows are stable, private equity finance still plays an important role. During the mature age entrepreneurs modify their needs and, while almost all priorities were driven by sales development and size increasing, in this period the problems come from governance or corporate finance decisions.

Expansion financing	
Definition	Financing of the fast growth phase of a firm that aims to consolidate the position in the market.
	Money is used only to sustain the gap existing between cash flow and money needed.
Risk–return profile	Money is used to finance sales growth. Risk is moderate (and linked to the business) because the trend of development of the business is well known. It is possible to calculate the expected IRR.
Critical issues to manage	To give strong support; To face risks linked to a fast process of growth (i.e., accurate selections of the new markets to enter, inventory choices, etc...).
Managerial involvement	Mentoring and advisory activity in defining the right assumptions of strategic decisions. The percentage of share is not very high and it does not represent a specific characteristic in this type of deal.

FIGURE 2.4

Expansion financing.

Replacement financing — the typical support from private equity finance for firms in their mature age — funds companies looking for strategic decisions associated with the governance system and the firm's status, rather than the firm's approach to finance. This kind of investment may be realized in different ways:

Listing on a stock exchange
Substitution of shareholders
A new design for the company governance

Replacement financing is never used to boost sales growth or to realize investment in plants. Instead it is used for strategic or acquisition processes. Replacement capital is the proper solution to fund spin-off projects, equity restructuring, shareholder substitution, IPOs, family buy-in or family buyout, etc.

For investors the risk profile of these deals is moderate because

The firm business model is successful
The firm governance is settled even though it is in a shifting phase
Entrepreneurs usually remain and work for the company development

The effective risk depends also on the whole sector/market risk and the quality of the process to be put in place.

Financial institutions operating in this environment could be used as just an investor or as an advisor and consultant. The role of the private equity operator is to support managerial strategic decisions and the implementation of the entire deal design.

At this point managerial involvement from the investor is extensive. When the financier acts as more than a financial operator, industrial knowledge and previous expertise become very important. Entrepreneurs need to skillfully manage corporate governance issues and corporate finance deals.

In this case, private equity operators buy a large number of shares issued by the firm they are working with. This makes the whole deal easier to implement, and very often the private equity operators turn into prime shareholders. However, even though they hold the majority of the company's shares, they do not participate in the current management allowing the entrepreneur to retain the top management role.

Compared to the types of financing used by private equity operators and venture capitalists, replacement financing is the most independent from the actual business; instead it is related to the personal and private needs of entrepreneurs (see Figure 2.5).

2.2.6 Vulture financing

Even when firms are declining or are in crisis, private equity operators are suitable partners. When a firm is financially distressed, private equity operators can offer vulture financing. This is used to restructure firms enabling companies to improve their financial performance, exploit new strategic opportunities, and regain credibility. In extreme situations, restructuring can make the difference between a company surviving or folding.

Replacement financing	
Definition	Financing of a mature firm that wants to face strategic decisions linked to the governance or to the corporate finance decisions. Money is used only to sustain the strategic or the acquisition processes.
Risk–return profile	Money is used to finance sales growth or investment. Risk is moderate and linked to the quality of the strategic process that is necessary to be put in place. Examples are: IPO, turnaround, LBO, restructuring of family governance. It's possible to deeply calculate the expected IRR.
Critical issues to manage	To give strong support to manage strategic decisions. The role of the private equity moves from a simple financer job to an effective consultant activity.
Managerial involvement	Very high and qualified, in terms of deep industrial knowledge and strong capability to manage corporate governance issues and corporate finance deals.

FIGURE 2.5

Replacement financing.

There has been a great deal of research done on the causes and consequences of corporate restructuring, but little is known about the actual practice: this topic can be very difficult to analyze, because the issues involved are often politically and competitively sensitive. Moreover, many managers are reluctant to discuss the difficult decisions and choices made in these situations. It must be emphasized that the description of vulture investors in the press is often critical; similar to the description of corporate raiders in the context of hostile takeovers. The relevant issue, however, cannot be the public or personal perception of vulture investors, but rather the role they play in financially distressed firms.

For investors, vulture financing is very risky; there is no assurance the business will be revitalized by the survival plan. The risk is linked to the "nature" of the crisis: a business crisis is different from an audit fraud crisis because it is due to macroeconomic factors and not mismanagement of funds.

Vulture investors frequently gain control by purchasing senior securities, and they often become board members or managers of the target company. From this position they can propose a survival plan, implement it, and monitor the growth of the firm. Vulture financing serves to discipline managers of companies in financial distress (see Figure 2.6).

Many skills are required of financial institutions operating in this environment, because their intervention forces them to act as advisor and consultant, or, more often, as entrepreneur. The fundamental role of the private equity

Vulture financing	
Definition	Financing of a firm that faces crisis or decline. Money is used to sustain the financial gap generated from the decline of growth.
Risk–return profile	Money is not used to finance sales growth or new perspective but to launch a survival plan. Risk is very high and linked to the "nature" of the crisis. Example of different typologies of crises are: debt restructuring, turnaround or failure. It is hard to calculate the expected IRR.
Critical issues to manage	To give strong support; To manage strategic decisions; The role of the private equity moves from a simple financer job to an effective entrepreneur activity.
Managerial involvement	Very high and qualified, in terms of deep industrial knowledge and of strong capability to manage corporate governance issues and corporate finance deals.

FIGURE 2.6

Vulture financing.

operator is to support managerial strategic decisions and the implementation of the entire deal design. This requires deep industrial knowledge or the ability to manage corporate governance issues and corporate finance deals.

2.3 THE IMPACT OF PRIVATE EQUITY OPERATIONS

In the last few years while private equity deals and operations have grown both in size and geographic diffusion, research activity on their growing global impact is still limited.

The World Economic Forum invested in a study called the "Global Economic Impact of Private Equity." It evaluates private equity transactions that occur during equity investment realized by professionally managed partnerships including leveraged buyouts, which link equity investment with debt. It also evaluates the impact of this type of investment worldwide and covers these main topics:

Demography of private equity firms: number, duration, and outcome of this type of deal

Willingness of private-equity-backed firms to realize long-term investments, in particular in high innovative industries

Impact of private equity activity on employment

Consequence of private equity investment for the governance of private equity firms

Key highlights include:

Demography — Considering the holding period of these operations, the study has verified that, first, almost 60% of the investments are exited more than 5 years after their beginning and, second, the length of the holding period has increased in recent years.

Bankruptcy — The weight of buyout transactions ending in bankruptcy or financial distress is 6% of the total deals realized. This is translated into a low default rate of 1,2% per year when compared to an average default rate of 1,6% for US corporate bonds.

Innovation — The positive relationship between buyouts and patent level demonstrates little change after private equity operations but a higher economic impact.

Employment for existing target — The study illustrated how the employment growth is affected by private equity deals. It demonstrates that employment growth follows a "J-curve" pattern in the years pre and post deal. During the two years before the operation, employment in the target company grows more slowly than in the control group. This is similar to two years after the buyout when the difference between the two growth patterns is around 7% lower for the target than the controls. In the fourth and fifth years following the transaction, employment in private-equity-backed firms becomes consistent with the employment of the control groups.

Employment growth at new business launch — In these cases, the study discovered an opposite trend; firms backed by private equity had 6% more job creation than the control group two years after the buyout.

Governance — The outcomes indicate that private equity board members are most active in complex and challenging transactions. Private equity groups appear to fine-tune their board composition based on the anticipation of investment challenges.

Theoretical foundation of private equity and venture capital

INTRODUCTION

There are many theories explaining the birth and development of the private equity and venture capital industry and many schemes developed to help understand financing problems and their solutions. This chapter describes theories about financing selected by corporations; for example, whether debt or equity financing is (or should be) chosen. This is different from today's explanation about how venture capital and private equity works within companies.

3.1 THEORIES ABOUT CORPORATION FINANCING

Leading theories of capital structure attempt to explain the proportion of debt and equity on a corporation's balance sheet. Most research assumes that the firms requiring sources are public, involved in non-financial business, and raising capital primarily from outside investors rather than from the firm's entrepreneurs, managers, or employees.

There is no universal theory of capital structure, and there are no reasons to expect one. There are useful conditional theories, but they differ in their relative emphasis on the factors that could affect the choice between debt and equity, such as agency costs, taxes, differences in information, and the effects of market imperfections or institutional or regulatory constraints. These factors could dominate a firm or be unimportant for other corporations.

Leading theories of capital structure are

Capital-structure irrelevance. This theory refers to the initial works of Modigliani and Miller from the mid-1950s. Their work states firm value and investment decisions are independent and not linked to financing decisions. The choice between debt and equity is not totally unimportant, but it indirectly effects real decisions.

Trade-off theory. This idea follows the Modigliani and Miller framework, but focuses on fiscal consequences. Firms choose target debt ratios by trading off the tax benefits of debt against the costs of bankruptcy and financial distress. Actual debt ratios move toward the target.

Agency theory. This approach was initially proposed by Jensen and Meckling. It theorizes that decisions have direct and real effects on firms and managerial behavior, because they change manager incentives and investment in operating decisions. Agency costs drive financing, or at least they explain the effects of financing decisions.

Pecking order theory. According to Myers and Majluf and Myers, financing decisions mitigate problems created by differences between insiders (managers) and outside investors. The firm turns first to the financing sources where differences matter least.

These theories may be useful when explaining capital structures with data and findings that confirm they work.

Economic problems and incentives that drive these theories do not explain financing strategy, thus they offer only a partial understanding of the conditions under which each theory, or some combination of the theories, works. Zingales says that a "new foundation" for corporate finance is needed to effectively understand financing decisions. This new approach requires a deeper understanding of the motives and behavior of managers and employees of a firm. For example, all standard financing theories assume the manager pursues a simple objective. The manager's actual objectives depend on how he is rewarded for his actions. Managers used to be thought of as the agents of stockholders, but managers and employees also invest their human capital, which comes in the form of personal risk-taking and specialization. A general financial theory of the firm would model the co-investment of human and financial capital. In small and medium companies there is no difference between managers and shareholders because the entrepreneur represents both.

Because venture capital and private equity fund firms with both financial and non-financial capital, their motives cannot be understood by standard theories. Instead, a deeper analysis of the perspectives of the firms and financiers would lead to a more accurate motive that drives the private equity and venture capital decision process.

3.1.1 Remarks on the approach of Modigliani and Miller

Modern theory of optimal capital structure starts with Modigliani and Miller (M-M) proving financing decisions do not matter in perfect capital markets. Their proof states the market values of the firm's debt and equity, D and E, add up to total firm value, V. V is a constant, regardless of the proportions of D and E, provided that assets and growth opportunities on the left side of the balance sheet are held constant. Financial leverage or gearing (the proportion of debt financing on the right side of the balance sheet) is irrelevant. This irrelevance results in a mix of securities issued by the firm. According to this approach, financial decisions are unable to increase or decrease the value regardless of who finances the deal.

For corporate finance, M-M propositions are benchmarks, not end results. Compared to investment and operating decisions, most financing decisions affect value: idiosyncratic financing decisions may not be harmful, and managers may not be able to discern the affects of financing on volatile stock market values.

M-M propositions are based on the perfect efficiency of capital markets and, consequently, on the perfect behavior of firms and the rational behavior of managers whose interests are aligned to those of the financier.

If this was a proven approach, private equity operators and venture capitalists would be no different from other financial institutions and would be considered only during reliable value growth of the left side of the balance sheet. Replacement and vulture financing could only be applied when the re-organization of financial sources generates an expansion of the firm's value.

3.1.2 Remarks on the trade-off theory approach

Trade-off theory changes M-M's proposition about firm value. In this approach the total value of a firm is still the sum of equity financing and debt financing (D + E), but these two elements must be considered:

1. Present value of future taxes saved because of interest tax deductions
2. Present value of costs of financial distress; i.e., the present value of future costs attributable to the threat or occurrence of default

Firms choose the level of debt that maximizes the whole value; the optimum level requires the firm to borrow up to where the present value of interest tax shields and the present value of financial distress costs are equal at the margin.

Trade-off theory therefore explains moderate, cautious borrowing. It identifies firms that face especially high costs of distress; for example, firms facing higher business risk and firms with growth opportunities and mostly intangible assets. The trade-off theory predicts that firms or industries with these characteristics should be especially cautious and operate at low target debt ratios.

This theory has been tested cross-sectionally using proxies for tax status and the potential costs of financial distress. This research reinforces that large, safe firms with tangible assets tend to borrow more than small, risky firms with mostly intangible assets (because they are usually linked to expenditures on advertising and R&D expenses). Firms with high profitability and valuable growth opportunities tend to borrow less. These factors make sense under the trade-off theory.

It must be emphasized that trade-off theory results are mostly qualitative; for example, lower borrowing for firms with valuable growth opportunities is predicted, but not the amount borrowed. At the same time, the theory does not specify financial distress probability as a function of leverage, nor does it quantify the costs of financial distress, except to say that these costs are important.

Trade-off theory explains the presence of venture capitalists and private equity operators among financial institutions, and how they help firms modify their value or their ability to calculate the probable costs of distress and/or their ability to support leverage. Trade-off theory also suggests that the private equity industry may represent a better solution for firms that are unable to use traditional financiers because of high financial risk or large amounts of intangibles and growth opportunities.

3.1.3 Remarks on agency theory

Agency theory describes the ever-present agency relationship in which one party (the principal) delegates work to another party (the agent) who performs the job. The fundamental idea is that the relationship is similar to a contract.

The following articles further explain agency theory.

Jensen and Meckling explore the relationship between owners and managers and underline the way to align interests of all subjects.

Fama discusses how efficiency of labor and capital markets plays an important role when monitoring the behavior of managers.

Fama and Jensen conclude that an effective board may reduce management's opportunism.

Agency theory solves two sets of problems: difficulties in monitoring and attitudes toward risk. In the first case, agency theory tries to solve conflicts between the principal and agent or if there is a real problem verifying the agent's actions. In the latter case, agency theory proposes solutions when principal and agent act differently because of their risk preferences (see Figure 3.1).

Agency theory framework	
Cause	There is a substantial difference among aims and goals of principal and agent; that is, between shareholders and managers, firm owners and firm financiers, firms and fininicial institutions, majority shareholders and minority shareholders
Basic idea	The relationship between principal and agent may be improved and made more efficient
Role of information	There is a problem of information asymmetry between subjects, so information is a valuable item and may become a clause in an agreement
Analyzed items	Contract between principal and agent
Contract problems	Moral hazard
	Adverse selection
	Monitoring and controlling
	Risk sharing

FIGURE 3.1

The agency theory framework.

Agency theory offers an understanding of the relationship between financiers and existing shareholders. This becomes important if financiers are venture capitalists or private equity operators since they may also act as shareholders and managers.

During a deal entrepreneurs and private equity operators have information asymmetry: one party has more or better information than the other. This creates an imbalance of power, which can cause transactions to go awry. Problems may manifest before, during, and after the deal.

The typical problem before the deal is adverse selection. This is a financial deal process where "bad" results occur when financiers and funded subjects have asymmetric information and the bad subjects are more likely to be selected. For example, a financial institution that sets one rate for all its products runs the risk of being adversely selected against by its low-balance, high-activity (and hence, least profitable) entrepreneurs.

A typical post deal problem is moral hazard — a party insulated from the risk may behave differently than it would if it were fully exposed to the risk. For private equity operators and venture capitalists this a problem, because they do not know how entrepreneurs will use the financial sources they have been given.

During financing, problems can occur with the monitoring and controlling of a firm's performance. For venture capitalists and private equity operators, contracts must consider verification and disclosure costs. This is defined as the "costly state verification" (CSV) approach. Here the contract is designed so a lender has to pay a monitoring cost. The pre-deal contract structure specifies auditing and certification conditions. It must be emphasized that without an audit, the entrepreneur would be unable to raise money from investors because the financier anticipates the entrepreneur will falsify information about the company's performance.

Principal and agent, or entrepreneurs and private equity operators, are willing to take on different types of risk (the so-called risk-sharing problem) such as the type of financing (i.e., equity, debt, mezzanine), type of remuneration (i.e., interest, dividend, etc.), and the selection of a counterpart (i.e., new vehicle, existing company, etc.).

Previous theories are unable to explain why and how firms and institutions realize a deal, while agency theory states that entrepreneur's choices are not automatic and both parties emphasize that financiers are not just part of the financial support mechanism.

Deals between private equity operators or venture capitalists and firms might be more expensive and complicated than traditional financing contracts (i.e., mortgage), but their interests and opportunistic behaviors must be aligned or at least considered. Reputation is more important for venture capitalists and private equity operators than for traditional financiers because bad business behavior may reduce the future development opportunities.

According to the agency theory, private equity operators and venture capitalists represent a valuable counterpart for firms, but complicated agreements and specific clauses must be settled to realize the deal.

3.1.4 Remarks on pecking order theory

The pecking order theory states that companies prioritize their sources of financing (from internal financing to equity) and consider equity financing as a last resort. Internal funds are used first, and when they are depleted, debt is issued. When it is not prudent to issue more debt, equity is issued. This theory maintains that businesses adhere to a hierarchy of financing sources and prefer internal financing when available, and debt is preferred over equity if external financing is required.

As noted by Berger and Udell, the hierarchy depends on the firm's size and level of development, because there is a particular level of information asymmetry and financial need for every phase of growth. This is also known as the "financial growth cycle."

During this cycle, venture capitalists and private equity operators may improve the efficiency of the entire financial system, because they tend to work with informationally opaque firms. For this reason, they represent the proper solutions for start up because of the lack of information, the uncertainty of future results, and the organizational structure that is likely to develop. At the same time, firms that want to make strategic decisions linked to the governance or to the status of corporate finance decisions may find that the private equity industry is right for them.

According to this theory, private equity operators and venture capitalists revolutionized the pecking order system, because equity finance comes before debt financing in some cases. This occurs because of the need for more transparency and the reduction of information asymmetry among traditional financiers, such as banks and firms where the need for financial sources is just a part of the whole problem to be solved.

The pecking order theory explains the role of the private equity industry and, more important, highlights the reasons why it operates regardless of the level of development or size of a company. Different from traditional financiers that usually support firms only with money, the private equity industry brings management capabilities to the firms and information to the whole financial system. These elements set this industry apart from credit or banking institutions.

3.2 A REVIEW OF THE VENTURE CAPITAL (AND PRIVATE EQUITY) CYCLE

Empirical evidence clearly shows that private equity and venture capital deals cannot be considered "traditional" financial deals for two reasons: the different evaluation system and the above average risk profile. As Benveniste et al. underlined, this industry develops where a greater informative opacity exists, because of sectors considered (i.e., venture capitalists tend to specialize in high tech and high growth sectors), the agreement characteristics (i.e., private equity operators and venture capitalists usually define the exit strategy before the deal), and the traits of issued securities (i.e., warrant rather than preferred shares), apart from the expectations of the entrepreneurs and financial institutions.

Gompers and Lerner stated that all difficulties found in the private equity industry analysis may be attributed to informational problems and to the different incentives of the subjects involved in these deals. Private equity operations are concentrated in sectors with a high degree of uncertainty and where informative gaps are common among investors, entrepreneurs, and financiers. Moreover, Gompers and Lerner believed firms requiring private equity interventions had problems connected to intangible valuations whereas investors care about how to fund the firm and how the funds are used.

Gompers and Lerner wrote about the "venture capital cycle" and further expanded the idea: from a financial standpoint, private equity financing or venture capital financing may be described as a process that starts with funding, followed by investment and monitoring phases, and concludes with the exit. They further stressed the venture capital cycle can be applied to private equity deals, even though the typical information concerns are more prevalent in venture capital.

Gompers and Lerner are not the only ones analyzing the private equity and venture capital process. Reid and Smith analyzed the relationship between financiers and entrepreneurs in a "principal–agent framework" where the entrepreneur is the agent and the financier is the principal. They underlined the different typologies of risk faced in the private equity industry, and explained agency and non-agency reasons that lead to the signing rather than to the abandonment of initiatives.

Nevertheless, the analysis proposed by Gompers and Lerner represents a clear reference point for the analysis of the entire sector because of its simplicity and ability to subdivide the venture capital (and private equity) cycle into standard phases: fundraising, investing, and exit.

This is the right way to analyze private equity and venture capital because it does not depend on the characteristics of investors, deals, and level of involvement.

Analysis of the private equity cycle considers at least three different types of subjects: suppliers of financial sources, private equity operators, and beneficiaries of financial sources. The first group supplies funds to financial institutions because they are not skilled enough to analyze deals or they cannot bear the risk. The second group is made up of financial institutions whose tasks are to define, select, control, and monitor investments. Finally, beneficiaries are companies that receive financial sources, implement expansion projects or turnaround or change of ownership, and accept all conditions and clauses provided by financial institutions (see Figure 3.2).

Furthermore, analysis has to focus on the characteristics of each step to evaluate the activities emerging in the typical relationships created during deal evolution. In this sense, fundraising, which involves suppliers and investors in venture capital and private equity, presents issues intended to respond to specific needs of the involved subjects. Thus the comprehension of which players are involved, their needs, their fears, and the characteristics of agreements they sign is the first step in understanding how to improve the first phase of the private equity process and the first step to developing a successful private equity deal.

The investment activity (and subsequent management and monitoring) is based on the results of the previous phase and must also provide solutions to the typical problems incurred in this step. It must be emphasized that most

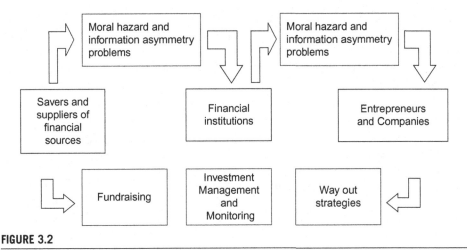

FIGURE 3.2

The private equity cycle.

of the potential troubles of this phase present the same structure as those addressed during the fundraising phase but, at the same time, they present internal variables that make them difficult to standardize and more complicated. All issues regarding the evaluation of the counterparty must be resolved as well as the quantification of non-financial involvement of financial institutions or the definition of characteristics of individual securities that must be issued. In addition to the characteristics of the subjects involved, the most important items to be analyzed include the vehicle, the characteristics of each contract, and the relationships among investors involved.

The third phase of the private equity cycle is the exit of investors from companies. Here the analysis focuses on modalities used for the way out, the time of exit, and on the role played by operators. Relationships between entrepreneurs and venture capitalists or private equity operators, and between providers of financial sources and financial institutions, are very important for the process of liquidation and exit from the investments.

3.3 FUNDRAISING

The financing of entrepreneurial projects cannot be separated from collecting the necessary funds to realize investments. This activity is essential regardless of the legal status of the deal, the organizational structure of subjects involved, and the characteristics of firms or projects selected later.

Unfortunately, this issue has never attracted any academic interest so there has been little research done to understand the phenomena that drive the business and the success of fundraising.

The elements of fundraising are classified by the

Players involved
Problems and risks
Objectives

In this phase, the most important players have the financial sources to invest in risky projects. Typically, there are two broad categories of investors: individuals and institutional. Individuals are ordinary savers who have a significant amount of resources available for investments, the propensity and the preference for high-risk investments, the desire for portfolio diversification, and who search for high returns. However, the individual investor is less significant than the institutional investor who typically is in the financial industry. They know the market environment and are able to accurately understand the risk and expected return of an investment or financing. These investors are known as professional investors. Typically, the professional investors have more resources to invest and operate in a medium/long term, because they can ensure private equity operators or venture capitalists a substantial flow of sources and are able to wait a reasonable period of time to achieve their performance targets.

Investors and venture capitalists (financiers and money collectors) deal with different types of risks. Business risk is borne by venture capitalists or private equity operators, because they identify opportunities and exploit economies of scale. The components related to agency risk are similar with different nuances. The resource providers face information asymmetry and the risk of opportunistic behavior by financial institutions. Financial institutions, at least in theory, are at risk for opportunistic behavior by suppliers of funds that cannot make the agreed payments, change the terms, alter expectations, etc. An appropriate contract structure can overcome these difficulties, but they cannot be totally eliminated.

Problems related to the nature of risks and potential troubles that arise in the relationship between groups involved in the fundraising phase are attributed to the different objectives they are each trying to achieve. Unfortunately no empirical tests have been done on specific objectives of financiers and private equity operators during fundraising limiting the conclusions drawn on this vital topic.

Marti and Balboa concluded that investments made the year before the fundraising and fundraising activity from the following year are strongly connected as well as the divestment of assets, the earnings history of transactions, and the amount of sources available for these deals. Kanniainen and Keuschnigg stated that the size of a private equity investor is directly connected to its capacity to collect money. Based on these assumptions, Cumming postulated that the size of the portfolios held by institutional investors in risky deals was a function of the market conditions, organizational structure of financial institutions, types of investments, level of development, and sector of funded companies.

3.4 INVESTMENT MANAGEMENT AND MONITORING

When fundraising is complete, the next objective is how to use the accumulated resources. This objective kicks off another phase of the private equity cycle. The investment (and management and monitoring) phase also can be divided into stages with features such as

Groups involved
Problems and risks
Objectives

Groups involved in the investment phase include venture capitalists (private equity operators) and entrepreneurs (companies). The venture capitalists focus on techniques and activities carried out by firms asking for money, while the latter group is considered for projects to be financed.

Contrary to the fundraising phase, the relationship between the reception of funds from private equity operators (or venture capitalists) and the level of performance of the funded company has attracted greater interest, although attention is often limited to the business of venture capital.

Jain and Kini demonstrated that companies financed by venture capital and listed on a regulated stock exchange had an above average level of cash flow and sales growth. Lerner investigated the issue and showed that enterprises funded through measures aimed specifically at increasing size, rates of employment growth, and sales were higher than in other companies. Engel and Keilbach, analyzing the German market, concluded that for venture-backed companies growth rates were higher than non-venture-backed firms.

As in the fundraising phase, different interests, information, behavior, and purposes converge in the second step of the private equity cycle. Gompers and Lerner proposed an interesting analysis of the risks and problems during this step. They stated that the problem of risk should be interpreted as a "limited capacity" of companies to raise capital. At the same time, they recognized four factors that affect whether financial institutions are interested in investing: uncertainty, information asymmetry, the nature of the assets of the company, the state of target markets and/or financial markets.

Problems related to the risk nature and problems arising in relationships between groups involved in this phase are attributed to the different objectives that these groups are trying to achieve. In an interesting study of the British market, Reid and Smith showed that financial institutions and entrepreneurs are able to assess the risk level of a private equity deal. Consequently, the broad division between venture capital and private equity, as well as the more specific early stage financing and expansion (MBO), turnaround, replacement, and vulture financing are adequately shared by the world of financial practitioners. From a purely economic point of view, this means that companies and financial institutions similarly interpret the same investment opportunities.

From the same study, financial institutions are shown to be particularly sensitive to the organization of funded companies and to the concrete chances of project realization. As such, they are subject to agency risk. Entrepreneurs demonstrate their primary interest is solving the business risk, even in a venture capital or private equity deal.

These results are consistent with the findings reported by MacMillan et al., but do not match the results of Fried and Hisrich, where the expected return on investment seems to play as important a role (if not even higher) as the capacity of management.

Manigart et al. studied the investment process put in place by British venture capitalists for transactions with companies operating in the biotechnology sector. The study found that management and its capabilities are important only when the projects are already started. If the investment still has to be defined (i.e., seed or start-up financing), the financial variables, market, and technology come first. However, the structure of contracts and initial requirements asked by financial institutions for such transactions are no different from sectors with a high degree of risk (i.e., the high-tech or Internet projects).

3.5 THE EXIT PHASE

Divestment and the subsequent exit of the financial institution from a company is the last phase of the private equity cycle. The interventions of venture capitalists or private equity operators are temporary and linked to the company's trend. If the situation were different, private equity and venture capital would not be assumed as transitional. The study phase of disinvestment is important because it represents a fundamental step by which the venture capitalists can realize their profits or value, in monetary terms, their commitment and activity in favor of the counterparty.

For private equity, exiting is an extremely important step. It requires two fundamental aspects: determination of the channel to be used and identification of the best time for divestment.

Disinvestment has been significantly studied and represents the most interesting element of research in private equity. However, as noted by Gompers and Lerner and Povaly, most of the tests carried out were focused on IPOs. During the second half of the 1990s the most important issue was identifying differences between the venture-backed and non-venture-backed companies. Since the beginning of the new millennium, the scope of research has broadened and today more extensive and detailed studies analyzing this phase can be found.

Schweinbacher et al. have attempted to rationalize the issue of exit strategies considering the sector, the investment length, the external economic environment, the stage of development, etc. The final results are quite interesting: the sector is a very important variable in the definition of both timing and kind of exit. Cumming, in contrast, linked the issue of exit strategies to the characteristics of individual agreements and found that the governance, the dividend policy, and the existing financial leverage have a significant effect on exit strategies. Gordon Smith discussed the question of the agreement terms and forms in private equity transactions. He concluded that the prediction of an exit strategy in the initial agreement is an incentive for the financial institutions, and that private equity operators tend to sign agreements in which there are clauses that give them the opportunity to increase their power when the time for exit is near.

Schweinbacher compared the exit strategies of both American and European private equity operators to test if a "common strategy" exists. Results showed that the most used exit strategy in both markets is the trade sale, even if all players consider the IPO more profitable and a better solution for developing a solid reputation for future deals. It also showed that the length of the investment is almost equal in both markets, and the involvement of financial institutions is similar in operations based on the same assumptions. The main difference is that the Europeans showed a lack of liquidity in all of the deals; in particular, the length of divestment is higher, the financial instruments used are less modern, and the syndicated deals are poorer with fewer participants.

Povaly proposed a deep analysis of private equity exit studies focusing on the exit management process for leveraged buyouts. He found a number of studies on portfolio company exits related to types of exits, timing, and process. He underlined that the reports had findings that could be relevant for other studies.

Legal framework in Europe for equity investors

INTRODUCTION

In the European Union (EU), private equity is considered a financial service and is supervised by the appropriate authorities. Because it is supervised private equity financing is considered safer, more stable, and easier to control than unsupervised financing. The negative impact of supervision is higher costs and specific constraints.

The first section in this chapter introduces options available for private equity finance throughout Europe, while the following section underlines differences and common rules of the EU. The most remarkable aspects of the fund–asset management company system are outlined in Sections 4.3 and 4.4.

Section 4.5 explains the relationship between closed-end funds and asset management companies (AMCs) and defines management fees and carried interest. The last section describes the vehicles available for private equity finance in the EU.

4.1 DIFFERENT FINANCIAL INSTITUTIONS THAT INVEST IN EQUITY: AN INTRODUCTION TO THE EU SYSTEM

According to EU rules, private equity is considered a financial activity and must be supervised. Private equity firms must comply with rules that regulate the entire European financial system. For example, in Italian market organizational structure, investment in equity is regulated by the Banking Act (1988–1993) and the Financial Services Act (1998).

It must be emphasized that there is no other EU law regulating the financial system. However, each country in the EU has ad hoc rules in place to apply the above Acts and different laws for going public as well.

Different vehicles for setting up an equity investment legislated by the EU are

Banks
Investment firms
Closed-end funds (or limited partnership, based on the UK or US models)

Banks and investment firms deal in credit intermediation, so investment in equity is only one of the activities they undertake. In Italy, the Banking Act helps these financial institutions. On the other hand, investment in equity is the core activity of closed-end. There are differences between the funds themselves and the funds' investors; for example, there are a number of specific domestic laws throughout Europe supervising fund investors.

4.2 BANKS AND INVESTMENT FIRMS: COMMON RULES AND DIFFERENCES IN THE EU

4.2.1 Banks

According to EU legislation, banks can develop any kind of financial business except

Asset management activity
Insurance activity
Non-financial activities unrelated to financial activities

Nevertheless, banks are allowed to hold equities of AMCs, insurance companies, and non-financial firms. Some countries have fixed rules due to the specific relationship between banks and non-financial firms. According to EU rules, if a bank invests in equity, it must cap the investment because equity investments, as well as other banking assets, impact regulatory capital.

The caps applied are similar throughout Europe, with the exception of Germany where there are no caps. This comes from the tradition of the German "Hausbank" relationship between firms and banks. There are two groups of constraints applied to private equity investment:

Capital adequacy
Cap rules

Bank type	Concentration cap	Global cap	Division cap
Ordinary bank	3%	15%	15%
Bank with permission	6%	50%	15%
Specialized bank	15%	60%	15%

FIGURE 4.1

Constraints applied to banks when investing in private equity.

Ordinary banks have regulatory capital under €1 billion, banks with permission have regulatory capital over €1 billion and manage equity, and specialized banks have regulatory capital over €1 billion and manage long-term equity and liabilities.

Caps applied to each category of bank have these distinctions:

Concentration cap is related to every private equity investment and is calculated on the bank's equity.

Global cap also refers to the bank's equity; however, it is related to the portfolio of investments held by the bank and includes the sum of all equity investments the bank holds in its portfolio. The cap is calculated using the equity of the bank.

Division cap (or specific cap) refers to the owned company's equity. It is a specific investment using the equity of the company being invested as the variable instead of the bank's equity (see Figure 4.1).

We should emphasize that there are further divergences because, in the Banking Act, there are no fixed parameters and the decision to apply caps is left to the regulator of each country. So we find two groups of countries:

1. Germany and France apply constraints. Banks can hold as much as 100% of a company's equity.
2. The rest of Europe allows a maximum investment of 15% of a company's equity.

Figure 4.2 illustrates the calculation formulas related to the above mentioned caps.

4.2.2 Investment firms

To start up an investment firm in Europe a company should be regulated and supervised.

Investment firms cannot develop banking activity, but they can develop

Equity investment
Lending

Payment services and money transfers
Currency brokerage and dealing

According to EU legislation, all of the above listed activities are carried out with no limits and no caps.

$$Concentration\ cap = \frac{Each\ investment}{Regulatory\ capital}$$

$$Global\ cap = \frac{\Sigma\ Investments}{Regulatory\ capital}$$

Regulates the money invested in private equity

$$Division\ cap = \frac{Investment}{Company's\ equity}$$

FIGURE 4.2

Calculation formulas for caps.

Box: An example of investment firms: the Italian case

There are three types of investment firms in the Italian Banking Act:

Ex art. 113 class
Ex art. 106 class
Ex art. 107 class

Investment firms organized as ex art. 113 are not responsible for the management of the investment firm. Investments and management are concerned only with the manager's personal wealth. The advantages of setting up this kind of firm are no constraints after receiving permission from the banking authority and no regulatory capital required.

Investment firms classified as ex art. 106 have no specific constraints, very little supervision, and no constraints applied to regulatory capital. These are relatively small firms composed of a limited number of investors. Its managers are allowed to manage the money of other investors. Nevertheless, some conditions must be met such as permission to start operating.

Investment firms classified as ex art. 107 face the same constraints set for banks and there is strong supervision since every investment generates regulatory capital usage like a bank. These operators function the same as the ex art. 106 class but are much larger in size, have a larger amount of investors, and must be supervised.

4.2.3 **The role of Basel II on private equity investments for banks and investment firms**

The Basel II framework describes a comprehensive measure and minimum standard for capital adequacy that national supervisory authorities are asked to implement through domestic rule-making and adoption procedures.

It is not the purpose of this book to explain the effects of Basel II financial systems, but it must be emphasized that, according to the European directive on the capital adequacy of investment firms and credit institutions adopted in each country by ad hoc rules, private equity finance does not represent a profitable business for either investment firms or banks.

Among all assets, private equity (and venture capital) is declared as one of the most risky, and for this reason it must be weighted more to reflect risks associated with the investment. The Basel Committee suggests that national authorities use a risk weight of 150% or higher.

At the same time and according to the same principles, participations in firms denominated as equity exposures follow similar rules. For regulatory and supervisory purposes, participations must be deducted from the capital base for the risk-weighted capital ratio calculation or must be risk-weighted at no lower than 100% independent of the approach used by financial institutions.

These rules do not ban direct and indirect investments in equity. Instead they enormously reduce the opportunities, because banks and financial institutions find this type of deal very expensive compared to other transactions. In summary, the Basel Committee (national authorities) assumes that banks and investment firms are not the right vehicles for promoting private equity and venture capital finance among countries.

According to the Bank Act, caps always must be respected. The Basel II framework creates new limitations for the capital ratio calculation for investments in insurance and financial companies. Participations in these firms, for regulatory and supervisory purposes, must be deducted from the capital base. For general equity exposures a special risk weight system is provided.

Private equity and venture capital deals are contemplated as "high-risk" exposures so they must be risk-weighted at 100% (under the standard approach option). If the company the bank invests in shows negative net earnings for two years, the risk-weighted percentage is 200%.

If banks adopt the internal rating base (IRB) approach the treatment is the same and the high-risk assumption remains. For equity participations different from those deducted from the capital base, there are three models. The simplest model, which is also the most wide-ranging, calculates the exposure at default (EAD) using these percentages:

190% for private equity instruments only if diversification is adequate
290% for listed equity instruments
370% for all others equity instruments

Contrary to the loss given default (LGD) factor of 45% that is a reference point for certain debt exposures, private, well-diversified equity instruments have an assumed LGD of 65% and 90% for all other cases.

Box: Equity investments through banks and investment firms

"Golden rules" followed by banks and investment firms regarding equity investment:

Equity investment is free (has no limits in place) for investment firms, while it is capped for banks
Banks can operate wider than investment firms by giving deeper assistance to participating firms
No caps for holding equity investment
For both banks and investment firms, the investment in equity generates a usage of regulatory capital
Rules generated by the Basel II framework make private equity finance costly for banks and investment firms
The usage of regulatory capital means the internal rate of return (IRR) of the investment must be compared and correlated to the cost of used regulatory capital.

Investment firms classified as ex art. 106 or ex art. 113 have no supervision because the national authority (Bank of Italy) has chosen to only supervise investment firms that are more organized and bigger. Because of this, there are a different set of rules applicable to ex art. 107 institutions. They are very similar to those defined for banks with some differences such as reduced capital ratio for investment firms whose sources are not collected from retail investors and the chance to adopt an easier standard approach methodology.

With ex art. 107 institutions exposure in private equity and venture capital deals is contemplated as high risk so they must be risk-weighted at 100%. For investment firms adopting the IRB approaches, the same rules provided for banks must be followed.

4.3 CLOSED-END FUNDS AND AMCs: PRINCIPLES AND RULES

According to the definition of financial services proposed by the EU, there are some activities that cannot be offered by banks directly[1] but can be managed by specialized organizations such as funds, special investment firms, and other structures accepted by single country regulations.

In private equity business, the most relevant non-banking activity is asset management, because it assumes a direct or indirect investment in firms. The following sections provide more detail about the most common structures used throughout Europe to invest in private equity.

There are two reference structures used to manage investment in firms:

Limited partnership
Funds and AMCs

Limited partnerships are available in both the UK and the US and will be presented in Chapter 5. The fund structures are presented next.

4.3.1 Funds

Funds are financial institutions where a separate manager or firm (AMC) manages a specific amount of money. The operating structure of a fund is seen in Figure 4.3.

Because European legislation requires supervision of financial institutions, control of the responsible managers becomes inevitable. Managers created a separate entity, the so-called AMC, so they can be supervised. In countries where

---

[1] According to the EU, there are six activities that banks cannot manage directly. They are also known as financial services and are regulated by the Financial Services Act:

- Dealing — buying and selling securities to obtain a profit

- Brokerage — buying and selling securities on a customer's behalf; in this case no risk is taken from the financial institution's side, therefore the profit derives from fees only

- Selling — selling the customer's securities in the primary market

- Underwriting — buying the securities in the primary market; the financial institution assumes the whole risk of the percentage of securities underwritten

- Individual (personal) asset management — managing the assets of private investors on an individual basis

- Non-individual asset management — managing private individuals' wealth on a non-individual basis; best used for its diversification advantages (since the wealth of a single investor might not be enough to appropriately diversify the portfolio of investments) and its related benefits

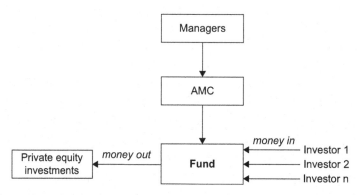

FIGURE 4.3

The organizational structure of funds.

the fund system is adopted, the AMC is one of the financial institutions included and defined by acts providing for financial services management.

There are three main groups of funds:

Open-end
Closed-end
Hedge fund

An open-end fund is defined as the floating size fund; investors are able to exit continuously whenever they want to. The most relevant features of this fund are

Liquidity. It should be able to manage its liquidity at any time, which is the reason it invests mainly in listed securities.

It is principally dedicated to the retail market.

It cannot invest in private equity.

Since the intention is to describe private equity business, the detailed description of this type of fund is beyond the scope of this book.

A closed-end fund includes non-floating size funds; investor are able to invest only at the initial phase of the fund (during the fundraising process described in Chapter 3) and exit only at the life-end of the fund. This fund can invest in private equity because private equity business needs resources and liquidity without any kind of exit pressure from the investor's side. Closed-end funds are a separate entity that invests money for a community of investors. The relationship between parties involved is mainly based on mutual trust. Investors invest their own money in a specific fund because they trust the manager's ability to successfully manage this money.

A hedge fund is able to leverage unlike the other two types of funds described above. It can be either an open- or closed-end fund depending on its purpose. The fund supervisor decides who invests in the fund (i.e., according to EU regulations, retail investors cannot invest in these funds due to the high risk). The vehicles used to invest in private equity are a double level system containing the

AMC
Closed-end fund

4.3.2 AMC

An AMC is a financial institution that hosts funds (both closed- and open-end) and manages financial services as defined by the Banking Acts (i.e., AMC may supply personal management of savings, dealing, brokerage, or advisory).

Rules concerning AMCs are the same throughout Europe. The set of rules for closed-end funds is very short with regulatory activity delegated to the country's supervisor and the internal code of activity of each fund created. This will be explained in more detail in the following paragraphs.

AMCs can manage only one type of fund, either an open- or closed-end. This country-specific rule is in place to better regulate the typical relationship between companies and the financial system.

Rules for AMCs:

Minimum requisites to operate
Governance
Management

The application of these rules is verified from the supervisor of the country in which the AMC operates, and they can be partially modified from one country to another. Supervision is carried out for the life of the AMC.

4.3.2.1 *The minimum requisites to operate for AMC*

The minimum requisites to operate for AMCs are similar in all EU countries:

Regulatory capital should exceed €1 million or should be over €0.12 million for the so-called "short capital asset management company" (junior asset management company).

Should prepare a detailed business plan that clearly shows

- Activities
- Services and products
- Organizational structure

■ Future development of the company
■ Economic and financial forecasted statements

Shareholders must show requisites of capability to manage the company.
AMC has to allow easy supervision.

According to the law, junior capital AMC is very similar to standard AMC, but there are some fundamental differences:

Junior capital AMCs should manage and promote closed-end funds only.

Majority shareholders should belong to universities, research centers, public institutions, public or private foundations, and chambers of commerce.

The amount of money managed at the start up must be under €25 million.

Subscribers of the closed-end fund must be qualified and not retailers.

The minimum subscription must be €0.25 million.

The mission must be venture capital financing and/or high-tech venture financing.

Junior AMCs are set up by municipalities and regions encouraging investments in seed and start-up financing phases. In Europe no university owns a junior AMC.

Nevertheless, the disadvantage of a junior capital AMC is the elevated risk to investments. These investments require more invested equity to benefit from diversification. Therefore, considering their "short" capital determined by law, they are unable to diversify, so the risk borne by investors is quite high.

4.3.2.2 *Governance rules for AMC*

All minimum requisites are actively controlled and monitored by a supervisor:

Board of directors must show, at any time, requisites of "professional attitude, honor, and independence" (this is the only constraint applied by the Financial Services Act for the AMC, which is not used for any other financial institution regulated by the same act).

Shareholders must grant fair management within the company.

No caps or limits applied for any category of shareholders (i.e., the shareholding structure can be composed by banks, insurance companies, etc.).

Management must be clear and based on strong organization.

4.3.2.3 *Management rules for AMC*

The supervisor also controls and monitors requisites for management activity (see Figure 4.4):

The AMC can develop a range of financial services as outlined in the Financial Services Act.

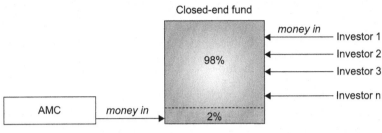

FIGURE 4.4

The organizational structure of funds.

The AMC develops (and sells) consulting services in the field of corporate finance and strategies only for closed-end funds.

The AMC has to subscribe to at least 2% of every fund managed (closed- or open-end), creating a commitment to investors' interests.

Regulatory capital is driven only from operational and financial risks.

4.3.3 Closed-end funds

As previously mentioned, funds are a separate[2] amount of money given from the subscribers and managed by the AMC. This money is used to invest in financial assets or in other assets such as real estate, gold, etc. The funds can be open- or closed-end. The distinction is driven by two parameters:

Maturity (fixed or not)
Amount of money to invest (fixed or not)

Closed-end funds have a fixed maturity and a fixed amount of money to invest and are used to invest in private equity. Because of the strong distinction between open and closed-end funds, it is typical to find that:

Open-end funds are mostly retail oriented and their securities representative are listed on the stock exchange.

Closed-end funds are most often wholesale oriented and their securities are rarely listed.

Investors in open-end funds take their profit or loss from selling the securities continuously and when they want.

---

[2] This amount of money, invested by the fund's investors, is separated from the asset management company.

Investors in closed-end funds take their profit or loss at the end of the fund's life, after the total disinvestment has taken place and after the fund has been closed.

Rules for closed-end funds include

General framework:

- Maturity
- Disinvestment process
- Certificate
- Loans
- Amount of investments

Internal code of activity:

- A clear pattern of rules
- A complete set of rules
- A synthetic approach

Investment policy:

- Assets fund may invest in
- Assets fund may not invest in
- Limitation on asset allocation
- Limitation on asset management

Relationships with the market:

- Presence of public offering
- Absence of public offering

In Europe the internal code of activity, according to the AMC funds system, is not a contract but an act approved by the supervisor defining the relationship between the AMC and the fund investors. It is a set of managerial rules supervised by authorities to be used during the life of the fund: it is a strong expression of the freedom of an AMC.

4.3.3.1 *General framework for closed-end funds*

To create a structure for the development and use of closed-end funds, a number of general variables must be defined; for example, rules concerning maturity and amount of investment loans and securities grants to financial institutions and investors so they can evaluate the strategic consequences of their involvement.

Typically, the closed-end fund maturity is no longer than 30 years and has to be strictly linked to the profile of investments. In Europe the average maturity is around 10 to 12 years.

The total disinvestment cannot be realized all at once and, for this reason, general rules provide for extra time to complete this phase. The EU average disinvestment process can be extended for three years after the fixed maturity of the fund. The AMC can disinvest without investor approval, but investors should be notified at least six months before the fund closure. There are specific rules about the investment process. It must last for a maximum of 18 months and at the end it is possible to revise down the amount of money of the fund.

Specific regulations are also provided for securities issued by closed-end funds. The original securities have to be listed on the stock exchange if their value is under €25,000. However, the IPO and the listing in a stock exchange are very unusual for closed-end funds, because the portfolio of investments is mainly composed of private companies so the value of the securities cannot be fairly measured. The average value of each investment certificate size is of €1 million.

It must be underlined that the value of securities is fixed by the AMC. By law, there is a floor of €50,000 when investments are concentrated on unlisted assets.

The general framework is particularly severe about lending. Loans can be used only when the AMC registers a lack of liquidity due to the transfer of disinvested amounts (the lack of liquidity is only a matter of days and occurs when the transfer of money requires a number of days; to respect the deadline date, this gap is covered by a loan). Through leveraging, the AMC gives the money back to fund subscribers before the end of the fund's maturity, but the amount of loans cannot exceed 10% of the overall investment.

There are provisions for investments. The amount of investment is fixed and decided by the AMC (in Europe the average size of a fund is around €200 million to 400 million, while funds exceeding the amount of €1 billion are called mega-funds). No caps or floors are set by law, since this is mostly a matter of negotiation between the AMC and the supervising authority.

Finally, the general framework for a closed-end fund is characterized by the commitment plan: the investor commits himself to meet the percentage of the investment required by the AMC when investing. This is necessary because investments are not undertaken immediately after the fundraising phase, but during the first 2 to 3 years of the operating life of the fund. Investors must commit to paying the required amount during the investment period. This is mainly based on the mutual trust between parties.

4.3.3.2 *Internal code of activities for closed-end funds*

In the presence of a very detailed general framework, EU regulations still allow the AMCs independence and self-determination to define the closed-end funds they want to manage. According to the law, the AMC regulates each closed-end fund regarding certification size, maturity of the fund, geographic area of investments, etc.

These items represent the internal code of activities; the specific set of rules followed by a closed-end fund. Generally the internal code of activity can be divided into three parts:

1. Detailed scheme for each of the managed funds
2. Technical and legal profiles of the managed funds
3. The way the fund works

The internal code lists critical traits that distinguish vehicles:

Typologies of investments (typologies of shares, liquidity percentage, geographic areas)

Use or no use of loans (percentage, goals, maturity)

Governance rules within the venture-backed firms

Amount of fees given to the AMC

Criteria of subscribing the certificates

Criteria of divesting

Criteria of payback for subscribers

Criteria of calculation (at least every 6 months) of the current value of certificates

4.3.3.3 *The investment policy for closed-end funds*

The closed-end fund internal code is the most important document for closed-end fund strategy and management. It is not only related to the general characteristics of the fund, but it also disposes policy.

The internal code defines instruments, securities, and deals in which the fund can or cannot invest. Closed-end funds *can* invest in

Financial instruments

Real estate

Commercial credits

Other goods that have a market where quotations are available at least every 6 months

Banking deposits

Cash

Closed-end funds *cannot* invest in

Forwards
Securities issued by the AMC
Securities issued by (or goods sold by) AMC shareholders

The investment policy is also related to asset allocation and use of voting rights. For closed-end funds there are several limitations:

20% cap to invest within the same issuer for unlisted securities

5% cap to invest within the same issuer for listed securities (up to 35% if securities are granted from a EU government or from an international institution)

20% cap to invest in the same bank's deposit

10% cap to invest in OTC derivatives

30% cap to invest in financial assets issued by subjects belonging to the same group

At the same time, AMCs have to consider their limits:

10% cap of voting rights within a listed company

No possibility of full ownership on a listed company (except for LBO deals, where the maturity of the investment is short)

4.3.3.4 *Definition of public and "reserved" offer*

For AMCs or closed-end funds, the relationship with potential investors is key in order to distinguish when a public offer occurs.

Here the law is very simple: a public offer can never occur when the closed-end fund is "reserved." A closed-end fund is considered reserved if

1. It is dedicated to less than 100 investors
2. The value of the certificate is higher than €50,000
3. Investors are all professional investors

When there is a public offer it is necessary to set up a circular offer and an information memorandum, applying local country rules.

Securities can be listed on the stock exchange, if the internal dealing code anticipates this possibility. However, the minimum amount to go public and trade on the stock exchange is €25 million for each fund. It is then necessary to follow domestic procedures to enter the stock exchange, which are the same as for an IPO (in Europe, a specialist is required).

4.4 **REASONS FOR CHOOSING A CLOSED-END FUND RATHER THAN BANKS OR INVESTMENT FIRMS**

The "golden rules" for equity investment in closed-end funds are different when compared to banks and investment firms:

Equity investment is not capped for closed-end funds.

Closed-end funds can operate wider as banks only if they are related or joined with a banking group.

There is a cap to the holding period for the equity investment related to the maturity of the closed-end fund.

The investment in equity does not generate a usage of regulatory capital.

The IRR of the investment must be compared and correlated to the cumulated IRR of the portfolio and to the target IRR of the closed-end fund.

4.5 **THE RELATIONSHIP BETWEEN CLOSED-END FUNDS AND AMCs: ECONOMIC AND FINANCIAL LINKS**

The relationship between the AMC and the closed-end fund is quite complex both economically and financially (see Figure 4.5). Groups with a significant role in this relationship include

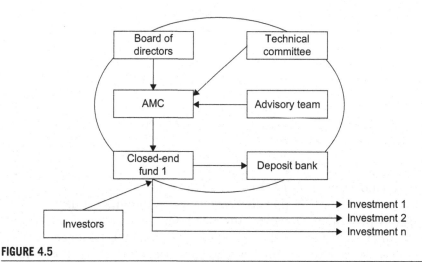

FIGURE 4.5

The relationship between the AMC, closed-end fund, and the main groups involved.

AMCs
AMC's board of directors
Closed-end fund(s)
Investors
Deposit bank
Advisory team (or company)
Technical committee

The AMC is composed of

1. Board of Directors — Oftentimes agrees with its shareholders who decide to launch the AMC
2. Advisory company — External company that by law must be completely separate from the AMC
3. Technical committee

Tasks and duties for all groups involved are quite clear and stated:

AMC has the responsibility to manage the closed-end fund, even though the assets coming from investors are separate from AMC assets. AMC is responsible within the investors.

AMC's Board of Directors is responsible for managing the AMC.

Closed-end fund(s) are owned and managed by the AMC.

Investors purchase certificates issued from the closed-end fund.

Deposit bank receives the money raised by the fundraising process from the fund.

Advisory team (or company), if it exists, is a company chosen from the AMC to analyze potential investment, develop due diligence, and evaluate exit strategy.

Technical committee is a team of technicians operating inside the AMC. It supports the Board of Directors to define strategies, to monitor the market, and to share the recommendations coming from the advisory company.

4.5.1 General overview of costs and revenues

The closed-end fund is the origin of costs and revenues for all groups. Its revenues include

Capital gain from investments
Dividends and interests from investments
Interest from deposit bank

Its costs include

Losses from investment
Interest due for loans
Management fee to AMC
Carried interest to AMC

The AMC distributes costs and revenues created from the closed-end fund and receives as revenues:

Entrance fee from investors
Management fee from the closed-end fund
Carried interest from the closed-end fund

The costs it bears are

Operating costs
Deposit bank fee
Percentage of management fee for the advisor
Percentage of carried interest to advisory company for its efforts with help-ing to identify the best possible opportunities in the market

4.5.2 Management fee

The management fee[3] is due annually[4] and is calculated as a percentage of the net asset value (NAV)[5] of the closed-end fund. However, the higher the manage-ment fee, the lower the amount of money left for investment activity. Defining the percentage of the management fee is negotiated between the AMC and investors, since it is in the best interest of the investor to pay a lower percent-age of fixed costs, while the opposite holds true for the AMC.

This fee cannot be too low, because it is meant to cover all operating costs incurred by the AMC. The management fee is a gross fee, since it covers operating expenses, pays the Advisory Company and the Technical Committee and fixed costs, and in the end the remuneration[6] for the AMC director.

[3] The average amount could range between 2 and 3.5%.
[4] It can be computed at the initial phase at time 0.
[5] Net asset value is the total value of the portfolio of investments less any liabilities. But, as men-tioned previously, closed-end funds cannot leverage.
[6] Salaries but not the capital gain.

4.5.3 **Carried interest**

Carried interest is due only at the end of the closed-end fund and it is a percentage[7] of the difference between the global IRR of the closed-end fund and a fixed interest rate ("hurdle rate" or "floor IRR") as defined at the starting date of the closed-end fund. It is computed as follows:

$$Carried\ Interest = \%[Final\ IRR - Hurdle\ Rate]$$

It is the percentage of profits the AMC receives from investors in the form of capital gain and it goes to the directors/managers of the fund itself.

Carried interest and the floor rate are fixed at the beginning of the fund's life and they appear at the internal code of activity of each fund. They are determined through long negotiations between investors and the AMC.

Sometimes, by using a private agreement, a predetermined percentage of both the management fee and the carried interest is transferred by the AMC to the advisory company. There is a strong link between the reputation of the advisory company and the percentage it can obtain by the end of the disinvestment phase as capital gain.

Consider the situation in the table in Figure 4.6, where the floor rate (hurdle rate) is 7,5%, carried interest is 30%, and at the end the global IRR generated NAV is 178%. This represents 30% of (178% − 7.5%) revenues obtained by the AMC at the maturity of the closed-end fund. The final carried interest earned by the AMC is of 68,50% (or 51,15% of the final NAV of the fund after payment of management fees), while the remaining amount to be distributed to the fund's investors is 165,42, showing a global IRR of 65,42% of the initial amount invested.

4.6 **USABLE VEHICLES FOR PRIVATE EQUITY FINANCE IN THE EU**

Despite all attempts to standardize the regulatory approach in the EU, several financial institutions may be used as vehicles for the realization of private equity finance in each country. For example, in Italy, a closed-end fund is the best way to manage private equity finance, despite banks or investment firms that may also realize these deals.

The same conclusions may be reached for every European country. Throughout Europe, a double system is evident:

Limited partnership model (similar to the UK and US)
AMC funds scheme

---

[7] Typically ranging between 15 and 40%.

Data entry	time 0									
Management fee	2,50%									
Floor IRR	7,50%									
Carried interest	30%									
Forecast	**Year 1**	**Year 2**	**Year 3**	**Year 4**	**Year 5**	**Year 6**	**Year 7**	**Year 8**	**Year 9**	**Year 10**
Net asset value (NAV)	100	103	115	178	180	195	245	247	278	
Management Fee	2,50	2,58	3,05	2,88	4,45	4,50	4,88	6,13	6,18	6,95

Global IRR on NAV[8]	178%
Difference between IRRs[9]	170,50%
Carried Interest	51,15%
Final profit & loss account	**Year 10**
NAV y-10	278
Cumulated management fee[10]	44,08
NAV y-10 after management fee[11]	233,93
Carried interest[12]	68,50
NAV y-10 for investors[13]	**165,42**

FIGURE 4.6

An example of the way to calculate management fee and carried interest earned by the AMC, along with the final return delivered to a fund's investors.

According to the EVCA, the legal and tax environment is not homogeneous (see Figure 4.7).

4.6.1 The legal framework for private equity finance in France

France provides several structure typologies for private equity finance.

"Fonds commun de placement à risques" (FCPR)
"Fonds commun de placement dans l'innovation" (FCPI)
"Fonds d'investissement de proximité" (FIP)
"Société de capital-risque" (SCR)

The first three are organized as funds in a collective investment scheme, while the SCR are commercial companies that have opted for special tax treatment with specific requirements. Among these options, the FCPR is the most common.

FCPR is a closed-end fund, but it is not a separate entity, therefore, it has no legal capacity to enter into agreements. Any agreement must be executed by the management company on the FCPR's behalf.

Management companies have to be approved by the Autorité des Marchés de France (AMF) and comply with organizational and conduct of business rules intended to ensure investor protection and the legality of transactions. The equity capital must be at least €125,000 and once authorized, it must be at any time equal or higher than

€125,000 + 0.02% × asset under management in excess of €250,000
25% of general expenses of the preceding financial year

Moreover, the FCPR and SCR must meet several quotas and ratios regarding their invested assets.

4.6.2 The legal framework for private equity finance in Germany

In Germany there are no specific laws regarding private equity, but there are laws regarding promotion of venture capital (WKBG) and equity investment companies (UBGG). Thus, under German law, there is no specific vehicle for private equity.

Theoretically, all legal corporate forms are available for private equity finance development. The most common and suitable form is the limited partnership where a limited liability company (GmbH) is a general partner (so-called GmbH & Co. KG). There are no restrictions on foreign entities who want to invest in Germany or want to market themselves to German investors.

German corporate law establishes that the minimum share capital depends on the legal form of entity: €25,000 for a limited liability company and €50,000

Country	Presence of a regulation and vehicles for private	The preferable structure for private equity finance	Freedom on undue restrictions on	EVCA global score (1 = highest; 3 = worst)
Italy	Yes	Closed-end fund (Fondo chiuso)	Yes	0,088194444
Austria	Yes	Mittelstands-finanzerungs-gesellschaft (MiFiG)	No	2,00
Belgium	Yes	Private PRICAF	Yes	1,00
Chyprus	n.a.	n.a.	n.a.	n.a.
Czech republic	Yes	Qualified Investor Fund	Yes	0,088194444
Denmark	Yes	Limited Partnership (K/S)	Yes	1,17
Estonia	Yes	Limited Liability Company	Yes	2,17
Finland	Yes	Limited Partnership (Ky)	Yes	1,00
France	Yes	Fonds Commun de Placement à Risque (FCPR)	Yes	1,00
Germany	Yes	Limited Partnership (GmbH & Co KG)	Yes	1,33
Greece	Yes	AKES	No	1,33
Hungary	Yes	Private Equity Fund	Yes	1,00
Ireland	Yes	Limited Partnership	Yes	1,00
Latvia	Yes	Latvian Limited Partnership (Komandits-abiedriba)	Yes	1,00
Lithuania	Yes	Investment Fund	Yes	1,00
Luxembourg	Yes	Société d' Investissement en Capital à Risque (SICAR)	Yes	1,33
Netherlands	Yes	Commanditaire Vennotschap (CV)	Yes	1,33
Norway	Yes	Limited parnership (KS) and Limited liability company (AS)	Yes	1,17
Poland	Yes	Closed-End Investment Fund for Non-Public Assets (CEIF)	Yes	0,088194444
Portugal	Yes	Fundo de Capital de Risco (FCR)	Yes	1,00
Romania	n.a.	n.a.	n.a.	n.a.
Slovakia	Yes	Limited Liability Company	Yes	0,099305556
Slovenia	Yes	Venture Capital Company (VCC)	Yes	2,17
Spain	Yes	Sociedad de Capital de Riesgo (SCR) and Fondo de Capital de Riesgo (FCR)	No	2,00
Sweden	Yes	Swedish Limited Partnership	Yes	0,088194444
Switzerland	Yes	Fund under the KAG	Yes	1,17

FIGURE 4.7

Preferred vehicles for private equity finance in Europe according to the EVCA.

for AG. Also, companies qualifying as either a venture capital company or equity investment company need a capital of €1 million.

4.6.3 The legal framework for private equity finance in the Netherlands

There are no Dutch laws solely concerning private equity finance. The Financial Service Authority (AFS) interprets private equity operators as investment institutions that must be licensed and regulated under the existing financial laws.

Private equity deals may be realized using the available forms for non-financial companies. The options include public company (NV), mutual funds (FGR), private company (BV), or limited partnership (CV). Limited partnership is the most common.

AFS regulated investment managers must have an equity capital of at least €225,000 if assets under management are above €250 million, €125,000 if below.

4.6.4 The legal framework for private equity finance in Spain

In Spain non-regulated private equity vehicles (NRV) follow rules provided for commercial companies and regulated private equity vehicles (RV). RVs enjoy favorable tax treatment but have to comply with a number of regulatory requirements such as investment and concentration limits, reporting, and all regulatory rules issued by the market authority (CNMV).

Within RVs, the two structures most suitable for private equity finance are

Regulated private equity entities under corporate form or SCR
Regulated private equity entities under contractual form (i.e., funds) or FCR

RVs have their own law and regulations, and they can be run by

Regulated private equity management companies (SGECR), which are regulated by specific private equity regulation and must have an initial capital of at least €300,000

Investment collective scheme management companies (SGIIC), which are regulated and must have an initial capital not lower than the highest of the following amounts:

1. €300,000 + specific amount depending on the executed activities
2. 25% of the structure costs of the previous fiscal year

There are no specific capital requirements or regulation rules for NRVs.

Legal framework in the United States and United Kingdom for equity investors

INTRODUCTION

In the UK, investment in equity is not regulated by the financial system laws because of the common law framework and the general idea that a market discipline that is more powerful and important than regulating financial players. Hence, private equity investment is not recognized as a financial service, unlike in Europe where it is unsupervised. These are reasons why British legislators do not supervise private equity investors:

The private equity market in the US is the largest one in the world, therefore it is able to identify the proper rules governing its activities.

The UK is the most important market in Europe with rules very similar to the US market.

This chapter describes the regulating frameworks of the US and UK financial markets. The first section introduces the topic and underlines different options available for private equity investments and causes that lead to the different financial environments of continental Europe and the UK. Sections two and three illustrate which financial vehicles are used in the US and the UK. Section four presents definition and calculation modalities of carried interest and management fees in the UK environment. The last section analyzes the most important legal clauses signed in a limited partnership agreement (LPA).

5.1 WHY THE US AND UK DIFFER FROM THE EU: THE COMMON LAW VERSUS CIVIL LAW SYSTEM AND THE IMPACT OF SUPERVISION AND REGULATION

There are different vehicles/investors used to set up equity investments:

Banks (and investment firms)
Private firms
Business Angels
Specialized vehicles to invest

In each country's framework these vehicles/investors have different organizational structures and different involvement profiles as direct investors in equity investments.

Analysis of the private equity sector cannot be generalized. The most important feature depends on how the policymakers create the legislative environment for the whole industry development, and how financial institutions interpret the industry and its capacity to create concrete opportunities for growth.

In both the US and the UK no special discipline for equity investment exists. However, it is possible to summarize some equity investments in the UK that differ from the European framework:

- No limits on holding shares for shareholders
- No distinction in investment based on the European "banking system" and "financial services system"
- Usage of rules for
  Market discipline (corporate governance)
  Investors, duties and rights

5.2 RULES FOR US EQUITY INVESTORS

The US financial market is common law driven, and great importance is placed on laws from both local as well as federal courts. Federal laws have created a general framework for a financial system based on relevant financial activities, not financial institutions.

The pillars are

- Discipline for stock exchange and securities — The stock exchange represents the financial market and there are no financial market laws in place.
- Corporate governance rules — Rules concerning the governance of each company issuing securities.

- Discipline for insurance and pension funds — These are the most important players in the US market; pension funds are the largest investors followed by insurance companies.
- General rules for banks — In the US banks do not collaborate with investment firms, so rules concern only banks; in the EU there are no equity holding constraints.[1]

In US fiscal history there are three main Acts that drive trends in equity investment development.

- Small Business Investment Act (1958) — Created small business investment companies (SBICs). These investment vehicles were set up as public–private partnerships to invest in private equity. The federal government backed the SBICs by giving them the financial support needed to invest in private equity and therefore enhance the development of the country.
- Revenue Act (1978) — Introduced the mark down for capital gain taxation. The federal government decided that private individuals investing in private equity are exempt from paying tax on capital gains when they are reinvested in private equity.
- Employee Retirement Income Security Act (1979) —This act wrote off the "prudent man rule"[2] facilitating investment in private equity for pension funds.

Despite these laws it is still impossible to find a specific discipline for equity investment, and a specific discipline for equity investment for the bank sector does not exist. However, from a legal point of view, equity investors in the United States could be

Venture capital funds
SBICs
Corporate ventures
Banks
Business Angels

---

[1] This decision was made in 1999 after The Glass-Steagall Act was dismantled. This Act, passed by Congress in 1933, prohibited commercial banks from collaborating with full-service brokerage firms or participating in investment banking activities.

[2] The Prudent Man Rule is based on common law stemming from an 1830 Massachusetts court decision, which adopted a standard to guide those responsible for investing other people's money. Per the standard, such fiduciaries (executors of wills, trustees, bank trust departments, and administrators of estates) must act as a prudent man or woman would be expected to act, with discretion and intelligence, to seek reasonable income, preserve capital, and, in general, avoid speculative investments.

Today, venture capital funds along with SBICs constitutes approximately 60% of the US private equity market, while the other investment vehicles (corporate ventures, banks, and Business Angels) constitute the remaining 40%.

5.2.1 Venture capital funds

Venture capital funds are not based on the European system of closed-end funds, instead they are limited partnerships (LPs). The name refers to the limited liability of the providers (limited partners) of capital. A venture capital fund is a typical way to create a company in the United States and its common forms include:

Sole proprietorship (SP)
Partnership (P)
Limited-liability partnership (LLP)
Limited partnership (LP)
S corporation (S-Corp)
C corporation (C-Corp)

This means that equity investment is considered simply as a business and not a financial activity, unlike the European framework.

LPs show a fixed life equity investment; LPs with a maturity of 10 years are the most common since US regulation states a maturity of 10 years (plus 2 years of extra time[3]) creates a tax exemption for these companies. The shareholding structure of LPs (see Figure 5.1) is made up of two different categories of partners (shareholders):

- Limited
- General

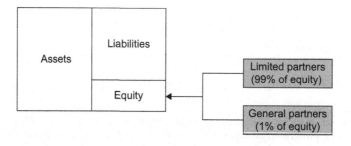

FIGURE 5.1

Shareholding structure of LPs.

---

[3] This extra time is given to the private equity funds for the disinvestment process so they can take advantage of different market opportunities.

In an LP the investment manager is the general partner, while providers of capital are the limited partners. The partnership is governed by an LPA negotiated and signed by the parties involved. This agreement is similar to the EU internal code of activity introduced in Chapter 4.

When drafting an LPA keep in mind

- The state[4] where the fund is established, since it is crucial that the environment understands the business
- The contract must include everything because this type of business is unsupervised.

Limited partners are investors of funds, they do not manage the company and their liability is limited to the extent of their investment. However, their participation in the company's equity is consistent (99% of the stake). In the American private equity funds, each limited partner must be an "accredited investor":[5] a person or legal entity, such as a company or trust fund, that meets certain net worth and income qualifications and is considered to be sufficiently sophisticated to make investment decisions about complex securities and businesses. If there is no accredited investor, then it is necessary to use the protection of Securities Act for common investors.

General partners are managers of the company and they are fully liable for business debt. General partners control the company and manage investments. The investment of general partners is about 1% of invested funds. Due to the high-risk exposure of general partners, these partners operate as limited partners of an advisory company set up as a limited liability partnership (LLP) to reduce their risk. In the LLP, the liability of partners is limited to the extent of their investments; nevertheless, the partnership is fully liable for business debt. General partners cover their risk exposure by signing insurance contracts with insurance companies. These rarely used contracts considerably reduce risk but they are very expensive[6] and negatively impact the final IRR of the overall investment portfolio (see Figure 5.2).

The great success of limited partnerships is twofold: they are simple and characterized by a transparent taxation profile. There is full flexibility regarding earnings distributed and the allocation of capital gains and losses to the limited partners. Therefore, each limited partner keeps its specific fiscal profile with no exemption.

---

[4] California, Delaware, and Massachusetts are the only states that understand the environment.

[5] Regulation D of the Securities Act of 1933 permits accredited investors to invest in a private partnership without the protection of a registered public offering under the Securities Act. Qualifications for a person are $1 million net worth or annual income exceeding $200,000 individually or $300,000 with a spouse.

[6] Generally the total cost is around 2% of the overall fund managed.

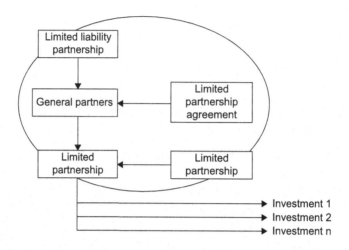

FIGURE 5.2

Organizational structure of venture capital funds.

LPs typically attract investors such as banks, insurance companies, pension funds, private investors, etc.

These companies are able to leverage, unlike their European counterpart. Because of this, they combine equity and debt to reach a higher IRR.

General partners should be able to manage fundraising with the limited partners and financial institutions that provide debt to the fund. American LPs also allow extra time for the disinvestment phase. As established by law, the maximum extra time allowed is two years after the maturity of the fund.

5.2.2 Small business investment companies

The Small Business Investment Act, enacted by the US Congress in 1958, created a partnership between the federal government and private capital to finance the country's small business community.

SBICs are financial institutions that provide equity capital to small businesses. They are licensed by the US Small Business Administration but are privately managed. In return for pledging to finance businesses, SBICs qualify for long-term financing from the public authority. Therefore, SBICs are partnerships between private and public investors in an equal percentage. The federal government gives loans with a fixed low interest rate with a cap of one-third of the total debt and capital gains and other revenues are not taxed. Taxation starts with the distribution of earnings. Features of these companies include:

- Two different categories of shareholders each with 50% of the stake: public authority[7] and private investors
- Only private investors can manage the SBICs.

Today SBICs finance about 25% of the US private equity market ranked second behind venture capital funds.

5.2.3 Corporate ventures

Even though no specific laws are dedicated to corporate ventures, direct investment in equity made by corporations is quite developed. This vehicle usually is a subsidiary of a large corporation that makes venture capital investments. Corporations invest in teams, ideas, and projects that could be launched successfully. They invest in this type of vehicle to create new businesses and new companies that could prove useful for market positioning and competitiveness. In most cases corporate ventures are business related and represent a tool to sustain seed and start-up financing to increase their presence in the market.

5.2.4 Banks

It is rare to find banks involved in direct investments in equity, instead they invest through LPs. The banking system is involved in the equity market through dealing and brokerage rather than advisory and placement.

5.2.5 Business Angels

Business Angels are private investors that directly invest in private equity. They do not represent a legal cluster, instead they are equity investors devoted to sustaining seed and start-up financing but do not seek profit. In the United States these investors are exempt from taxation on capital gains generated by their private equity investment (transparency principle).

Examples of Business Angels are high net worth individuals, foundations, research centers, non-profit societies, corporations acting as donors, etc. They usually invest in a start-up, early-stage, or developing firm. They are significantly sustained by private equity investors, because they generally enhance investment possibilities and bear most of the risk. They often have managerial and/or technical experience to offer the management team as well as equity and debt finance. Furthermore, their investment view is medium- to long-term oriented and principally concentrated in high-risk situations.

5.3 RULES FOR UK EQUITY INVESTORS

The financial market in the UK is common law driven like the US, and great importance is given to laws from both local and federal courts. These laws have created a general framework for the UK financial systems; however, laws designed by the EU Banking and Financial Services Act are also available. This means that there is a great variety of legal solutions/typologies for equity investors. In the UK social and political attention is given to the "equity gap."[7]

These laws are considered crucial for equity investment development in the UK:

- Industrial and Financial Corporation Act (1945) — Created public funds to sustain small medium entities (SMEs) and start-ups.
- Business Start-Up Scheme (1981) and Business Expansion Scheme (1983) — Gave fiscal incentive for both corporations and private individuals to invest in equity. The intent of these schemes is to support and promote new, small businesses as well as expanding businesses to bring vacant retail units back into the investment stage.
- Enterprise Investment Scheme (1994) and Venture Capital Trusts Act (1997) — The Enterprise Investment Scheme (EIS) was designed to help small, higher-risk trading companies to raise financing by offering a range of tax reliefs to investors who purchase new shares in those companies. The Venture Capital Trusts Act was designed to encourage individuals to invest indirectly in a range of small, higher risk trading companies whose shares and securities are listed on a stock exchange by investing through venture capital trusts (VCTs).

Today, these Acts still work for companies as well as for private individuals. It is impossible to find a specific discipline for equity investment, and a specific discipline for equity investment and banks does not yet exist.

Equity investors in the UK use these vehicles:

- Venture capital funds
- VCTs
- Merchant banks

---

[7] See MacMillan Committee, Report of the Committee in Finance and Industry, London, 1931.

- Business Angels
- Dedicated public institutions

As in the US private equity market, venture capital funds along with the VCTs constitute over 50% of the UK private equity market, while the other investment vehicles (merchant banks, Business Angels, and dedicated public institutions) constitute the rest of the market.

5.3.1 Venture capital funds

This investment vehicle is structured as an LP, exactly like its American counterpart. In the UK these vehicles have a long operating history. The first venture capital fund operating in the UK started in 1907, and these early LPs are still operating today. Like the US framework, they have a fixed maturity of 10 years plus 2 years to take advantage of the tax transparency principle.

As in the United States, limited partners include:

Banks
Insurance companies
Pensions funds
Private investors
Corporate Investors

5.3.2 Venture capital trusts

First introduced in 1997, VCTs were created by the Venture Capital Trust Act and have met with great success in the UK market. Their relationship is defined through the mutual trust agreement between parities involved (see Figure 5.3).

The organizational structure of VCTs (see Figure 5.4) is based on a Trust defined as an amount of money separate (or separate amount of wealth) from the owner managed by professionals indicated as Trustee.

1. Trust — Group of investors (private individuals) investing their personal wealth

2. Trustee — Group of individuals managing the wealth of the trust

VCTs are companies listed on the stock exchange.[8] They are based on the concept of UK Trust, where the Trustee[9] has the same function as general partners in

---

[8] In the London Stock Exchange.
[9] They are fund managers that run the VCT, and are usually members of larger investment groups.

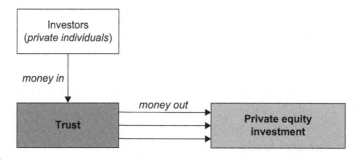

FIGURE 5.3

Investing process structure of trusts in the UK.

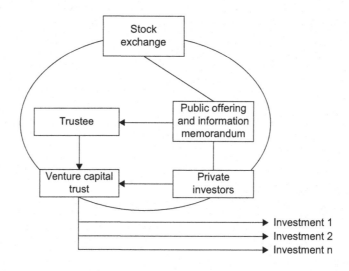

FIGURE 5.4

Organizational structure of VCTs.

LPs. Because they are listed companies, VCTs have no fixed maturity, hence they are considered as perpetual investments.

Only private individuals can subscribe to or buy shares in VCTs, which invest in trading companies by providing them with funds to promote development and growth. VCTs realize their investments and make new ones periodically; however, at least 70% of their investment portfolio is composed of unlisted companies. Fiscal incentive like participation exemption and reduction on earnings tax operates wider. VCTs are exempt from corporation tax on any gains arising from the disposal of their investments.

The main difference between the VCT and the European closed-end is their transparency level. After investors have transferred their personal wealth into a

VCT, they are unable to influence decisions made by the trust or trustee managers. Closed-end funds are completely transparent as defined by the EU regulating framework, whereas the VCT is completely blind because investors are uninformed about the composition of the investment portfolio. Therefore, there is no disclosure of the trust's investment activities. Another difference is that a VCT's trend cycle shows no correlation with the London Stock Exchange.

5.3.3 Merchant banks

Direct investment in equity is developed, even though they it is declining in volume, within banks dedicated to merchant banking business.[10] Like the United States, the UK banking system is much more involved in the equity market through dealing and brokerage rather than advisory and placement. However, private equity investments through merchant banking are common during seed, start-up, and early stage financing.

5.3.4 Business Angels

As in the US market, Business Angels do not represent a legal cluster but are identified as equity investors devoted to sustaining seed and start-up financing without a profit goal. Since these investors do not generate profit, they are represented by

- High net worth individuals
- Foundations
- Research centers
- Non-profit societies
- Corporations acting as donors

5.3.5 Dedicated public institutions

These are joint ventures between private investors (corporations or financial institutions) and public partners supported by a special local act dedicated just for them. Management rules are totally private, but some legal/fiscal ad hoc incentives are still in place. Unlike the SBICs operating in the US market, this type of investment vehicle operates at local levels under local laws with direct involvement by municipalities. Even though there is a profit goal, social valuations are considered during investment decisions.

---

[10] Financial institution that engages in investment banking, counseling, negotiating mergers and acquisitions, and a variety of other services including securities portfolio management for customers, insurance, the acceptance of foreign bills of exchange, dealing in bullion, and participating in commercial ventures.

5.4 CARRIED INTEREST AND MANAGEMENT FEE SCHEME: US AND UK SYSTEMS

The only complete integration of UK countries with the EU framework occurs during the origin of costs and revenues. As described in Chapter 4, vehicles through which investments generate revenue include:

- Capital gains from investments
- Dividends and interests from investments
- Interest from a deposit bank

While costs include:

- Losses from investment
- Interest due for loans
- Management fee to managers[11]
- Carried interest to managers

Considering the case of venture capital funds, revenues to general partners are the

- Entrance fee from investors
- Management fee
- Carried interest

While the costs general partners bear are the

- Operating costs
- Deposit bank fee
- Percentage of management fee for the advisor
- Percentage of carried interest to the advisory company for identifying the best opportunities in the market

5.4.1 Management fee

This is a fee charged by the general partners to the limited partners. Management fees in a private equity fund are annual and calculated as a percentage of the

---

[11] When considering LPs, the management fee goes to general partners who manage the company.

NAV[12] of the fund. Typically the fee ranges between 2 and 3.5% of the NAV, depending on the type and size of the fund.

The general partners' management fee may vary over the life of the fund; it might decrease over time as the limited partners' original committed capital is paid back from investment returns. However, the higher the management fee, the lower the amount of money left for investment activity.

The percentage of the NAV is a matter of negotiation between the general partners and limed partners, since it is in the investors, interest to pay a lower percentage of fixed costs, which is just the opposite for general partners. Since the percentage is meant to cover all operating costs, it should not be too low. The management fee is a gross fee covering the operating expenses as well as paying the Advisory Company, the Technical Committee, fixed costs, and the managers' remuneration.[13]

5.4.2 Carried interest

Carried interest is the general partner's share in the profits of a private equity fund. Typically, a fund must return the capital received from the LPs before the general partner can share in the fund's profits. The general partners then receive a percentage ranging from 15 to 40% of the net profits as "carried interest."

Like the EU framework, it is due when the fund matures. Carried interest is a percentage of the difference between the global IRR of the closed-end fund and a fixed interest rate (hurdle rate or floor IRR) as defined at the starting date of the closed-end fund.

$$Carried\ Interest = \%[Final\ IRR - Hurdle\ Rate]$$

Hurdle rates typically range from 5 to 10%.

Carried interest and the floor rate are fixed by the parties involved before the LP agreement is signed. They are determined after long negotiations between limited partners and general partners.

By using a private agreement, a predetermined percentage of both the management fee and the carried interest can be transferred by general partners to the advisory company. There is a strong link between the reputation of the advisory company and the percentage obtained at the end of the disinvestment phase as capital gain.

---

[12] NAV is the total value of the investment portfolio less any liabilities.
[13] Salaries but not the capital gain.

5.5 CLAUSES SIGNED IN AN LP AGREEMENT

Contrary to the EU countries, in the UK and the US there are no legal requirements dictating private equity investment agreements. However, for the US and
the UK, the national association of venture capitalists and private equity operators have proposed some "models" of legal documents and agreements that can
be used for private equity deals. The most common vehicle for private equity
investment is the LP. Clauses typically signed in an LPA include:[14]

- Parties — Identifies each person or institution who takes part in the initiative
- Introduction (or Recitals) — Explains why the LPA is signed
- Definitions and Interpretation — A list of references and terms used throughout the LPA
- Name and Place of Business — These self-explanatory statements are required by law, because an LP must have a name; the name and the principal place of business, together with other details, must be reported in the LPA
- Establishment — Information in this section is related to the most impor-tant features of the LP organization and key people proposing the deal
- Purpose of the Partnership — Fund description and the way general part-ners will carry on the fund's investment activities; description of invest-ment strategy constraints and limitations
- Duration of Partnership - Termination of Partnership — Life period of the partnership and rules or conditions for its termination
- Capital and Loan Contributions — Specifies the role and financial commit-ment of LPs
- Allocations, Sharing, and Distributions of Partnership Profits — Governs the order in which partners are repaid, partnership profits are allocated, the ratio in which the partners share profits between themselves, and how the profits are to be distributed to the limited partners and general partner
- Carried Interest — How the manager calculates the general partner's share of a private equity fund
- Appointment and Removal of the General Partner — Specifies under what conditions a general partner is appointed and/or removed from his position

---

[14] See the British Venture Capital Association Web site (http://www.bvca.co.ukwww.bvca.co.wk)
and the American Venture Capital Association Web site (http://www.nvca.orgwww.nvca.org).

- Powers, Rights, and Duties of the General Partner — Rights and duties of the general partner; the general partner is authorized to do everything necessary to operate the partnership

- Powers of Limited Partner — Limited partners are excluded from managing the partnership to ensure their limited liability against creditors; other powers cannot be generalized and are specified in every agreement

- Withdrawal of Partners — Rules for when a partner wants to leave the partnership or the partnership wants to expel the investor from the partnership

- Borrowing and Bridge Financing — Rules for the LP financial management

- Fees and Expenses — Rules concerning the calculation of the management fee, establishment costs, transaction costs, fee income

- Accounts and Reports — Documents and information prepared by the manager for the limited partners and investors

- Consents, Meetings, and Votes — Constraints on the general partner's powers or topics requiring the limited partners' consent before the execution

- Representations and Warranties

- Deed of Adherence — An extra form (not compulsory) attached to the back of the LPA; it is the formal means by which most investors become limited partners specifying the number of commitment units and how these commitments are divided between capital contribution and loans

- Miscellaneous Legal Issues — Governs law and jurisdiction, power of attorneys, confidentiality, notices, etc.

Taxation framework for private equity and fiscal impact for equity investors

INTRODUCTION

This chapter presents the role of taxation in private equity and venture capital throughout Europe and the US. A deep theoretical and analytical analysis country by country will be demonstrated in the following sections The first section shows how the private equity and venture capital industry is tax sensitive, underlining the role of policymakers, and that the taxation technique and its application must always be considered together. In Sections 6.2 and 6.3, analyze taxation models and define areas of taxation for investors, vehicles, and companies requiring funds who conduct private equity and venture capital deals. Section 6.4 proposes a comparative analysis of the tax system for European countries and the United States underlining the differences between corporation taxes, withholding taxes, and personal taxes applicable to financial incomes. Focusing attention on the private equity and venture capital industry, the EVCA position is analyzed and reviewed. Finally, the last section analyzes taxation on vehicles used to implement private equity and venture capital deals and the interrelation of taxation on vehicles, investors, and companies in the EU.

6.1 FUNDAMENTAL ROLE OF TAXATION IN PRIVATE EQUITY AND VENTURE CAPITAL

Policymakers play a fundamental role in private equity and venture capital development. They must address regulatory and administrative barriers and ensure coherent policies. This enables investors to provide a continuous financing cycle for start up, spin off, company development, transition, and buyout investments to create taxable value or returns (see Figure 6.1). Investors should be considered in the valuation framework of investment strategies used to allocate financial sources, taxation, and the entire country taxation system.

Private equity and venture capital portfolios are structured to trade off the risk and return from diversified combinations of assets and are influenced by institutional and regulatory factors where taxation is essential.

As noted in previous chapters, the private equity industry is regulated on a national basis in most EU member states: there is no cohesive framework for private equity at the EU level, and a number of EU legislative measures indirectly

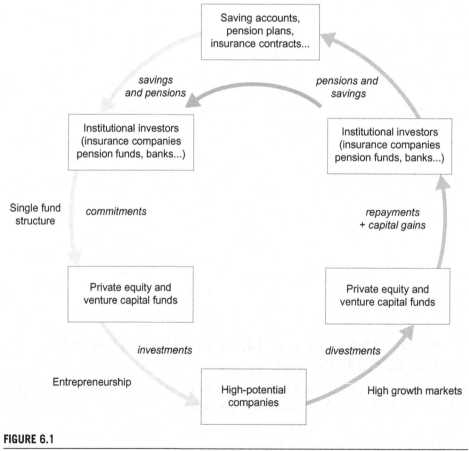

FIGURE 6.1

Financing cycle of private equity and venture capital (http://www.evca.com-www-evca-com).

affect the industry, such as MiFID, UCITS, the Pension Funds Directive, and the Basel II Principles or Capital Requirements Directive. The entire fiscal policy is local, so every government and every country legislates autonomously.

In this environment, it is very difficult to find a strictly defined tax system for investments of private equity operators and venture capitalists, because the fiscal systems are wider than the regulations of this industry. In a general structure, government policies supporting the development of private equity and venture capital industry may be direct or indirect and related to the supply side rather than the demand side.[1]

Figure 6.2 illustrates how important the fiscal environment is and how governments can make investing easier for both firms and financial institutions. Tax policies shape incentives for private equity and venture capital to approve particular types of financing. Whatever these firms decide, i.e., capital gains taxes or investment subsidies, it has to solve a double moral hazard resulting from a joint effort.

Entrepreneurs tend to focus on technological aspects such as product development, whereas financial institutions draw on their commercial experience and industry knowledge to provide managerial support and to promote the development of the firm. To reduce all potential risks and biases, an equity contract becomes necessary. However, it is inefficient when both parties equally invest in a deal, but must share the total results and each party is taxed differently. The effects of taxation are interesting to evaluate; for example, the introduction of a uniform capital gains tax on both entrepreneurs and financiers delays entrepreneurship, while increasing incentives for the financier. On the other hand, an investment subsidy boosts entrepreneurship but depresses total returns thereby diminishing incentives for private equity support.

	Demand side	Supply side
Direct intervention	Public incubators	Public private equity or venture capital funds
Indirect intervention	Tax policy Promotion of enterprise, management, technology park, incubators	Tax policy Downside protection scheme Upside leverage schemes Promotion of financiers' network Exit or fund's operating scheme

FIGURE 6.2

Government options to improve the private equity and venture capital industry.

---

[1] See Caselli S., Gatti S. (2004). *Venture Capital. A Euro-System Approach.* Springer-Verlag, Berlin London.

Taxation for private equity and venture capital is analyzed considering the

- Taxation technique
- Application area

Section 6.2 analyzes the taxation technique and taxation, while Section 6.3 defines areas of taxation for investors, vehicles, and companies requiring funds who conduct private equity and venture capital deals.

6.2 TAXATION AND EQUITY INVESTORS: LESSONS FROM THEORY AND RELEVANT MODELS

There is a strong relationship between taxation rules and private equity market development; evidence demonstrates a strong, worldwide correlation between specific tax benefits and the increase of private equity volumes. Examples include:

Taxation on capital gains
Taxation on earnings and dividends
Fiscal incentive to start up
Fiscal incentive to R&D investment

Capital gain is a value greater than zero defined as the difference between the final and the initial value of the equity participation bought by private equity operators. Earnings are usually defined as the gross difference between revenues and all monetary and non-monetary costs. However, the definition of earning may be a little different and considers only some of the types of revenues and costs. For example, the EBITDA is a type of earning — more precisely, it is the earning before interest, tax, depreciations, and amortizations — while EBIT is the earning before interests and taxes.

Taxation of both capital gains and earnings may be different, so there are various modalities of realization:

- Participation exemption (PEX) schemes
- Dual income taxation (DIT) schemes
- Flat tax approach
- Transparency taxation approach

Participation exemption schemes provide shareholders with an exemption from taxation on dividends received and potential capital gains arising on the sale of shares. Dual income tax schemes consider two types of income to tax. For every fraction of the whole income a particular percentage of taxation is applied, so the taxation rate depends on the income composition. Usually, dual income tax schemes are applied to reduce the firm's leverage and spur equity financing.

A flat tax is a tax system with a constant tax rate. Flat taxes are used for specific cases such as household income or particular corporate profits that are taxed at one marginal rate. This is different from progressive taxes, which may vary according to income or usage levels.

In transparency taxation systems generated income is not taxed thus becoming transparent from the tax system's perspective. These incomes are relevant for people (or organizations or entities) who receive them, and they are taxed by different rules.

There are various modalities of fiscal incentives to start up a business:

Carry back and carry forward
Temporary taxation rate mark down
Shadow costs usage

Carry back and/or carry forward are tax benefits that allow business losses to be used to reduce tax liability in previous and/or following years. In many cases, there is a maximum number of years to recover losses or use tax benefits. Another entrepreneur incentive is the temporary reduction of the whole tax rate, where the cut is often linked to the amount of invested sources. A third way to spur entrepreneurs is the creation of a shadow cost system. In this system, the fiscal provision supports the indirect cost, which is often concealed and linked to investments. Examples of shadow costs are downtime, administrative costs, learning costs, etc.

6.3 TAXATION PLAYERS: INVESTMENT VEHICLES, INVESTORS, AND COMPANIES DEMANDING CAPITAL

Taxation and incentive rules may be applied to all companies, vehicles, and investors participating in a private equity or venture capital deal. Usually, there is a distinction between rules for companies and rules for vehicles and investors. A different set of rules is applied if one or both of the deal participants are domestic or foreign.

Among the companies, investors, and vehicles, companies are the easiest subwhole to identify. Companies are the demand side of private equity business, and from the government's perspective, they develop deals with the intention of improving the private equity and venture capital industry. So fiscal policies increasing the entrepreneurship trend are specific and implemented as fiscal incentives for start up, investments in R&D, or investments in general assets.

Fiscal policies for companies may be planned not only from the investment and asset side of the balance sheet, but also to provide incentives or disincentives to use a particular source of funding, i.e., debt rather than equity.

Taxation rules for investors and vehicles are primarily defined by earnings and incomes related to private equity or venture capital investments and capital gain or loss, potential or effective, coming from the purchase and the sale of a firm. In Figure 6.3 the links between domestic and foreign groups are outlined.

Relevant models of both taxation and incentives can be linked to many players in the private equity market (see Figure 6.4):

Vehicles to invest (closed-end funds, limited partnerships, etc.)
Private and corporate investors
Corporations demanding private equity capital.

Generally measures implemented as incentives to start up or R&D investments are not relevant for investors and vehicles. They are only relevant for

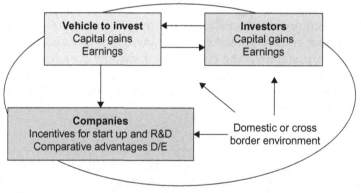

FIGURE 6.3

The link between taxation and private equity players.

	Vehicles to invest	Investors	Company demanding capital
Taxation on capital gains	Relevant to increase NAV and IRR	Relevant for personal taxation profile (final net IRR)	Not relevant
Taxation on earnings and dividends	Relevant to increase NAV and IRR	Relevant only for gains given through earnings	Not relevant
Incentive to start ups	Not relevant	Not relevant	Relevant to reduce company tax rate
Incentive to R&D investment	Not relevant	Not relevant	Relevant to reduce company tax rate
Comparative incentive D vs E	Relevant for equity pooled investment	Not relevant	Relevant to compose capital structure within net WACC

FIGURE 6.4

The link between tools of taxation and private equity players.

companies because they reduce the entire company tax rate and enhance the potential demand for private equity intervention. If these measures are meant as incentives for companies to use equity, then they must face a disincentive to use debt often realized by a rise in the tax rate. Along with these measures vehicles also have to deal with an artificial environment; for example, if the vehicle is an equity pooled investment these incentives may make the deal easier.

A firm's choices are not affected directly if taxation concerns capital gain and earning, but investors and vehicles are. Taxation on earnings and capital gains reduces the IRR of vehicles, whereas they may diminish the final profit for investors.

6.4 TAXATION FEATURES AROUND THE WORLD: A BRIEF COMPARATIVE ANALYSIS

The most important characteristics of European and American fiscal schemes are reported in this chapter.[2] The focus is not on the private equity industry, but the entire economic system; however, only financial taxable incomes (i.e., interests, capital gains) are considered.

For each country, three types of taxes are analyzed:

1. Corporate tax
2. Withholding tax
3. Personal tax

Corporate tax (or corporation tax) is a tax levied by each jurisdiction on profits made by companies or associations. It taxes the value of the corporation's profits. This analysis examines the taxes levied on dividends and capital gains paid to firms, rather than the fiscal and R&D incentives provided for companies.

Withholding tax is an amount withheld by the party making payment to another and paid to the taxation authorities. The purpose of withholding tax is to facilitate or accelerate collection by collecting tax from a small number of payers rather than a much greater number of payees, and by collecting tax from payers within the jurisdiction rather than payees who may be outside the jurisdiction. This section analyzes taxes withheld by dividends, interests, and royalties. Because of its importance for the domestic and international development of private equity and venture capital, the analysis will focus on the presence/absence of any remittance tax.

---

[2] See http://www.evca.comwww.evca.com, http://www.ec.europa-eu/taxation_customs/taxinu www.ec.europa.ev/taxation_customs/taxinv, and publications about taxation of KPMG and PWC.

Personal tax is the last tax scheme to be analyzed. The items compared are the tax rate, the concept of taxable income, the taxation of capital gains, and the presence or the lack of any net wealth or net worth tax.

6.4.1 Taxation in Italy

The Italian tax system is one of the most difficult to analyze, so a general overview is necessary to define corporate, withholding, and personal taxes. For corporations, the standard tax rate is 31,4%; the sum between the IRES (27,5%) and the IRAP (3,9%). However, some local authorities (i.e., regions or municipal authorities) may increase the total amount with a spread.

In Italy, principles of tax exemption are applied to firms, so dividends are 95% exempt, except when the subsidiary distributing dividends is directly or indirectly a resident of a country on the Italian black list (countries with a privileged tax system). Capital gain benefits from the 95% exemption only if the participation is held for at least 12 months and is recorded as a financial asset, the company is not resident in a country on the Italian black list, and the company is run effectively. Otherwise, capital gains are taxed at the standard rate.

A number of incentives are available for firms in Italy, but there are requirements to satisfy regarding location, size, and type of business. The Italian fiscal system offers companies the chance to carry forward losses for five years, while carry back is not permitted.

The Italian withholding tax system is detailed and intricate because of the presence of tax treaties and the application of an EC parent–subsidiary directive. In general, dividends paid to non-resident companies are taxed at 27%, but tax treaties or EC parent–subsidiary directive may reduce the amount. Interest may be taxed at 27% or 12,5%, which is applied to all government bonds and bonds with an expiring maturity exceeding 18 months, rather than to interest on loans paid to a non-resident company. Management fees are exempt from withholding tax, and for payments to non-resident companies the standard final rate is 22,5%, even though the EC interest and royalties directive or specific tax treaties may reduce the amount.

In Italy there is neither net wealth tax nor net worth tax, but the taxation system is progressive and rates are up to 47,5%. Nevertheless, it must be underlined that private investment incomes are subject to a rate of 26,375%, while capital gains may see a reduction in the standard rate in many cases.

6.4.2 Taxation in France

Even though the standard tax rate for companies is 33% and a surtax of 3,3% is paid by some companies, SMEs and new firms have some benefits. The principles of tax exemption are applied to firms and if this system does not apply, dividends and capital gains are subject to the standard tax rate and surtax. The participation exemption applies if the participation is at least 5% of equity capital and the holding period is at least 2 years. Losses from French companies may be carried forward and, under certain conditions, carried back for 3 years. The most important incentives concern R&D investments, which are usually allowed as tax credits.

The withholding tax system depends on the presence of tax treaties or the provisions of the EC interest and royalty directive that may reduce the amount, rather than applying the participation exemptions. It must be emphasized that there is a branch remittance tax of 25%. Dividends paid by a French company to a non-resident shareholder are taxed at 25%, while interests and royalties are taxed at 18 and 33,33% respectively.

Regarding personal taxes, all incomes, including investment incomes, are considered taxable and the applied tax rate is progressive up to 40%. Capital gains follow different rules and, if they derive from the sale of securities, the applied rate is 18% plus a special surcharge amounting to approximately 11%. The French system also provides a net wealth or net worth tax applicable to non-residents in certain cases.

6.4.3 Taxation in Germany[3]

German corporate taxation is based on a rate from 30 to 33% including a calculated surtax of 5,5%. The participation exemption system leads to a tax exclusion of 95% of dividends and capital gains received by German resident companies. Many aid programs are available for German companies, and, in case of losses, the fiscal system provides an unlimited carry forward and a one year carry back. However, a minimum tax is applied.

There is neither a withholding tax on interest nor a branch remittance tax. If the application of the parent–subsidiary directive does not reduce the amount, there is a statutory rate of 26,375% applied to dividends, with a possible refund of 40% for non-resident corporations. For royalties the potential rates are 15,825% or 21,1%, depending on the case.

German personal tax rates are progressive (up to 47,5%) and consider only incomes because net wealth or net worth is not taxed. Private investment incomes are subject to a rate of 26,375%, while the normal tax rate applies for capital gains, even though different scenarios are provided by law to reduce the total amount.

---

[3] In late 2008 an important tax reform, with substantial consequences on private equity and venture capital was discussed in Germany.

6.4.4 **Taxation in Spain**

The standard corporate tax rate in Spain is 30%, which may be reduced for SMEs. Dividend and capital gains are subject to this rate, even though the participation exemption rules or tax treaties may reduce the effective amount of tax. When applicable, tax exemption is equal to 100% and, to exploit all benefits, Spanish companies must hold a participation of at least 5% (or more than €6 million) and for at least 12 months. Incentives are available for investments and export activities, and the tax system allows companies to carry forward losses up to 15 years, but it does not allow carry back.

The withholding tax system is particularly complicated because of the presence of domestic rules, tax treaties, and EC directives that may reduce the applied rate. Generally, dividends[4] and interest paid to non-residents are taxed at 18%, while royalties are taxed at a rate of 24% by law. There is also a branch remittance tax equal to 18%. The Spanish personal taxation system is based on a general progressive rate from 24 to 43%, and saving incomes, such as capital gains, are taxed at 18%. Taxation concerns only income and no net wealth or net worth tax is applied.

6.4.5 **Taxation in Luxembourg**

Companies in Luxembourg are asked to pay a standard rate of 20% plus a surtax of 4%, and municipal authorities may request a further spread. Dividends and capital gains are exempt from tax if the shareholder holds at least 10% of the share capital or there is an acquisition value of at least €1,2 million, and the holding period lasts at least 1 year uninterrupted. Otherwise, there is a standard rate of 15% for dividends and the standard tax rate is applied to capital gains.

In Luxembourg tax credit and other measures for venture capital and tangible and intangible investments are available, and for losses, laws provide for unlimited carry forward, while carry back is not permitted. The withholding tax system is extremely clear: there is neither a remittance branch tax nor taxation on interest and royalties, while dividends paid to non-resident companies are taxed at 15% or less in the presence of tax treaties or an EC parent–subsidiary directive. The benefits of the EC directive may also be exploited for companies in countries where tax rules are similar to those in Luxembourg.

Personal incomes are subject to a progressive rate up to 38% with no net wealth or net worth tax. Income tax is further increased by a contribution of 2,5% for the employment fund. There are special rules for dividends that are taxed at a rate of 15% or long-term capital gains that receive favorable tax rates

---

[4] Inter-company payments intra-EU are exempt if the foreign company has continuously held at least 10% of the equity for 1 year before distribution.

depending on the kind of asset and the length of holding period, while short-term capital gains are subject to standard tax rates.

6.4.6 **Taxation in Netherlands**

The Dutch fiscal system regarding withholding taxes is easy to understand, while it is a little more difficult when companies or people are considered. The withholding system is clear: no remittance branch tax nor taxation on interest and royalties is applied, but there is a 15% tax on capital gain. Reductions or exemptions are available if tax treaties exist or an EC parent–subsidiary directive is applied.

The corporate tax rate is progressive up to 25,5% and a participation exemption system for dividends and capital gains is provided. Dividends received by a Dutch company are exempt, unless the subsidiary pays an effective tax rate lower than 10% or has over 50% of passive assets. Otherwise, a tax credit is provided. Capital gains exemption is granted if they derive from a participation of at least 5%, the participated company pays an effective tax rate higher than 10%, and the participated company has less than 50% of passive assets. Otherwise, they are taxed at about 25%.

There are various incentives for investments and financing in different cases. For losses, rules provide a carry forward for 9 years and a carry back for 1 year, apart from some special restrictions for financial firms or holding companies.

In the Netherlands, there is neither a net wealth nor net worth tax.

6.4.7 **Taxation in the UK**

The British tax rate for companies is 28%, but SMEs pay a lower rate (21%). There is no participation exemption scheme in the UK (it is effective from September 2009) but at the moment there is already a system of tax credit calculation.

For dividends a full exemption is only available to resident companies that receive these sources from a resident company. Dividends received from a foreign company are taxed, but a tax credit is available for the amount already paid abroad.

Generally, capital gains are taxed, but an exemption exists for companies disposing substantial shareholdings. The conditions for exemption are ownership of at least 10%, a holding period of at least 12 months, and both companies trade before and after the deal. Incentives are available for certain R&D expenditures. For losses the carry forward is unlimited and the carry back is admitted for 1 year.

The British fiscal system states that there is neither withholding tax on dividends nor a branch remittance tax. Interests and royalties paid to non-residents are taxed at 20%, but tax treaties or EC interest and a royalties directive may reduce the amount.

For personal tax purposes, all income, including capital gains and interest, must be considered. In the UK the personal tax rate is progressive up to 40%, but dividends from UK companies are taxed at 25%, whereas capital gains are taxed at 18% (10% on the first £1 million).

6.4.8 **Taxation in the United States**

In the US the corporate tax is progressive up to 35%, and branch profits are taxed with an additional tax of 30%. Other surtaxes are provided by law and an alternative minimum tax scenario is available for firms and are used by foreign corporations engaged in American businesses.

The participation exemption scheme is not available in the US, so gains derived by companies on assets held for investment are taxed at the same rate as ordinary income. A deduction is available for dividends paid and received between US corporate shareholders.

Laws provide a number of tax credits related to R&D investments and for a carry forward and carry back system for losses. Carry forward is admitted for 20 years and carry back for 2.

The general withholding tax is based on a rate of 30% or lower if a tax treaty exists, so dividends, interests, royalties, and branch remittance paid to foreign subjects are taxed at a rate of 30%. It must be emphasized that in certain circumstances, linked to the export profile of firms, dividends are tax exempt or that certain interest (mainly paid by government bonds) are exempt from withholding tax.

Personal taxes encompass all forms of remuneration that are not specifically exempted, while net wealth is not taxed. The rate is progressive up to 35%, and there is special treatment for long-term capital gains (investment held for more than 21 months) that are taxed at a flat rate of 15%.

6.5 **FISCAL FRAMEWORK FOR EQUITY INVESTORS AND VEHICLES: THE EU CONDITION**

Chapters 4 and 5 demonstrated that many differences among EU countries persist despite efforts to create a standardized legal environment for the private equity industry. Tax procedures are different because of dissimilar legal systems and the level of country development.

Previous chapters showed that EVCA proposed a way to appraise the ability of a country's fiscal system to spur the private equity and venture capital industry: calculate a comprehensive score from 1 (the best) to 3 (the worst) by rating these items:

- Tax environment for most usable fund structure
- Presence of fiscal or incentive schemes for private equity and venture capital investment

- Tax environment for companies requiring sources
- Tax environment for fund managers and private individuals

Items considered regarding aspects related to vehicles and investors include the

- Availability or the accessibility to any tax transparency option
- VAT environment for the private equity and venture capital industry
- Necessity of permanent establishment
- Presence of any fiscal incentive meant to encourage investments in private equity and venture capital
- Capital gains and income tax for private individuals and entities
- Taxation of carried interest

Figure 6.5 illustrates that the European fiscal system is still far from being standardized. The fiscal policy does not develop the private equity and venture capital industry, instead it is the result of variables linked to each country's fiscal approach that are satisfying a greater number of objectives.

There is a negative relationship between taxation for private individuals and entities and taxation of carried interest. When the taxation of carried interest is profitable, the negative relationship between taxation for private individuals and entities appears to be expensive. Taxation of carried interest is also negatively related to the presence of fiscal incentives for the private equity and venture

Country	Tax transparency option	VAT environment	Permanent establishment request	Fiscal incentive to the industry	Taxation for private and entities	Taxation of carried interest
Italy	3	1	1	2	2	2
Austria	3	1	1	1	3	2
Belgium	1	1	1	1	3	2
Czech Republic	3	1	1	3	1	2
Denmark	1	1	2	3	3	1
Finland	1	1	1	3	3	1
France	1	1	1	1	3	1
Germany	1	3	1	3	3	2
Ireland	1	1	1	1	3	1
Luxembourg	2	1	1	1	1	2
Netherlands	1	1	3	1	2	3
Norway	1	1	2	3	3	2
Poland	3	1	1	3	3	2
Portugal	1	1	1	1	2	3
Spain	3	1	1	1	3	2
Sweden	1	3	3	3	3	1
Switzerland	1	1	2	1	2	3
UK	1	1	1	1	3	1

FIGURE 6.5

EVCA comparative analysis of European fiscal systems.

capital industry: it seems that governments tend to separate the encouragement of investments in private equity and venture capital from tax rules for investors. A negative relationship is also evident between the availability of a transparency rule and the VAT environment as well as the permanent establishment restriction. This confirms that vehicles and investors are considered separately by governments.

There is a positive correlation between the VAT environment and the presence of incentives for private equity and venture capital investments; i.e., the relationship between the VAT environment and the permanent establishment restriction. These items run together and are available just for businesses operating with a domestic and enduring headquarters in the country of choice.

Box: Effective corporate taxation around Europe

World Bank — IFC proposes an annual study measuring the ease of paying taxes for small to medium-sized domestic companies in countries around the world (in the last version, 181). There are three indicators:

- Total tax rate (TTR; the cost of all taxes borne by the company)
- Time taken to comply with the major taxes
- Number of tax payments for major taxes

Considering the theme of this book, the TTR is the most interesting if the corporate taxation system is attractive for domestic or foreign entrepreneurs. In general, the study confirms that corporate income tax is only one of many taxes that businesses have to bear. It accounts for only 13% of payments, 26% of compliance time, and 37% of the TTR. Any reform needs to look beyond corporate income tax: companies make important tax contributions as employers, and they are also influenced by taxes on consumption (VAT).

Country	TTR (% of corporate profits)	Rank
UK	35.2	59
Netherlands	39.1	77
Portugal	43.6	96
Germany	50.5	128
Austria	54.5	141
Spain	60.2	152
France	65.4	164
Italy	73.3	166
United States	42.3	92

6.5.1 **Taxation of the most important private equity and venture capital vehicles**

The fiscal framework for private equity and venture capital vehicles depends on the legal framework and the organization of the fiscal system. In each fiscal system private equity deals may be realized in a different way.

Figure 6.6 illustrates the tax profile for the vehicles used most often in private equity investments.

6.5.2 **Vehicle taxation: Italy**

Italy's fiscal framework is highly volatile due to the political cycle and the use of taxation as a short-term tool of political economy. However, taxation related to financial investments and its vehicles is not so volatile (see Figure 6.7).

Investment vehicles, investors, and companies demanding capital round out the fiscal picture. Private equity and venture capital investment each have different vehicles (i.e., closed-end funds or investment firms) and the presence of two fiscal frames:

- Flat tax system for closed-end funds
- Participation exemption on capital gains and earnings for investment firms

Closed-end funds do not pay ordinary Italian tax (i.e., IRES and IRAP) but pay a flat tax fixed at 12,50% instead. Italian fiscal law considers capital gains, interest, and others earnings on both the revenue and cost side in the calculation framework as well as other types of costs and revenues.

If private equity and venture capital deals are made by investment firms, they are forced to pay Italian corporation tax (i.e., IRES and IRAP) as well as other legal entities. A participation exemption scheme for 95% of dividends and capital gains is exploitable only under certain conditions, including a holding period longer than 18 months where the main activity of the company acquired is not real estate.

There are two ways to compare investment vehicles in Italy. Investment firms have higher revenues coming from capital gains and earnings, whereas closed-end funds have a higher increase in market value of shares during the holding period. This is related to the behavior and strategic plan of investors: if there is a short-term strategy, the better choice is an investment firm, but if the strategic view is long-term, closed-end funds are more appropriate. A different amount of tax is paid if income comes from closed-end funds rather than investment firms, and if investors are private or legal entities.

Country	Preferable vehicle	Tax profile
Italy	Fondo chiuso	Italian closed-end funds follow a particular treatment. A flat tax rate of 12.5% is applied on the fund results.
France	Fonds Commun de Placement à Risques	FCPR itself is not subject to any taxation. In particular: No corporate income tax is payable by an FCPR on any dividend income remitted by a target company in which the FCPR has a participating interest; No capital gains tax is payable by the FCPR on any profitable sales of its shareholding in a target company.
UK	Limited partnership	Capital gains are de-taxed, while other revenues and costs are tax sensitive.
USA	Limited partnership	Capital gains are de-taxed, while other revenues and costs are tax sensitive.
Spain	Sociedad de Capital de Riesgo (SCR) and Fondo de Capital de Riesgo (FCR)	SCR and FCR are taxable according to the 30% corporation tax. Nevertheless, there are special tax arrangements established in the Corporation Tax legislation and their principal characteristics and requirements are as follows: Participation exemption of 99% of revenue obtained from the sale of securities representing equity of companies in which they have invested; The application of the deduction for internal and international double taxation of dividends on 100% of the tax base relating to dividends.
Germany	Limited partnership (GMbH & Co KG)	Corporation and solidarity tax is payable on profits and another trade tax on trade earnings. Business expenses, interest, trade tax, and amortization are deductible.
Luxembourg	Société d'Investissement en Capital à Risque (SICAR)	Profits realized by a SICAR are subject to corporate income tax and municipal business tax. However, income derived from portfolio items consisting of securities, capital gains derived from the sale of such securities, and income from temporary investment in liquid assets held for a maximum period of 12 months before investment in risk capital are excluded from the tax base.

FIGURE 6.6

Tax profile of the most important vehicles in Europe.

	Vehicles to invest	Investors	Company demanding capital
Taxation on capital gains	Participation exemption for investment firms and flat tax for closed-end funds	Different profiles for companies and private individuals	Not relevant
Taxation on earnings	Participation exemption for investment firms and flat tax for closed-end funds	Different profiles for companies and private individuals	Not relevant
Incentive to start ups	Not operating at 2008	Not operating at 2008	Not operating at 2008
Incentive to R&D investment	Not operating at 2008	Not relevant	Not operating at 2008
Comparative incentive D vs E	Maximum amount of deductible interest. No specific rules for equity.	Not relevant	Maximum amount of deductible interest. No specific rules for equity.

FIGURE 6.7

The fiscal framework in Italy.

If income originates from closed-end funds, private investors (domestic or foreign) do not pay taxes on capital gains, whereas domestic legal entities pay taxes using a tax credit of 15% on the capital gain. Foreign legal entities do not pay taxes in Italy, only in their domestic country. If incomes originate from investment firms, private investors (domestic or foreign) pay a flat tax of 12,5% on the earnings, whereas legal entity investors use the participation exemption scheme for earnings.

Companies in Italy are asked to pay IRES and IRAP. There are many ways to calculate this taxable income. Private equity and venture capital deals may be realized with debt instruments so there is a rule defining the maximum amount of interest that may be deducted. Simply put, the sum of interest that may be deducted is based on a value equal to 30% of EBITDA.

At the moment, no special domestic law provides incentives to start ups or R&D investments.

6.5.3 **Vehicle taxation: United States**

Principles for taxation in the United States include:

- Transparency, i.e., taxation on investment vehicles is simple: excluded or partially excluded
- Investors sustain, i.e., provisions from specific schemes dedicated to private investors or to Business Angels
- R&D support, i.e., provisions of rules that reduce the actual expenses for a start-up company, rather than for investing in R&D

In the United States different ways to invest in private equity and venture capital can be found. Deals can be run by

- Venture capital funds
- SBICs (small business investment companies)
- Business Angels

Venture capital funds refer to a pooled investment vehicle, very often a limited partnership (LP) that primarily invests the financial capital of third party investors in enterprises that are too risky for the standard capital markets or a bank loan. To gain benefits provided by law, venture capital funds must be structured as a 10-year LP.

In 1958, the Small Business Investment Act officially allowed the licensing of private SBICs to help the financing and management of small entrepreneurial businesses in the United States. It was believed that fostering entrepreneurial companies would spur technological business to compete. This federal program used public funds to develop the economic system by supporting SMEs. Today, rigid regulatory limitations minimize the role of SBICs.

Business Angels are private entrepreneurs who provide capital for a business start up. The tax profile of venture capital funds organized as 10-year LPs can deduct capital gains, whereas other revenues and costs are tax sensitive. According to the law, all SBIC revenues are de-taxed. The tax profile of Business Angels is more complicated and can be summarized by the following:

Capital gains are de-taxed in case of reinvestment of money in 60 days in qualified small business stocks (QSBS) or SBIC shares

Capital gains are de-taxed for 50% if the holding period of QSBS is higher than 5 years

Taxes are paid differently if investors are considered a private rather than a legal entity. For private investors, capital gains and earnings are taxed at 5% or 15% depending on global revenues and state, whereas the capital gains of legal entities are always taxed (in the United States the participation exemption principle is not applied), and earnings are taxed from 0 to 30% depending on the held quota.

Unlike Italy, in the United States there are low incentives for companies, especially for start-up and R&D expenditures. Start ups are provided with a mark down of the company tax rate between 15 and 35% related to the amount of revenues. For R&D costs and investments, exiting rules order a tax credit equal to 20% of the difference between yearly R&D costs and the average R&D costs of the last 3 years.

No DIT or thin cap schemes are operating in the United States.

6.5.4 Vehicle taxation: the UK

The principles for taxation in the UK are similar to those in the United States, but the actual tax systems are different; for example, the British scheme for private equity and venture capital deals is more complicated. In the UK, private equity and venture capital deals are run by

- Venture capital funds
- Venture capital trusts
- Business Angels

Venture capital funds are pooled investments in companies believed to be too risky by banks or other financial institutions. In the UK the most common vehicle used to create a venture capital fund is the LP. To obtain benefits provided by law, the LP must run for 10 years.

A venture capital trust (VCT) is a highly tax efficient closed-end collective investment scheme designed to provide capital finance for small expanding companies and capital gains for investors. First introduced by the Conservative government in the Finance Act in 1995, VCTs have proved to be much less risky than originally anticipated. The Finance Act created VCTs to encourage investment in new UK businesses. VCTs are companies listed on the London Stock Exchange that invest in other companies who are not listed.

Business angels in the UK, must act as individuals, so they can only be investors.

In both the UK and United States venture capital funds organized as 10-year LPs can deduct capital gains, while other revenues and costs are tax sensitive. For VCTs capital gains are de-taxed if the holding period is longer than 3 years, whereas earnings are always de taxed.

There are different tax structures for investors considered as Business Angels, legal entities, or private or corporate investors. Business Angels in the UK can only be private investors, and their investment generates a tax credit of 20% if the holding period is longer than 3 years and the amount of the investment is lower than £150,000. Capital gains are de-taxed (and losses are deductible) if the holding period is longer than 3 years.

If the investor is a corporate venture there are general restrictions: they are allowed only to be unlisted companies or quoted for a maximum of 30% of their total shares. Corporate ventures generate a tax credit of 20% and capital gains are de-taxed if money is invested in the same investments within 3 years.

For private individuals the system is less intricate, because capital gains and earnings are taxed at a level of 10% or 32.5% depending on the amount of revenue (under or over £29,400). Legal entities are unsuitable vehicles for private equity and venture capital deals, because costs can be higher than other vehicles: capital gains are always taxed (in the UK the participation exemption principle is not applied) and earnings are always taxed.

Like the United States and contrary to Italy, there are many incentive schemes for start ups and R&D expenditures in the UK. Fiscal rules allow a mark down of the company tax rate within a range of 0 to 19% of the amount of revenues for a start up, and for R&D costs and investments there is a tax credit of 50% for unlisted companies.

In the UK there is a strict thin cap scheme and interest rate costs are not deductible.

6.5.5 Vehicle taxation: reform in the German market

After long political debate, the German legislature produced a new set of laws reforming the private equity and venture capital financial framework.

This reform is under review by the EU Commission regarding its fiscal aspects and by German financial institutions as far as the implementation feasibility is concerned.

Two of the most important items created by the reform are

- Classification of a company as a venture capital company or equity investment company
- Tax profile for incomes related to equity investments

The new tax framework will change the actual subjects and vehicles operating in the private equity and venture capital industry apart from their fiscal profiles.

Vehicles that will be available in Germany include:

- Venture capital companies
- Equity investment companies

Venture capital companies are recognized by BaFin[5] only if they meet these requirements:

- They must manage acquisition, holding, administration, and divestiture of venture capital participations
- Their headquarters must be in Germany;
- Minimum capital must be at least €1 million
- Management must be made up of at least of two managers
- Investments must be in "target companies," i.e., in companies with particular characteristics

Equity investment companies are classified by the competent Supreme Federal State Authority and not by BaFin.[6] In Germany, equity investment is a very broad term that includes participations in domestic and foreign companies, all mezzanine financing, and all investment that may be related to equity.

The German law distinguishes between an open equity investment company and an integrated equity investment company. The integrated equity investment company still qualifies as a subsidiary after the expiration of a 5-year start-up period during which investors can hold a participation of more than 40% of the capital or voting rights. However, the company may only invest in companies managed by at least one person who directly holds at least 10% of its voting rights. All equity investment companies may hold participations for a period of 15 years.

---

[5] The German financial authority.
[6] This aspect is one of the most criticized fiscal reforms.

The taxation profile of venture capital companies depends on its classification: asset manager or commercial company. If it is classified as an asset manager, the company is completely "transparent" for income tax purposes so all income is not taxed. If the classification of asset manager does not apply, all tax advantages are lost and corporation tax must be paid. However, capital gains, under certain conditions, may result in tax exemption.

For equity investment companies there is no special treatment and general taxation rules are applied.

Since 2009, for all operators, tax exempt carried interest is reduced from 50 to 40%.

The Process and the Management to Invest

The management of equity investment

7.1 EQUITY INVESTMENT AS A PROCESS: ORGANIZATION AND MANAGEMENT

Equity investment satisfies two different needs: (1) companies collect funds because their entrepreneurs do not have sufficient financial resources to support and increase the development of their businesses and (2) these financial resources are held by investors who finance high-risk high-reward projects.

Equity investment can be developed through vehicles that allow institutional venture capital activity. These funds are split up between different companies that are potential sources of high economic return.

Different vehicles for investment activity include:

1. Partnership — Shareholders are responsible for the management of the private equity fund and they respond directly with their personal assets; in some cases, the management of the fund can be delegated to external professionals (management company), but the total funds reserved for shareholders and the fund are equal, and the fund does not represent an autonomous legal entity. This partnership has a life of about ten years that can be extended for two more years depending on the shareholders.

2. Limited partnership (LP) — Similar to a general partnership, there are two clearly defined categories of shareholders. The limited partners are institutional and individual investors who provide capital. They have limited responsibility in the fund's management and investment decisions, which only extends to the capital they contribute. The general partners, apart from transferring capital, are responsible for organizing the fundraising, managing

the funds raised, and the reimbursement of the quotas to the subscribers at the expiry of the fund. Their responsibility is extended to their personal assets. Almost all partnerships allow a single partner to close the partnership in case of a death or withdrawal of the general partners and/or fund bankruptcy. Usually the LPs include some private agreement allowing the limited partners to dissolve the partnership and replace the general partner if the limited partners represent more than 50% of the fund and the general partners are damaging the fund.

3. Corporation — A company where the shareholders are the investors. The main disadvantage, compared with the previous organizational forms, is that the corporation is subject to taxation on capital gains realized (and not distributed), whereas the partnership and the LP have full "fiscal transparency." The law does not allow specific parties to operate through partnership or LP in a corporation.

4. Closed-end fund — An autonomous legal entity independent from both the subscribers and the company that manages the resources. The subscribers, however, cannot interfere in the management or investment activities of the management company. The management of the fund can also be supported by one or more advisory companies.

Regardless of the legal structure, a set of common characteristics distinguish venture capital funds from other types of financial intermediaries:

1. Limited life — This fund has a predefined expiry date at which the redemption of the quotas subscribed are returned to the investors. This minimizes the risks to venture capitalists and investors during the timing and methods of redistributing the invested funds. Returning the subscribed quotas to investors is a powerful incentive to optimize the efficiency of management company investment policies. If the results are worse than expected, it will seriously compromise the fund's ability to raise money in the future.

2. Flexibility — A management company can launch several funds simultaneously, each one characterized by a distinctive duration, capital, and investment philosophy; therefore, it is possible to satisfy a variety of investor categories, each with a specific risk/return/liquidity profile, widening the depth of the risk capital market. This flexibility allows the manager to delegate (to advisor companies) some of their institutional activity (fundraising, identification of the target companies, investment selection and/or monitoring, analysis of the exit opportunities). Therefore the company is always able to supply the clientele with highly specialized and sophisticated products without possessing wide and specialized expertise.

3. Remuneration mechanisms — Parties appointed to the fund management receive a fixed management fee, generally between 2 and 3% of the total capital raised. The management company also participates in the final result of the fund, through the carried interest mechanism, allowing it to receive a certain percentage (usually 20%) of the total capital gains realized in the exit phase. Hence, venture capitalists are more responsible in the investment selection and management activities because this affects an important part of their own remuneration.

Venture capital funds constituted through LPs provide two distinct investment categories, general partners and limited partners, with a different level of involvement and responsibility in the management of the capital raised. This separation is typical in closed-end funds, but it does not occur between the reserves of the venture capital fund and the fund managers; the general partners allow the management team to act autonomously in the selection of the best investment opportunities, accelerating the decision-making process relative to the preparation and conclusion of the investments.

To avoid the risk of opportunistic general partners, they are explicitly prohibited from trading operations on their own behalf (self-dealing), which could allow them to receive benefits unavailable to the limited partners.

In contrast to the closed-end funds, subscribers can exit the investment before the end of the fund's life, i.e., the limited partners can ask at any time for reimbursement of the subscribed quota. It is thus possible that liquidity risks might arise within the LP jeopardizing the stability of the financial resources given to the companies financed.

An LP is not a company with share capital so it is not eligible, in the countries whose legal regulations provide for such a company structure, to be admitted for quotation on official stock markets. The quotas of a closed-fund, on the other hand, can be traded on a regulatory market, and in case of quotation, it is possible to subdivide the quotas to permit greater marketability of their certificates and increase the liquidity profile.

In the countries where it is possible to constitute an LP, the largest part of its success is related to favorable fiscal schemes. This is different from the schemes applicable to other intermediaries operating in the venture capital market, e.g., the closed-end fund.

7.2 THE FOUR PILLARS OF EQUITY INVESTMENT

Vehicles dedicated to equity investment have a specific value chain with phases and organizational functions that can be classified worldwide. For each phase there is a different contribution from management and the advisory board and the Board of Directors. The typical phases of equity investment are fundraising, investing, managing and monitoring, and exit.

7.2.1 Fundraising

Fundraising is the promotion of a new equity investment vehicle within the business community; the purpose is to find money and create a commitment. The main motivation, considered by investors during the selection of the funds, is based on obtaining returns higher than those offered by the financial market. Private equity investors normally want a premium of about 5% compared with the gain. This extra performance covers the extra risk connected with the minor liquidity of the fund and the higher risk connected with private companies. Also taken into account is the track record of the investment managers based on their competencies, their reputation, and their previous performances. Investment managers should demonstrate that past deals have been successful because of a series of good capital allocations not just one successful deal. Investors use IRR as a measure of success. The money multiple (the number of how many times the fund has been able to multiply the initial endowment of capital) is also used because it is influenced less by distortions over the duration of the investment. Investors also evaluate the terms and rules included in the corporate governance structure of the fund.

The fund subscribers consider not just the IRR realized by the investment, but also the performance of the fund netted by the costs, the fees, and carried interests paid. It is important to define carried interest: it is a part of the earnings generated by the fund and given back to the management team at the end of the fund. It is defined as 20% of the fund performance and can be calculated in two different ways:

1. The fund as a whole — The carried interest is based on the total performance and result of the fund and is paid only when the investors receive their total capital before subscribers.
2. Deal by deal — The investment manager receives a part of the profit obtained from the investment, but they have to avoid the eventual losses provoked by management activity.

Mixed solutions are also frequently applied allowing the investment managers to receive the carried interest deal by deal but only at the end of the fund after reimbursing the risk capital to the subscribers.

Fundraising is for all funds, especially ones without a track record, because many investors are reluctant to invest in an unproven team even if the partners have successful individual track records. There are many ways new private equity funds can solve this problem. The first solution is to identify and involve investors who are not only focused on financial returns but look for some strategic benefit from the fund. In this case the investors are willing to accept a lower return in front of the indirect benefit provided by the investment. The second strategy is to arrange a partnership with an existing institution such as an investment bank or another private equity fund providing a joint management of the funds raised. The main benefit of this strategy is improved credibility but, at the same time, there are some real costs; for example, investors should suspect that the institutional partner will affect the quality of the investment strategy. Another solution is to hire a lead investor. This is an institutional investor who leads the investment strategy. His is often called a special limited partner because he subscribes a relevant amount of capital and usually provides the financial resources needed by the fund to cover the costs of marketing (seed funding).

Fundraising activity is directly influenced and determined both by the supply of private equity (the relative desire of institutional investors to allocate capital in the sector), and the demand for private equity (the number of entrepreneurs with a good idea who want to be financed). Many analyses of fundraising activity have been performed, and one theory suggests that this activity is impacted, in inverse proportion, by the change in tax rates that should foment or lower fund demand. Other theories argue that fundraising activity depends on the public equity market status: during robust phases the market allows new firms to issue shares and entrepreneurs to achieve liquidity and monetize the value of their companies.

There are many sources of capital and the following are six of the most common investor types:

1. Family and friends are the most common source of seed money and probably the easiest way to raise funds, but are also the most likely to cause problems. If the business fails, the financial troubles of the parties involved may be dwarfed by the emotional consequences. Nonetheless, many of America's successful companies have been created from this type of financing.

2. Private placement funds are subscribed by private "amateur" investors instead of professional investors. There are big risks when playing such an important role in the development of major innovative firms.

3. Private pools of funds are partnerships between different shareholders who decide to invest part of their own assets.

4. Corporate funds are funds and financial resources managed by venture capital with the intention of financing companies in the development stage.

5. Mutual investment funds are financial vehicles that provide capital by issuing and placing participation quota with investors.

6. Bank financial intermediaries, in particular merchant banks, are entities most oriented to long-term investments and are prepared to sustain risk levels.

7.2.2 Investing

To reach his financial and competitive goals, a private equity investor creates value through the scouting and screening of available investments. The type of investment is chosen through the use of debt, because the private equity management team is involved in the governance of the venture-backed companies financed.

There are different practical types of investments: investment in a private equity fund, in a private equity fund of funds, or the direct investment in equity or the construction of a private equity fund and the involvement of the private equity fund in the firm-financed shareholders under the control of a single entrepreneur. The first two types of equity investments follow a logical financial strategy, whereas the last two follow an industrial strategy and the third one (direct investment in equity) has both a financial and industrial logic.

The venture capitalist investments, depending on the specific phases of the life cycle of the target firm, can be classified as three main clusters of equity investment:

Pre-competitive investment (seed financing)

Competitive investment including start-up financing, growth or expansion financing, and the public equity

Recovery investment realized through debt restructuring, turnaround financing and leverage buyout financing, and vulture capital.

Investors of risk capital must focus on the origination activity, which consists of a steady flow of investment opportunity. This is the key factor in starting the investment process. The origination phase includes selection of an investment opportunity realized through appropriate professional resources and information. This phase requires a lot of time due to the extremely selective nature of the investment decision through risk capital, especially if early stage expansion or the buyout of a small to medium family firm with a high level of innovation is selected. The selection is based on the industry and the position inside the industry of the target firm, the validity and reliability of the business plan, the entry price, the quality and skills of the entrepreneur and/or management of the target firm, and the exit strategy.

Scouting activity should create good proprietary deal flow and its strategy must be consistent with investment policies, the type of investor, and their cultural and industrial characteristics.

The scouting, screening, and eventual choice of the investment are realized using different tools:

SWOT analysis
Industry analysis
Future financials analysis
Valuation of the company by different techniques, i.e., comparables, fundamentals, net present value, adjusted present value, discounted cash flow
Industrial and human resources skills valuation
Valuation of management skills and track record
Due diligence (market, environmental, accounting, financial, legal, and tax)

During investment activity, it is important to have a clear entry and exit strategy as well as rules established between investors and the entrepreneur regarding transparency, involvement in the Board of Directors, and the general overview of company management. It is critical to define the timing and the privacy of the investment deal, to be fully engaged in the negotiation process, and to ignore the rumors and deal inside the financial market and with other equity investors.

When planning exit strategies in this phase investment managers should define covenants, the timing of divestment, contractual IRR expected, and identification of subscribers.

7.2.3 Managing and monitoring

Managing and monitoring selected vehicles help to create value and control opportunistic behaviors of the financed venture firm. Two different areas exist to create and measure value and establish rules. The first one is based on the availability of deep expertise and advisory skills; the second one is based on the valuable network of relationships owned by the financial investors.

The venture capitalist supports the financed company by participating in all activities concerning the Board of Directors and other committee meetings, with professional expertise, and the ability to impose severe discipline. Investors also help choose staff because they have a great depth of knowledge about specific companies and their sectors. Another source of value is the investors' network of customers, suppliers, governmental lobbying, and the ability to arrange additional financing.

According to the survey from MacMillan, Kulow, and Khoylian,[1] at the end of the 1980s there were three different types of investors directly involved in the management of target companies. The first cluster is represented by the "laissez-faire" investor who participates little in the firm's daily activity. This investor provides funds and advice used to improve the financial structure of the target company and the relationship with other financial supporters.

The second group is composed of shareholder investors with a higher level of involvement. Not only do they contribute money, but they also support management and operation choices. The third and last type of investor is fully involved in the daily activity of the target company. These investors take part in marketing and operation strategies as well as monitoring the strategies during the implementation phase.

The approach of the private equity investors depends on the specific type of project financed; for example, a minority or majority participation or if the project is in the testing or start-up phase.

7.2.4 **Exiting**

When exiting the decision to sell equity owned in the portfolio to gain the value added created during the managing of the investment is considered. It is a decision that has to be planned with broad vision, because it directly impacts the portfolio performance. This phase of the venture investment is critical and a good time and the best way to exit must be identified. The investment manager should have a clear idea about the potential disinvestment from the beginning, especially with minority participation where the team has to avoid any arbitral constraints connected with the financial partner's exit.

Exit decisions are not only based on the economic return created. Every investment implies the arrangement of specific rules and covenants regulating their relationship. This prevents and mitigates any agency problems and opportunistic behavior. Exiting is also directly influenced by external or internal factors related to the status of the company and its industry as well as the financial market.

Every exit strategy must have a concrete way out that transcends the logic and the legal structure of the investments. There are a number of common and widespread exiting strategies:

Trade sale happens when the private equity investor sells its participation to a corporation or an industrial shareholder.

Buy back strategy sells its stake to already existing shareholders or other people they choose.

---

[1] MacMillan I.C., Kulow D.M., and Khoylian R., "Venture capitalists' involvement in their investments: extent and performance," *Journal of Business Venturing,* 4, 1988.

Sale to other private equity investors.

Write off is the devaluation, partially or totally, of the participation value as a consequence of the loss of money unrelated to a transfer of property.

IPO, or sale post IPO, allows the private equity investor to exit by selling its stake through the stock exchange market.

It is important to plan the exit in advance because the timing of the exit strategy depends on when the economic return is monetized for both the subscribers of the private equity fund and the investment manager. Private equity investors are compensated by the potential revaluation of the participation in the venture-backed company, but the investor manager and his team are compensated in other ways:

Structuring fees are the costs directly connected with the creation and organization of the fund. They are also related to the fiscal and legal advisory activity; these costs are directly deducted from the total funds available for subsequent investment activities.

Management fee is a commission between 1,5 and 2,5% of the total capital subscribed.

Transaction fee is a commission for each single operation charged to the single venture-backed company where the investment has been realized; this commission can also include the aborted costs (costs connected to an uncompleted deal).

Carried interest is a part of the total gain realized by the fund, usually 20%, paid to the investment manager only if the rate of return of the fund has surpassed the hurdle rate agreed between the parties. This mechanism plays a double role: an incentive for the private equity manager to work hard and a signal that attracts potential subscribers fascinated by the explicit trust in the investment manager's dealing skills.

7.3 THE RELEVANCE OF EXPERTISE AND SKILLS WITHIN THE PROCESS

The expertise and attitude needed in the investment process (see Figure 7.1) is different depending on the specific stage. The specific skills necessary during the venture capital activity (Figure 7.2) include:

Company valuation skills are relevant during the investing and exiting phases. If the investment activity is to hit its economic returns target, then it is critical to wisely select the investment target and choose the right time and way to exit.

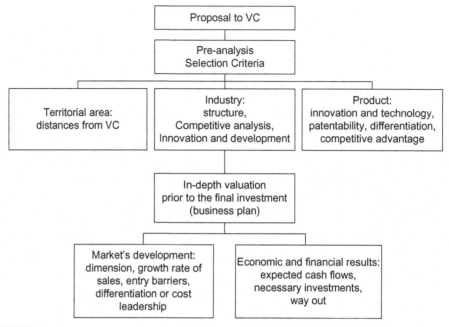

FIGURE 7.1

The process of equity investment analyzed in the pre-investment phase.

Skills / Phases	Company valuation	Legal & Fiscal	Governance	Reporting	Promoting & Selling	Recruiting	People management
Fundraising		◆	◆		◆		
Investing	◆	◆	◆	◆			
Managing & Monitoring			◆	◆		◆	◆
Exiting	◆	◆	◆		◆		

FIGURE 7.2

The skills along the private equity investment process.

Legal and fiscal skills are important during the deal structuring, closing, and exiting because they are the stages when the private equity fund has to define and respect specific legal and tax requirements balanced with the needs and desires of the investors.

Governance skills are relevant during all the processes because they allow the investment manager to structure and lead critical relationships early in the investment, during the phase of management and monitoring, and within the entrepreneur and/or the management team of the financed firm.

Reporting activities are concentrated during the core phases of investing and managing funds owned by private equity. They are important for solving or reducing agency problems between subscribers and managers of the fund and also to guarantee a higher level of transparency.

Promoting and selling skills are critical at the founding and at the closing of the fund, because they help realize the desired economic return at the exit.

Recruiting and people management skills are part of the soft support that a venture capitalist gives to the venture-backed company during the managing and monitoring phase. These skills try to satisfy the needs of a team that works well together while researching the success of the entrepreneurial initiative.

Because the level of competition is increasing and more challenges are faced by the European private industry, there will be a need for private equity players to focus on adding value to their holdings beyond financial engineering. As the world financial markets are facing a tremendous crisis of unpredictable dimension and duration, venture capital operators should first preserve the value of their existing portfolios. The recession should not hide opportunities to invest in valid firms that now are underestimated and underfinanced by traditional financial institutes due to the widespread credit crunch.

Fundraising

Fundraising sells a proposal or business idea to a particular market. The funds raised are used to create an invest equity vehicle that produces value shared between the promoters–managers and the investors. Funds may be raised over a period of one to two years. This can create information asymmetry and moral hazard problems between the venture capitalist and the individual investors that are typical for a principal–agent relationship.

The information asymmetry occurs because the investors have trouble monitoring the venture capitalist. Investments are generally made during the start-up stage so it is difficult to compare the investments with the market activity until the conclusion of this stage. Moral hazard is generated from the venture capitalists. They generally subscribe up to 1% of the capital so, to maximize their incomes, they invest in high-risk activities.

To reduce moral hazard and information asymmetry and to ensure a high probability of success, fundraising has to be studied and structured as a selling game where reputation, mutual trust, and love for gambling are the pillars of a risky job dedicated to the raising of large amounts of money.

The only way to solve the information asymmetry is to impose regular and smooth communication about the investment's performance. Moral hazard can be avoided through

Fixed deadlines for the return of the funds to the investors
Exiting revenues distributed to the subscribers
Gradually collecting equity subscribed

There are certain steps in the fundraising process that lead to a successful result:

Creation of the business idea
Venture capital organizations
Selling job
Debt raising
Calling plan
Key covenants
Types of investments

8.1 CREATION OF THE BUSINESS IDEA

The creation of a business idea starts by explaining the idea to the business community and catch the attention of potential investors. The business idea must include the following elements:

Choice of the vehicle
Target to invest (countries, sectors, life cycle stages)
Size of the vehicle and minimum for closing
Corporate governance[1] rules (i.e., relationship between promoters–managers and investors)
Size and policy of investments
Internal code of activity
Track record of the promoters–managers
Usage and size of leverage
Costs

In the UK and the United States, venture capitalists are generally structured as a single company that simultaneously manages different funds that are legally separated in a limited partnership (LP). There are fiscal advantages for this type of structure: the venture capitalist has unlimited responsibility by subscribing only 1% of the fund and investor responsibility is limited to the amount of capital subscribed.

The typical Italian structure for private equity activity is the closed-end fund.[2] Like LPs, it is impossible to subscribe after fund closure (when all shares have

---

[1] Instrument governing the rules for the nomination and function of supervisory boards, function of the business control, and greater control of particular acts.
[2] This term refers to the legal structures operating in the United States that are similar to closed-end funds; in Great Britain, the venture capital trusts; in France, the *fonds communs de placement à risque*; in Germany the *unternehmensbeteiligungsgesellschaft*; and in Spain, the *fondos de capital-riesgo*.

been subscribed) and investor exit[3] is possible only when the fund expires or by agreement. The normal duration of the fund is 10 years divided into 2 periods (investment and disinvestment period) lasting 5 years each.

Topics considered when analyzing the valuation of the target company:

Country the target is based in
Industry
Status of quoted company
Availability and reliability of data used for valuation
Life cycle stage

Each fund applies its own strategy when choosing the investment target. It is common to mix the previously listed elements, but valuation of the company can also be based on cash flow methods, market-based methods, or income-based and balance sheet methods. Different approaches to valuation of the target company depend on dissimilar industries (old vs. new economy), different weight of the intangible assets, and the opportunity for the target company to compare its value with the average value of similar public companies. In general,[4] income-based methods are often used in Italy,[5] France, and Germany, whereas the other methods are more prevalent in the UK and the United States.

During valuation of possible targets, regardless of the method, it is necessary to consider the position of the company along its life cycle curve (Figure 8.1); this affects both the value and the duration of the investment.

Creating or absorbing cash flow is strictly connected with a company's life cycle stage. A company early in its life cycle will not create cash flow for a long time so it will take a while to obtain the desired return on the high-risk investment. A mature firm, on the other hand, ensures a steady cash flow and lower risk because of the shorter payback period.

---

[3] The methodology used by the European Venture Capital Association (EVCA) subdivides the typology into initial public offering, trade sales, and write-off.

[4] Americans use the concept of enterprise value added (EVA), which is very close to the "goodwill" tradition of Europe. European venture capitalists and investment companies increasingly use free cash flow or multiples for valuing not only high tech firms but also old economy ones. This is not a surprise considering the globalization of financial markets and relative practices.

[5] In Italy, the use of net worth based methods or earning methods has been ratified at a statutory level by the Bank of Italy, which recommends these metrics for the valuation of companies included in closed funds portfolios. Cash flow methods are not openly recommended.

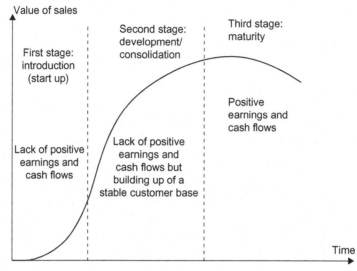

Value of sales

First stage:
introduction
(start up)

Second stage:
development/
consolidation

Third stage:
maturity

Lack of positive
earnings and
cash flows

Lack of positive
earnings and
cash flows but
building up of a
stable customer base

Positive
earnings and
cash flows

Time

FIGURE 8.1

Life cycle of a firm.

Each investment fund has its own investment policy, which is a consequence of the

1. Amount of capital collected
2. Strategy of the promoter
3. Composition of the total fund's portfolio managed

The amount of capital collected affects the flexibility of the fund's management. This allows fund promoters to choose between megadeals, which are pooled investments focused on very big, highly visible target companies on the market, and low risk investment with a diversified group of small to middle sized firms.

The financial market in which the fund operates influences its size; in Italy for a fund to be considered large it must have €500 million and in the UK and the United States it is necessary to collect at least €1 billion.

Fundraising is not money collecting. It also involves a relationship between the promoters–managers and the investors that can improve investor retention when it is conducted with transparency and involves all aspects of the business reducing the risk of moral hazard and agency costs.

Structured, well-planned, and exhaustive communication helps the temporary marriage between investors. It is executed through the investors plenum carried out at least annually and within six months after the closure of the fiscal year and through the quarterly performance report, which includes:

1. Fund summary describing structure, strategy, and relevant news
2. Executive summary detailing funds raised, investments, and changes related to fund managers
3. The trend of a monthly IRR and the actual value of the sum invested
4. Important news about target companies

Many funds have an advisory board and investors committee. The advisory board solves potential conflicts of interest and supports the managers, whereas the investors committee takes care of the relationship with the key investors. It is advantageous to avoid an excess of involvement in the daily operation without delegation of audit and planning authority.

The value of the investment is strictly influenced by a tax shield; the value created from financing through the debt allows the deduction of interest paid from the companies' incomes. This fiscal benefit allows companies to increase leverage up to the optimum value of the debt equity ratio, which permits the tax shield benefit without creating financial distress or reducing the value created.

It is impossible to conclude the analysis of the first step of fundraising without considering the costs connected with the creation of the deal in terms of time spent and economic resources and the due diligence that has to be executed. Preparation of the business idea involves an audit of the legality of the fund structure and the predisposition of the marketing presentation. The most expensive part of building a new private equity fund is the legal and fiscal advisors.

There are also the costs incurred by promotion fees from the placement agent. In Europe it is common to form a sponsorship with banks and consulting companies with well-known and widespread reputations. Sponsors of the fund are selected because of their professional track record and success with previously closed financial operations. The expertise and the high standing of the investment managers guarantees the interest of potential investors. It is also possible that sponsors can participate in investment decisions by selecting and evaluating investments and possible conflicts of interest. The purpose of sponsorship is to reassure investors the venture capital company, which is often small and little known, is valid.

It is important to underline the importance of investment managers who manage and maintain the relationship with the potential underwriter of the fund. They must organize several meetings (in general four or five) to inform potential investors about the fund. Fund managers must also manage and develop a relationship with financial markets. This is a fundamental element for the entrance and maintenance of the fund's position inside the financial market and for future successful fundraising.

The due diligence process allows investors to acquire all necessary information to make the investment and guarantee close quicker. When due diligence is done properly, it focuses on the market, environment, financial structure, and legal and tax position of the company financed.

8.2 VENTURE CAPITAL ORGANIZATIONS

Based on the business idea there are different venture options:

1. Business Angels — Private investors, with a large amount of available personal finance and a detailed knowledge of the sector in which they wish to invest, who finance new entrepreneurial initiatives. They take on high-risk, high-reward projects that have higher potential than the institutional venture capital companies. The principal limit of this type of investor is related to the limited dimensions of the assets invested.

2. Private pools of funds — Partnerships in which several shareholders (limited partners) have decided to invest a part of their own assets. Typically these funds originate from entrepreneurs or holders with substantial assets who are interested in jointly investing part of their wealth in new enterprises with potentially high returns. Historically, these entrepreneurs consolidated the success of their own company and decided to invest their own know-how and financial resources in new initiatives with excellent development prospects. Their solid financial background and expertise sustained high-risk projects in familiar or different sectors to diversify the portfolio. Transfers made between shareholders can range from $25,000 to $10 million individually. These are typically small deals.

3. Corporate funds — Funds and financial resources belonging to companies managed by venture capitalists that finance developing companies. Some companies also finance the start-up phase, but in certain cases the culture and interests of the developing company can block the development of new initiatives because they lack defined objectives and are incapable of managing rapidly evolving situations.

4. Mutual investment funds — Very important financial channels for venture capital because of the amount of capital raised publicly and the diversification requirements. They are financial vehicles that provide capital by issuing and placing a participation quota on investors (institutional and/or private). Closed-end funds meet the requirements of start-up companies, because the capital is stable for a medium- to long-term horizon and there is highrisk. In the UK and US markets fundraising for closed-end funds comes from pension funds, both public and private, whereas in Europe the largest investment

comes from the banking system and other institutional investors. Closed-end fundraising occurs during the initial formation phase through financial intermediaries until the capital requirement is reached. Therefore the fund is managed by a specialized intermediary who will invest in development projects whose returns will be distributed to investors on exit.

5. Public venture capital companies — They go public to obtain greater financial resources than those obtained from private investors. The greater inflow of capital is a consequence of the greater notoriety and transparency as well as the possibility for investors to exit from the operation due to a secondary market. In Europe the largest part of the capital in venture capital companies is held by founders and families belonging to the general partner.

6. Financial intermediaries (insurance companies, finance companies, investment banks) — Normally they have the necessary expertise to value industrial projects and raise funds for their realization. Merchant banks are entities most oriented to long-term investments and are prepared to sustain risk levels.

7. Public funds — Promote and satisfy objectives through the development of new company innovations such as research, creation of new employment, and growth of specific geographic areas. Some states have jointly accumulated wide-ranging funds from between $5 and $10 million reaching hundreds of millions of dollars. At the same time the size of the fund remains contained compared to the largest venture capital private companies with average investments from $100,000 to $500,000.

Academic foundations and institutions may invest in venture capital through the acquisition of holdings in closed-end funds, but their contributions are limited because of risk levels.

8.3 SELLING JOB

It is critical to identify the category of investors potentially interested in a fund, because the main channel for venture capital fundraising is the direct contact between company and investor. The fundraising strategy is profoundly influenced if the fund is new or it represents the continuation of a previous initiative; the absence of a track record and the necessity to develop a network of contacts makes the fundraising complex and burdensome.

The involvement of a placement agent increases the probability of success. The placement agent is a specialized operator with a big network of potential capital-raising clients. His experience contributes to the definition of the fund and the marketing strategy. It is necessary to hire a placement agent from the beginning because his expertise is important from the initial stages. Therefore the general partner or manager of the fund hires the placement agent to facilitate a quick end of the fundraising and attract a more effective segment of target investors. Another advantage of employing a placement agent is his ability to dedicate all of his time to investment selection. The placement agent is paid a significant commission, about 2% of capital raised, applied only in case of success.

After deciding the channel and the parties to be employed to raise funds, the next step is to identify the target market and develop the fundraising strategy (Figure 8.2).

To raise funds potential clients must first be defined. Domestic investors should be established first as their confidence in a fund attracts foreign capital who take into account the economic prospects of the fund's country, its capital markets, the presence of interesting entrepreneurial initiatives, etc.

The size of the fund becomes significant if large institutional investors are involved. When selecting potential clients it is also necessary to note the increasing role played by gatekeepers, i.e., institutional investors offering consulting management or services. Originating in the United States, but now prevalent in Europe, gatekeepers raise funds from small or medium sized institutions, large institutions without experts in the private equity sector, or high net worth individuals who wish to invest in private equity initiatives. The presence of a gatekeeper in a venture capital fund attracts further potential clients.

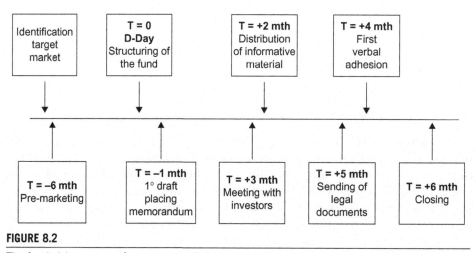

FIGURE 8.2

The fundraising process for venture capital.

In Europe banks or consulting companies who are wellknown and reputable often sponsor funds; the purpose of the sponsorship is to reassure investors the venture capital company is valid. Moreover, if the sponsor is a bank or a financial intermediary, they are likely to take part in investment decisions.

The pre-marketing phase focuses on understanding the potential market in order to evaluate interest and gather useful information for the investment proposal. This usually occurs through meetings to update existing investors about new possible initiatives. A purely informative meeting such as an international road show will be organized with new potential investors. Managers must be prepared to give precise information relating to the track record of past initiatives specifying details relative to the structure of the operation, cash flow, the growth of the investments, and the values and timing of exit. At the same time managers should offer a list of potential investors.

Once the fund has market approval, its structure must be defined in cooperation with legal and fiscal advisors. The project must remove any legal, fiscal, and technical factors that could discourage investors. This could cost a fund between €300,000 and €500,000.

Next is the preparation and sending of legal documentation to the probable adhering investors (partnership agreements, copy of contract, fiscal and legal matters, etc.); the operation will be closed once the final adherents are notified.

8.4 **DEBT RAISING**

As previously mentioned, the profitability of an investment is strictly connected to the value created by debt leverage. The financial structure of a venture capital deal is generally a mix of debt and equity (capital structure) used to acquire the target company.

Defining optimal capital structure is a topic that has always interested academics and market insiders. The most relevant and well-known theory about leverage use is formalized by Modigliani and Miller (M + M I) through three statements.

The first statement states that the mix of debt and equity does not create any impact on the company value in a world:

Without tax
Without any type of financial distressed costs
Without any form of information asymmetry
With flat investments
Without cost for the transaction

If one of the listed conditions is not present, it is very likely M + M I will not be supported. If the debt increases free cash flow raises proportionally with the tax rate applied to the interest paid (T × i × D), and as a consequence the debt creates a tax shield that increments the company value (M + M II).

Even if this second statement maximizes the weight of debt, the presence of financial distressed costs leads to the disruption of the company value due to the legal expenditures and the daily pressure on management to service the debt (M +M III).

In conclusion, if we visualize these three statements we have Figure 8.3:

The optimal capital structure is a range of D/E that ensures tax shield benefits and avoids any risk connected with distressed financial structure.

Assuming a target company is acquired with a mix of equity and debt, it is important to choose the appropriate type of debt and equity.

1. Equity is represented by the risk capital subscribed by investors as full power of corporate governance and the right to receive a fixed yield or priority in the dividend paying out.

2. The shareholder loan has the same risk profile as capital share, but it allows investors to receive a piece of their return without or before the selling of the share.

3. Management equity is an incentive to motivate management especially if it is used with a stock option plan that provides a premium related to company performance.

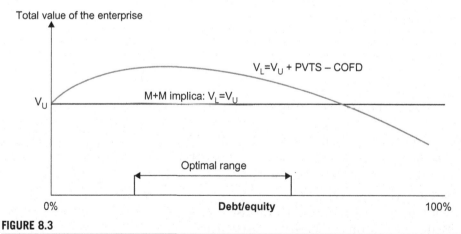

FIGURE 8.3

Optimal capital structure.[6]

---

[6] V_U is unlevered value; the value of a company without any debt. V_L is the value of a company with debt, PVTS is the present value of tax shield; and COFD is the cost of finance distress.

The other financing tool is debt. It can be divided into different categories depending on two main elements:

Seniority or the level of guarantee and protection ensured to the investors in case of default

Operational issue financed (acquisition finance, working capital facility, CAPEX facility)

Senior debt is the main part of the debt in a private equity deal that ensures the investor will be repaid before any other creditor. There are three different typologies:

1. Acquisition financing is generally covered by specific rights placed on the company's assets or facilities. It can also be granted by the expected future cash flow of the target company. Assuming the EBITDA is a good predictor of cash flow, investors apply a multiple to define the company's capacity to repay debt. This capacity is predicted by comparing the EBITDA to the total debt and/or the cash interest.

2. The refinancing facility is a turnover of the capital structure to reduce the number of creditors (banks).

3. Working capital facility is a tool that, along with a revolving structure, finances the daily company operations.

4. CAPEX facility is dedicated to the acquisition or improvement of the assets used by the company to develop their productivity.

If the senior debt does not cover the entire acquisition price or the promoter wants to reduce the level of equity, it is possible to recur the junior debt, which has a lower level of guarantee but a higher level of interest and duration of six and ten years. If these debts are traded on a public market, without collateral, they are called high yield bonds. This category of debt will be repaid only after the total satisfaction of the senior facilities.

Between equity and debt is the mezzanine debt. This is a sophisticated and complex financing instrument developed in the UK and US. It is covered by the same senior collateral, and its reimbursement always happens between the senior and the junior debts. The servicing of mezzanine debt is broken down into three different types: interest paid yearly, structured with a capitalization system with payment at the end of the loan, and represented by equity linked to company performance. This type of debt is used in competitive situations, because it allows the increase of the debt equity ratio while protecting the company from financial distress.

8.5 CALLING PLAN

The calling plan is a technique used to increase the internal rate of return (IRR) for investors without reducing revenues for the managers. The IRR is a measure of the net present value on the outgoings (purchases of quotas) and receipts (dividends, exits) of one or more operation. This method can be considered the most accurate because it is the only one capable of taking into account the time variable while calculating a single investment or a number of operations.

The calling agenda plans the time period investors have to wire the subscribed funds; at start up subscribers contribute only a percentage of their investment (commitment) and then complete the investment following the calling agenda. The venture capitalist carefully prepares the commitment agenda, because it is the only way to balance the short-term view of the investment, typical for the investors of the fund, and the medium long-term view of the investment that the deal needs.

8.6 KEY COVENANT SETTING

The fundraising phase cannot exclude the covenant setting; rules that settle and define the relationship between investors and managers. These rules underline duties and rights while minimizing opportunism, moral hazard, and conflict of interest. The covenant can be settled through a limited partnership (LP) agreement, which is an internal code of activity or a private agreement.

The covenant setting has three different classifications:

1. Overall fund management — These covenants regulate the general aspects of the investment activity in order to realize the expected return. Because significant financial and managerial resources are invested in innovative projects with high potential and high risk, it is critical to define the maximum dimension of the investment in a single firm to diversify resources into a sufficiently high number of initiatives (portfolio approach). At the same time capital gain should be realized within three to five years. Different types of debt are available so covenants need to define a suitable financial structure in terms of maturity, amount, collateral usage, and seniority. This is necessary to balance between the leverage benefit, the cost of the debt, and the risk of finance distress. The covenants clearly state that if the profits can be re-invested these criteria are to be applied.

2. The general partner must follow a policy that defines and limits the possibility of personal investing in portfolio companies to control conflict of

interest and ensure the minimum standard of professional care. Specific restrictions on the investment powers of the general partner include:

Diversification — No more than a specified percentage of total commitments (25%) are to be invested in a single or linked investment

Bridge financing — When the general partner intends to sell part of an investment within a specified period after its acquisition, the 25% limit is often raised to 35% of total commitments

Hedging — Not permitted except for efficient portfolio management

Publicly traded securities — Since investors are unwilling to pay private equity fees for the management of publicly traded securities, there are often strict limits placed on the circumstances in which these may be held by the fund

Fund documents — Regulate the terms and circumstances in which co-investment opportunities may be offered to investors

General partners' investment — Usually limited to a very low percentage of the investment such as 1% of the equity rule used in the United States

3. These contract rules settle the type of investment in terms of restriction on asset classes, defining amount and type of equity to be subscribed, and restriction due to conflict of interest with debt financers.

8.7 **TYPES OF INVESTMENTS**

Intervention in risk capital has different sizes, prospective, and requirements and is defined as the combination of capital and know-how. Intervention in risk capital is classified according to the target company's life cycle phase by operators, associations and research centers, and even for statistical purposes.

The types of venture capital interventions are based on the participation in the initial life cycle phase (early stage financing), which consists of

Seed financing (experimentation phase). The risk capital investor takes part in the experimentation phase when the technical validity of the product/service still has to be demonstrated. He provides limited financial contributions to the development of the business idea and to the evaluation of feasibility. The failure risk is very high.

Start-up financing (beginning of activity phase). In this stage the investor finances the production activity even if the commercial success or flop of the product/service is not yet known. The level of financial contributions and risk is high.

Early stage financing (first development phase). The beginning of the production activity has already been completed, but the commercial validity of the product/service must still be fully evaluated. This intervention consists of high financial contributions and lower risks.

The increasing complexity of financing and the problems in each of these stages means that the level of company development and the financial needs do not fit to the pattern. Additionally, investors of risk capital have developed advanced financial engineering tools that are more complex and sophisticated.

It would be useful to define a more analytical classification relating to the possible strategic requirements of a company considering the threats and opportunities faced by the sector and the final investors' objectives. We can group and classify the transfer of risk capital by the institutional investors in three principal types (following the types previously listed; Figure 8.4):

Expansion financing
Turnaround and LBO financing
Vulture and distressed financing

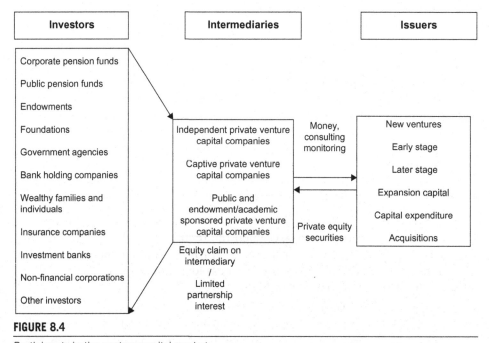

FIGURE 8.4

Participants in the venture capital market.
(Source: Fenn et al., Board of Governors of the Federal Reserve System Staff Studies, p. 168, 1995).

Investing

Investing is the core of private equity business and the way to develop a business idea for the investor. When investing the venture capitalist:

1. Acts within established time limits
2. Acquires only minority interests to control the entrepreneurial risk
3. Places emphasis on investment returns in terms of capital gain and goodwill; the participation in risk capital is only partially remunerated during the period of ownership from dividends or compensation for consulting.
4. May supply some services that the closed-end funds cannot due to statute clauses.

There are two main areas of investing:

Valuation and selection of opportunities and matching them with the appropriate investment vehicle

Target company valuation, the "core competence" of a private equity fund, is a proper blend of strategic analysis (about the business, the market, and the competitive advantage), business planning, financial forecasting, human resources, and entrepreneur and management team assessment.

Through acquisitions and participations, the venture capitalist finances new entrepreneurial initiatives or small non-quoted companies with the objective of sustaining growth to realize an adequate gain at exit. Venture capital operations are thus distinguished by returns expected, time horizon, and minimum size of the investment.

Private Equity and Venture Capital in Europe: Markets, Techniques, and Deals

Returns expected are normally very high, and only the prospect of attractive gains justifies the considerable risk of financing a start up. The duration of the investment is usually between four and seven years, and even if the venture capitalist qualifies as a medium long-term investor, he is not a permanent partner of the company financed. Instead, the venture capitalist expects to easily exit from the investment. The selection of projects to finance and the monitoring of the project require significant resources, which can only be justified for investments of a certain amount. At this point, it is necessary for the entrepreneur to seek financing. Significant variables that influence this choice include the:

Sector of the new initiative
Strategy followed
Level of preparation of the potential entrepreneur

The type of activity and strategy chosen affect the financial needs and potential growth of a new company, whereas the level of preparation of the potential entrepreneur affects the ability to attract external financing. When the launch of a new initiative occurs in traditional sectors by parties without a reputation, financial needs must be covered by the entrepreneur's personal resources. But the scarcity of financial resources can represent an opportunity rather than a restraint by motivating innovative behavioral strategies.

For new initiatives the involvement of institutional investors is unlikely because the financial requirements are too large and the involvement of a venture capitalist would not provide any real advantage. Value added by the institutional investor is very limited in terms of both knowledge and competitive dynamics as well as rapid growth. The intervention of an external financier would complicate the management of the new company undermining the flexibility that is essential during the start-up phase.

It is now necessary to distinguish between entrepreneurial commitments for seed financing and start-up financing. Involvement is possible and convenient during seed financing and only necessary in the process of venture creation (start-up financing). The development of the business idea requires research and development, analysis of the market, identification of potential collaborators and employees, etc. Financial requirements needed to select the appropriate investment are not large, and the risk of failure of the initiative is remarkable with an uncertain rate of success. Financial needs come from the promoter's personal resources as well as financing from state agencies. When financing new entrepreneurial initiatives, it seems that the start-up phase is better managed and financed by state agencies.

9.1 **VALUATION AND SELECTION**

Selecting investments made by venture capitalists is a complex process, because there is information asymmetry based on the interaction between impartial components, analyses with strong methodological rigor, and subjective experience and intuition. The first valuation step is the pre-investment phase where a series of critical factors are defined to see if and how they affect the investor. This screening is strongly influenced by the strategic orientation of the investor; for example, the geographic location, the sector, and the type of product (technology used, trademarks, leadership in differentiation or of cost, etc.). Fifty percent of proposals received by the venture capitalist in this phase are refused. The remaining proposals are examined in greater detail by analyzing the depth of the chosen market and its development, economic–financial results expected, and amount of financing required. After this stage, venture capitalists delete a further 35% of the proposals.

The real selection process follows the analysis of the entrepreneur's proposal. It concentrates on several key steps:

The business plan — detailed analysis of the pre-investment phases

1. Business
2. Market
3. Entrepreneur and management team
4. Competitive advantage of the initiative
5. Strategy
6. Economic–financial equilibrium
7. Timing

The investment process:

1. Capital budget
2. Pricing and the structure of the investment
3. Exit closing

The notoriety of this form of financial support from venture capitalists has made the search for funds increasingly difficult. The most critical element when choosing investments is the time the venture capitalist spends on evaluating proposals.

At the company level, the project plan is defined as a business plan; it is the first way to establish the relationship between entrepreneur and institutional investor as well as a request for risk capital. For those reasons the management of a target company prepares the business plan very carefully, communicating any relevant information that makes the project unique and interesting. An exhaustive business plan includes an executive summary that examines the basic elements of the project: opportunities, risks, expertise of the management team, and timing. The entrepreneur must communicate the concept of a feasible business idea that is missing only enough capital to start.

The first key aspect the venture capitalist wants to understand is if the business idea is related to a product or a service, a combination of the two, or the creation of an original and more complex model. The description of the product or trademark must be focused on the principal attributes that make it unique, because the investor is interested in knowing the limits of the product and the service offered. The venture capitalist also considers the target market in terms of boundaries, foreseeable market share, and total market value.

The investor must trust the management team of the target company. He will need information about its expertise, experience, cohesion and motivation focusing on capabilities, limits, interest, and commitment to the project.

A successful project can maintain its status over time defending its competitive advantages. It is useful to conduct a project analysis through the "five forces" as represented in Porter's model (Figures 9.1 and 9.2):

Strategy analysis is the most important part of the business plan, because it evaluates the company's targets, how they will be reached, and if the business

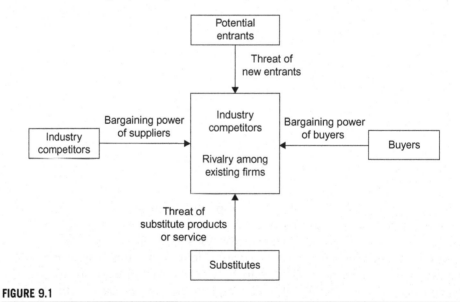

FIGURE 9.1

Porter's "five forces" model.[1]

---

[1] Porter M.E., *Competitive Strategy. Technique for Analysing Industries and Competitors*, New York, The Free Press, 1980.

Supplier power	Barrier entry	Buyer's power	Substitute product or services
Supplier concentration	Absolute cost advantages	Bargaining leverage	Switching costs
Importance of volume to supplier	Proprietary learning curve	Buyer volume	Buyer inclination to substitutes
Differentiation of inputs	Access to inputs	Buyer information	Price-performance trade off of substitutes
Impact of inputs on cost or differentiation	Government policy	Brand identity	
Switching costs of firms in the industry	Economies of scale	Price sensitivity	
Presence of forward integration	Capital requirements	Threat of backward integration	
Cost relative to total purchase in industry	Brand identity	Product differentiation	
	Switching costs	Buyer concentration vs industry	
	Access to distribution	Substitutes available	
	Expected retaliation	Buyers' incentives	
	Proprietary products		

FIGURE 9.2

Elements to be considered in Porter's model.

is coherently defined and consistent with the economic–financial forecasts. Financial forecasts explain costs and revenues, investments, and cash flow. They are the basis for the evaluation of the business idea because they help identify economic and financial equilibrium.

Business plan timing depends on the project or company. The time period of the plan covers the life of the project or it covers between three and five years with a very detailed degree of analysis in the first year and a more generalized approach for successive years.

Investment decisions are made based on several factors: the current and potential market shares of the company, its technology, and the creation of value during the exit phase. The negotiations step lasts three or six months after the preparation of the business plan, depending on the clarity and completeness of the information supplied by the entrepreneur. This information also defines the price and the timing and method of payment.

If there is agreement on the key points of the operation, the parties sign letters of intent in which the economic and legal aspects of the operation are defined (the value of the company, the presence of the investor on the Board of Directors, the informative obligations, etc.) and then refined in the investment contract.

Contract signing can proceed with the terms of the agreement regarding pricing, quota of participation, and administrative aspects, between the company, its shareholders, and the investor. Once the final agreement is achieved, the operation is formalized with the

Transfer of the shares
Payment of the price
Issue of the guarantees
Reorganization of the Board of Directors and the management team

The next phase, due diligence, refers to investor actions necessary to reach a final valuation. It also contributes to the protection of the institutional investors' capital. Good management of the due diligence phase guarantees a quicker closing of the deal and allows the investor to acquire all the necessary information for a professional investment.

There are five ways to classify due diligence:

1. **Market** — The way investors understand the positioning, the potentiality, and risks of the specific market in which the company operates. To check the consistency of the company data presented, market due diligence must be connected with financial due diligence.

2. **Environmental** — Comparison between company profitability, legislation and regulations, and the internal organization of environmental control and pollution. Identifies and verifies the impact on the environment and the pollution problems not yet resolved.

3. **Financial** — Final evaluation of the economic–financial aspects (cash flow and working capital) and definition of the necessity of funds (budget and business plan for three to five years) of the company financed with the historical economic trend of sales, margins, production costs, and fixed costs highlighting liabilities and risks connected.

4. **Legal** — Examines any legal problem such as lawsuits, commitments with third parties and relative risks, contractual guarantees, employee labor agreements, or stock option plans.

5. **Tax** — Analyzes fiscal aspects related to liabilities, structure of the acquisition operation, future fiscal benefits, and exit strategy.

The exit phase is the final part of the investment process. It is a sensitive and unpredictable step because it is the moment when gain should be realized. If successful, on exit the value of the participation increases. If the initiative fails, the exit is made when there is no possible way to solve the crisis. The exit can be realized through IPO, trade sale, sale to new (or majority) shareholders, or to the management as well as a merger or incorporation with other companies.

The investment process can be summarized in Figure 9.3.

Deal flow (origination)	The equity fund is able to generate opportunities from its network.
Screening	The preliminary analysis of opportunities made by the management and supported by the technical committee. The golden rule is that, starting with 100 investment proposals, only 10 will live through screening.
Valuation and due diligence	Three different activities take place: meeting with the entrepreneur and the management; use of financial and strategic techniques; due diligence activities.
Rating assignment	It consists of the transformation of the previous valuation and due diligence activities into a rating within the process chosen by the equity investor as per Basle II rules.
Negotiation (deal making)	Equity fund has "to sell" the valuation to the entrepreneur in competition (or in cooperation) with other investors.
Decision to invest money	The negotiation leads to a final price.
Contract designing	This process ends with three main choices: targeting, liability profile, and engagement.

FIGURE 9.3

The investment process.

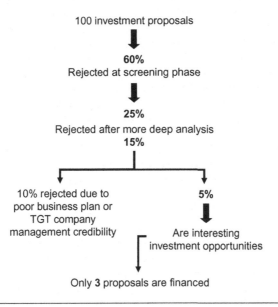

FIGURE 9.4

The golden rule.

9.2 THE CONTRACTUAL PACKAGE

The "contractual package" defines the commitment of the equity investor to the venture-backed company. It impacts and sustains value creation and allocates duties and rights between the equity fund and the venture-backed company.

The contract facilitates management and control and identifies the proper combination between risk and return. Contract design is developed through three different approaches:

Targeting
Liability profile
Engagement

Each approach is broken down in Figure 9.5.

The first approach is by targeting an investment vehicle; the valuation of the alternative investment or company or a special purpose vehicle (SPV) set up just for the deal. A direct investment is recommended when the investor is interested in the business, there is total control of the project, and there is a commitment between the investor and the company. An SPV is recommended when the investor wants only relevant assets or a branch, the investment is tailor-made on the business plan, there are no inefficiencies, and the SPV supports collateral schemes.

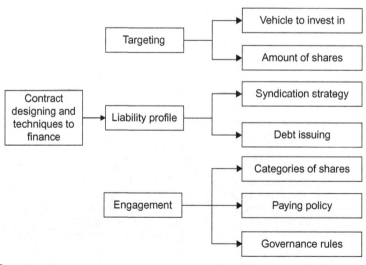

FIGURE 9.5

The contractual package.

Another way to choose an investment vehicle is based on the amount of shares or the percentage of shares to buy and the role of the venture capitalist within the shareholders. This decision is driven by

Majority versus minority participation in the risk capital
Relative and absolute size of investment
Capital requirement impact
Voting rights and effective influence within the Board of Directors

The liability profile of an investment vehicle should also be considered in the contractual package. Debt issuing can be realized through banking loans or bonds placement, and the most common scheme is an investment in an SPV through a leveraged buyout (LBO) to acquire a target company.

There are two financing tools available for this scheme:

1. Syndication strategy — The promoter finds other equity investors and builds a syndicate.[2] This tool is recommended because it increases investment power while sharing risk as pros and cons are blended.

   The pros are the
   Reduction of credit risk for each member
   Opportunity to diversify the portfolio of the investments in terms of industry, geographic area, etc.
   Opportunity to take part in a deal with international relevance
   Opportunity to increase services
   Huge amount of capital collected
   Cost reduction
   Timing and certainty of funds
   Flexibility
   The cons are the
   Hierarchy inside the syndicate
   Agreement between the investors
   Risk of losing market control and knowledge
   Duration is shorter then corporate bond
   The bank that organizes the syndication is named arranger and is selected according to its relationship status, speciality, queue, and open bidding.

   The financial structure can be fully underwritten, partially underwritten, or best effort. The syndicate can be a "direct loan syndicate," when the agreement is signed off by a group of banks or "participation syndicate"

---

[2] This tool started in the United States during the 1960s to satisfy the huge financial needs of big firms that could not be handled by a single bank.

when only one bank signs and then looks for other bank investors. Banks participating in the syndicate gain through management fees, commitment fees, agency fees, and interest charged.

After the syndication is organized, communication about the financial market and operation details and structure begins.

2. Debt issuing — The decision to combine equity investment (with or without SPV, syndicated or not) with leverage. Using leverage means multiplying the impact of equity investment, in terms of value, if the higher financial risk is sustainable.

   Placement can be public or private. Public placement debt servicing has an overall lower cost with a higher cost for marketing, legal representation, and management. Private placement has higher costs for the debt servicing, but it allows the issuer to be aware of the price that is fixed a priori with the institutional investors. Bond placement can be done through a syndication between different banks where the bank involved is named lead manager of the syndicated bonds and is responsible for the preparation of the offering circular. Within this document, the bond characteristics are explained and sent to other banks suitable to be the management group, underwriter, or seller.

   With public placement, the issuer understands and realizes the cost of the operation only at the closing.

   Advantages are the huge amount of capital provided and long duration financing. The high level of structure standardization is considered a disadvantage.

The last financial approach in the contractual package is engagement. It begins by choosing categories of shares or share class to buy guaranteeing the best way to support the investment and the managing phase.

Typically, the venture capitalist chooses between a range of shares with different rights and duties:

Common shares are securities representing equity ownership in a corporation, providing voting rights, and entitling the holder to share the company's success through dividends or capital gain. The holders receive one vote per share to elect the company's Board of Directors and to decide on company matters such as stock splits and company objectives.

Preferred stock usually does not include voting rights, or at least limited rights in extraordinary matters. This is compensated by priority over common stock in the payment of dividends and upon liquidation. Their dividend is paid out prior to any other dividends. Preferred stock may be converted into common stock.

Shares with embedded option provide different rights entitling the holder to buy company stocks issued at a predefined price due to an attached option. It is not traded by itself and it affects the value of the share of which it is a part.

Tracking stock is a security issued by a parent company related to the results of one of its subsidiaries or line of business. Financial results of the subsidiary or line of business are attributed to the tracking stock. Often, the reason for issuing this type of stock is to separate the high-growth division from a larger parent company. The parent company and its shareholders remain in control of the subsidiary or unit's operations.

Another investment choice during the engagement step is connected with the paying policy; the technique of issuing shares and the relationship of management within company corporate governance.

To ensure a useful and satisfactory paying policy, three basic questions need to be answered.

1. What is the usage of money? The investment can be obtained through new shares issued by the company or old shares sold to the venture capitalist by the entrepreneur.

2. What is the expectation of the entrepreneur? The entrepreneur can choose these types of financial operations for two reasons: just because he wants to earn money by selling company shares or because he needs financial or strategic support to sustain activity and its growth.

3. What is the relationship between the existing shareholders? The venture capitalist could invest in the company and keep total control of the risk capital or maintain all or part of the existing shareholders and negotiate the exit of those fired.

The last step in the engagement process is governance rules; the general agreement on shareholders duties and rights, Board of Directors activity, and information flow (see Figure 9.6). Governance rules can be formally written in the Limited Partnership Agreement, in the internal code of activity, or in a formal autonomous agreement designed to discipline the power of the shareholders.

The logic and the structure of the governance rules affect the

Percentage of shares owned
Effective power of shareholders

Corporate governance regulates the activity shared between the shareholder assembly and the Board of Directors as well as their relationship. These rules also define who has the power to appoint the executive director, the president, and the vice-presidents along with their duties and rights, generally fixing a special quorum.

Shareholders duties and rights	Discipline of activities shared between shareholder assembly and Board of Directors; Connection shareholders assembly – Board of Directors; Directors, executive directors, president and vice-president nomination; Special quorum policy.
Board of Directors activity	Power of executive director(s); Inner rules of Board of Directors activity; Non-executive directors presence and specific role.
Information flow	Content of information flow; Scheduling of information flow; Auditing activity rules to control information flow.

FIGURE 9.6

Corporate governance rules.

Good governance structure should provide a group of policies and processes that ensure smooth management from the Board of Directors, while settling key controls to minimize abuse of the power connected with the executive role. When the size or a particular industry where the firm operates suggests, a good rule is to give non-executive directors on the Board of Directors the ability to exercise control on executive members.

The last matter covered by corporate governance includes the auditing staff, its activities, and the information flow provided by the directors. These rules define the structure of the auditing staff in terms of number of people and their competencies and the power to look into company activities, as well as a planned list of controls to be executed.

9.3 PROBLEMS AND CRITICAL AREAS OF VENTURE CAPITAL OPERATIONS

Venture capital operations involve three key figures: the financier of the venture capital operations (pension funds, other types of institutional or private investors), the venture capitalist for managerial and financial support to the entrepreneur; and the entrepreneur who developed the highly innovative idea.

The typical structure of venture capital contracts, focusing on the relationship between institutional investor and the company financed, may suffer from asymmetric information or moral hazard, especially when the investment decision has been made because of the behavior of the entrepreneur or the venture capitalist. The entrepreneur is directly responsible for the success of the company's project. If a valid mechanism of control is missing, the possible and predictable consequence is opportunistic behavior; the entrepreneur follows personal interests. For example, if the entrepreneur is incapable of financing the idea with his own capital, he could motivate the risk capital investor to continue financing a project even when the conditions for its valid and effective development no longer exist. The opportunistic behavior of the venture capitalist exploits the entrepreneur's ideas by financing competitive companies similar to the initiative already financed.

Because of this opportunistic behavior, binding contracts are important. They solve and control possible interest conflicts between the entrepreneur who wishes to limit the possible leakage of information concerning competitive advantages, and the institutional investor who is interested in maximizing the motivation of the company's management for the most efficient development of the plan. The form of the financing selected solves these problems because it influences the incentives of both the entrepreneur and the venture capitalist.

Venture capitalists support high-risk initiatives with potentially high remuneration. It is necessary to identify the mechanism of fundraising and employment of the necessary financial resources for their initiatives. To raise funds, large institutional investors frequently agree to a significant quota of the capital gains obtained (approximately 80%) from the eventual positive outcome of the IPOs or merger operations. Pension funds are also used as a source of funds. From an employment perspective, the venture capital companies provide financing for a portfolio of companies, granting technical and managerial support and financial resources to the entrepreneur in exchange for becoming a minority shareholder (equity between 5 and 15%). The primary objective is to achieve high profit (capital gains equal to at least 20%), which results from the difference between the cost price of the participation at the moment of acquisition (subscription) and the sales price to third parties during the exit phase (with operations of IPO, LBO, or mergers).

Venture capitalists influence the development of investments in these three areas:

1. Closed ownership model of companies
2. Growth process of family companies
3. Innovative processes

Entrepreneurs do not always appreciate the participation of third party shareholders for fear of interference during the decision-making process, the definition of the strategic lines, and the selection of the managerial direction of the company. In the second area venture capitalists choose small companies with high competitive potential and adopt adequate operating strategies connected with the business choices of accelerated growth. Innovative processes are represented by the poor cooperation and collaboration between universities with scientific and technological centers and companies, which can delay the development of new companies with high technological content.

Venture capitalists affect investments by

1. Providing high technical qualification, level of experience, managerial expertise, and professionalism
2. Developing intermediation for risk capital inside the market

9.4 THE ROLE OF MANAGERIAL RESOURCES

The realization of a venture capital operation is a demanding task. To ensure success there must be a high degree of consulting, awareness of the high potential risk, and a high level of participation in all aspects of definition and organization of the final objectives of the operation starting with the set up of a Board of Directors.

Venture capitalists succeed because of the professional quality of the human resources dedicated to performing managerial activity with a highly innovative function. The wealth of knowledge and expertise brought to a project by venture capitalists is one of the principal requisites that guarantees the feasibility of a project. Venture capitalists also bring confidentiality, business intuition, flexibility, a critical mind, and a decision capacity based on a precise calculation and estimation of the risks to a project. It is also important that the resources utilized by venture capitalists to support entrepreneurial initiatives have proven experience evaluating companies. This guarantees a business analysis not limited to economic–financial aspects, but widened to include the strategic analysis of the sector (opportunities and threats of the possible product–market combinations), and to the study of the strengths and weaknesses, at competitive level, of the future development programs of the company.

The role of venture capitalists during the transfer of risk capital is more complex than just supporting and assisting activities. They provide a specific professional contribution that includes human resources that guarantee a service with a proven image of "active neutrality." The participation in the shareholding of small and medium sized companies by the institutional investors of risk capital must therefore be based on a responsible entry in the best entrepreneurial initiatives.

With a venture capitalist it is possible to combine the expansion of the company while maintaining its family character. Choosing venture capital allows the entrepreneur to place shares outside the family that are under his control, to issue preference shares, to trade on or outside the quota of minority shares in companies controlled by the holding company, and to create real and proper groups of companies capable of carrying out autonomous recourse to the capital markets.

Venture capitalists support and participate in companies that have:

1. An undisputed entrepreneurial expertise and experience
2. Analytical business plans and innovative market strategies capable of guaranteeing a potential level of development compatible with the dynamics of the market and with the situation of the company
3. New financial shareholders breaking down psychological and cultural barriers
4. High performance and high current and future profitability aligned with a level of risk-return, with a good economic–financial equilibrium guaranteeing a "secure" return of the investment
5. Absolute transparency

By choosing venture capital, the real and potential advantages for the company include:

- Providing new financial resources to develop the company's initiatives
- Access to new financing funds for family operated companies
- Entry of a prestigious shareholder, which permits greater contractual power between suppliers and competitors and greater guarantees for customers
- Improvement of the company image due to the presence of partners that assure the solidity of the company and its programs
- Strong distinction between corporate and personal interests for greater weight toward market policy and the business strategies adopted by management
- Possible synergies between the expertise of the company's management and the minority partner

The greatest advantage is the change in mentality that allows the small- or medium-sized entrepreneur to expand his financial horizons.

9.5 POSSIBLE UNSUCCESSFUL FINANCIAL PARTICIPATION

The principal reason for unsuccessful financial participation is related to management. Because management is responsible for finance, marketing, distribution, and production, they are considered the "dynamic element and the source of life of any business." If managements makes the wrong strategic choices related to the business in which it operates, financial participation could be unsuccessful.

9.6 INVOLVEMENT OF VENTURE CAPITALISTS IN THE BOARD OF DIRECTORS

It is difficult to control a venture capital operation because of information asymmetry between the entrepreneur and management. The best way to safeguard the transferred capital is to involve the venture capitalist in the management of the company. With their own people exercising control over the Board of Directors, it permits the institutional investors to participate in key decisions connected with suppliers, market policies, extraordinary financial operations, and ordinary management of the company. The theory of the financial intermediary labels this type of monitoring as "soft facet" and "hard facet." Soft facet monitoring merely supports management regarding principal operating choices and decisions. "Hard facet" is a form of monitoring that controls the entrepreneur with the purpose of limiting possible conflicts of interest between the objectives of the entrepreneur and the venture capitalists. The foundation of a positive outcome to an investment initiative with risk capital is based on the irreplaceable role of the venture capitalist in the support, assistance, and participation in the development of an entrepreneurial project.

Managing and monitoring

After closing the deal, both the investor and the venture-backed company need to organize, plan, and manage their partner, assuming that they will live a "temporary but important marriage." First, they have to define and share various details and agree upon both medium-long term and daily rules. Second, they must commit to working together and transparency when managing typical agency problems.

The goal shared between the investor and the venture-backed company (or the entrepreneur) is always the same: the creation of value. This condition divides successful operations from failures allowing the investor and company to reach the expected returns. Although they may have this common goal, many aspects, operations, and views can be completely different.

Critical topics that provoke debates and problems include:

Duration of investor involvement
Strategies used to increase company value
Financial and industrial alliances
New opportunities that modify the pre-investment situation

Both the investor and the entrepreneur try to solve all potential disagreements before the fundraising phase, corporate governance rules, and key covenant setting; however it is impossible to forecast the future and regulate everything. Conflicts also arise because the investor has his own portfolio to manage with constraints coming from the IRR objective, the residual maturity, the regulatory capital, and covenants settled between the fund's originators. On the other side, the venture-backed company (or entrepreneur) has its own industrial, financial, and personal goals that may differ from the investor.

10.1 PERFORMANCE DETERMINATION

Before analyzing specific monitoring and controlling activities, it is critical to define how funds evaluate the success of their investment activity. This is done by performance determinations consisting of a set of guidelines defined by industry associations and specific government regulations that are generally different in each country where the "directives" are acknowledged by the financial sector regulatory organizations. In Italy we follow the guidelines proposed in March 2001 by the European Venture Capital Association (EVCA).[1] These guidelines are a reference for all investors.

The huge increase of investments in risk capital has made other types of performance determinations inadequate. The model proposed by EVCA is not mandatory for operators, but in a business where reputation plays a fundamental role in the success of the initiative, not using EVCA's model could damage the operator's reputation and make fundraising much more difficult.

Problems determining an investment's performance arise when no efficient market exists or when trading is carried out in a non-transparent context. In these cases it is difficult to determine the final value of a company because not all operators are using the same calculation rules.

EVCA suggests calculating the investment's performance with the internal rate of return (IRR) or rate of internal return (TIR); it relates to the net present value on the outgoings (in particular, the purchases of quotas) and receipts (dividends, exits) for one or more operations. This choice, even if from a mathematical point of view the most difficult to perform, is considered the most correct because it takes into account simultaneously the time variable and number of operations.

Performance is calculated to provide an indicator of the manager's ability to select target companies and deliver success as well as to obtain an indicator of effective costs faced by subscribers. Because the starting data are not the same for all investments, we identify three different IRR:

Gross return on the realized investments — Net present value of the entries and exits of the investments made; for example, any pending write-offs or bankruptcies are not estimated or included.

---

[1]The European Venture Capital Association (EVCA) is the European association of investors in risk capital with the objective of standardizing the processes of acquisition, management, sale, and valuation of the quotas between the different operators.

Gross return on all investments — Includes the value of the operations still to be realized; for example, a quota yet to be invested or a write-down yet to be made excluding the liquidity reserve.

Net return to the investor — The most interesting measure for the subscriber because it clearly shows the final result and net of costs and commissions applied by the fund manager. The liquidity reserve is also taken into account during the calculation of the return.

Each closed-end fund manager decides whether or not to widen the data used in the IRR calculation; for example, when participating in foreign companies, the return calculation could use the exchange rates. The information of the net return, even if it includes all of the previous aspects, considers a series of information that does not allow the comparison among several managers; if the weight of the liquidity is different or the commissions and estimates are unequal, the comparison loses its significance. For these reasons the indicator most frequently used is gross return on the realized investments, because it offers a balanced vision of the operation analyzed.

The liquidity management process is a source of value for the investor, so it is relevant and critical, especially for the acquisition of a non-quoted company when realized in several stages. The financial deal promoter limits the importance of the liquidity by allowing fund subscribers to give their funds in different stages. This reduces the "mass" of liquidity initially held. If this option is not considered, the problem becomes urgent only for the short period necessary to make the investments.

The liquidity strategy is different between the open- and closed-end funds. Closed-end funds, not investing in non-quoted companies, usually place the liquidity in non-risk tools that are easily convertible to legal tender. Once the investments are realized, liquidity management problems decrease and become almost negligible because the quota subscribed cannot be turned into cash. With open funds, the problem of liquidity management is more important and difficult to manage because of the unpredictability of investors' requests. Over time these strategies have established a special trend in the liquid reserves. In the closed-end funds, for example, the trend is similar to a parabola. In the early period of activity researching opportunities and the technical timing cause the "supply of liquidity" to be high; whereas in the short and medium term, liquidity assumes secondary importance as the participations must be left to mature slowly. Problems managing the liquid reserves arise toward the end of the fund's activity when the previous investments made by the fund are transferred into cash for the redistribution of final returns to investors.

It is possible to draw a similar trend for open-end funds. First, the search for activities to invest in is much easier when a reference market exists because the amount of initial liquidity does not stay still for an excessive period. The same phenomenon happens at the end because the exit process of the quota is simplified by the same variables. However, throughout the process the manager of an open-end fund must pay attention to its liquidity, which is normally used to meet the subscribers' quotas and the commitments of the fund.

10.2 THE MANAGING AND MONITORING PHASE

The managing and monitoring of investors must ensure the creation of value and the control of any opportunistic behavior of the financed venture firm. There are two completely different areas of interest in the managerial phase that are relevant both to create and protect value (see Figure 10.1):

Area of actions to create and measure value
Area of rules to live together

10.2.1 Actions to create and measure value

Typically the actions involved qualify the presence and nature of the investor within the managerial process of the venture-backed company. These actions depend on

1. Stage of the investment — Depending on the phase of financing (seed, start-up, early stage, expansion, turnaround, buyout, vulture, and distressed) the deal faces different types of risks such as development, production, marketing, and growth risk (see Figure 10.2). The high amount of resources invested warrants a seat on the Board of Directors, even if the amount is not enough to ensure a real commitment.

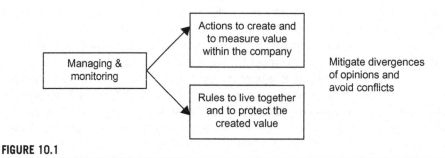

FIGURE 10.1

Activities of managing and monitoring.

2. Throughout the stages of investment the investor's involvement naturally decreases and changes. In both seed and start up, investor involvement could be industrial and strategic, while in expansion and replacement phases investor support could be reduced to an advisory capacity about financial and legal issues.

3. The quantity and the intensity of monitoring activities are linked with the duration of the participation in the target company. Because the investor and company management spend time together, there is a basis for a fair and trusting relationship with a decreasing need for control.

4. Style of the investor and the nature of the investment agreement — Generally these have different profiles:
   - Hands-on approach — A deep involvement both in corporate governance and financial and/or strategic decisions
   - Hands-off approach — A presence in the corporate governance and involvement only in financial decisions

5. Geographical distance and the expertise of the investor — The number of meetings between the investor and financed firm decrease over long distances. It is difficult to assess whether the impact of the investor's expertise is higher or lower with the frequency of contact between the directors and the other board members.

Regardless of the stage and style of investment, the key activities to manage and monitor are

Board services consisting of all activities concerning Board of Directors and meetings of other committees — Creation of value happens with

FIGURE 10.2

Risk during investment stages.

decision-making support, with the introduction of professional expertise, and with the imposition of severe discipline.

Performance evaluation and review — The investor fixes and plans a set of required processes used to monitor and measure the value inside the company and between the company and the investor.

Recruit management — Investor support is critical when hiring the right people for the management team. The management team coming from the ventured-back company is often inadequate in terms of skills and/or numbers for the development of the investment. The investor involves new people knowledgeable about specific companies and sectors or who have a professional background compatible with the project's entrepreneur.

Assistance with the external relationship — The investor usually has a network of customers, suppliers, and governmental lobbying that supports both current and strategic activities. The importance of the venture capitalist network is demonstrated by the direct correlation between the industries they invest in and the number of industries acquired. Consequently, there is usually a relationship between acquisition, dimensional growth, globalization, and internationalization when a venture capitalist takes part of a firm.

Arrange additional financing — When more financing is needed, the investor plays a critical role in finding the financer, arranging the deal, and negotiating its terms and conditions. The investor's reputation can enhance his ability to secure financing.

Mentoring — This is considered "soft assistance" with technical and human support to both the management and the entrepreneur (or shareholders).

The usual structure of management control is based on a set of rules and procedures that must be adhered to in order to obtain the desired results. Assigning tasks and objectives needed to accomplish the company's goals and a structure of rewards and punishment are critical to motivate employees during their daily activities.

Goal setting — Goals can change over time so the traditional five-year plans are not long enough. The first rule is to attach the company's goals to its operations and to identify measurable goals.

Setting standards — Once goals have been identified they have to be translated into standards to become effective.

Using motivators for the venture-backed companies — The main tools to motivate employees are money, status, and recognition.

10.2.2 **Rules to live together**

The participation of the venture capital investor, within the governance and management of the venture-backed company, requires rules to reduce conflicts and mitigate agency problems between the investor and management. The investment period is defined as a "temporary marriage"; a time when both the investor and the venture-backed company have very specific risks to avoid.

The investor must avoid these risks.

Wrong industrial decisions from management that affect the firm's performance and thus its value in the medium-long term.

Lack of commitment within the management can reduce the effectiveness of the target company strategy.

Divergence in timing to create value can directly impact the IRR created by the investment.

Entrance of new shareholders can create new conflicts between parties.

The venture-backed company must avoid these risks.

Exiting at the wrong time can impact the overall result of the investment in terms of less financial resources than expected (if the venture capitalist exits too soon) or excessive meddling from the financial partner (if the venture capitalist adopts a late exit strategy).

Lack of commitment from the investor can reduce financial resources or the advantages connected to his network or expertise and knowledge.

New shareholders entering the investment impact the balance reached between the entrepreneur and investor as well as the company strategy planned.

Exiting surprises interrupt the investment cycle and negate the realization of value for management and the entrepreneur.

Psychological constraints on management decrease its effectiveness due to external factors.

Venture operations are implemented in diverse industries, companies, countries, and in different stages of the life cycle of a firm. Because of this they are realized by different investors, in terms of participants, deal structure, and fund amount, the objectives are numerous. Consequently, the number and the nature of risks makes it impossible to forecast and solve all the possible conflicts. During the contractual design process there is a set of rules used to help reduce these risks.

First, mutual trust and patience are the best ways to avoid risks combined with a new integrated company culture created by a talented management team.

Secondly, with intelligence and wisdom the venture capitalist uses particular contractual rules that help sustain the mutual trust and patience.

These rules are usually created to fit the deal, but they are also used worldwide by financial investors and entrepreneurs often combined and blended.

The key element for a successful private equity deal is the trust the financial investor has in the expertise and management skills of the company's founder and the members of the Board of Directors. Thus it is reasonable to adopt a mechanism to ensure the stability of the property and the ongoing commitment and involvement of the management and the entrepreneur. This strategy is realized by using the best practice rules adopted by the firms through contractual schemes such as covenants and ratchets.

Covenants fall into two broad categories: positive and negative. Positive covenants are the list of things the company agrees to do including producing audited reports, holding regular board meetings, and paying taxes on time. The negative restrictions are usually included in the preferred equity agreement and they serve to limit detrimental behavior by the entrepreneur and, as a consequence, certain actions are expressly forbidden or require the approval of a super majority of investors. The ratchets are contractual agreements that provide the ability to change duties or rights in case those specific conditions occur.

These rules include:

1. Lock up — An agreement between the investor, existing shareholders, and/or the management that prohibits them to exit by selling their quotas to third parties. It is good to adopt a series of agreements connected with the transfer of the shares that start at the end of the lock-up period. The most important and frequent rule is the pre-emption clause, which gives the exiting partner the right to buy shares from an existing party. To ensure this rule is recognized, all parties assign their shares to an escrow agent, usually a trustee company, who will act according to the agreement signed by the parties so any opportunistic behavior is avoided.

2. Permitted transfer clause — A provision between the investor and existing shareholders that prohibits both existing shareholders and private equity investors from selling their shares without the approval of the other party. This rule protects the stability of the parties' commitments.

3. Staging technique — This makes sure that financial resources are invested in the firm with multiple installments. Investment of these installments is done after specific business targets are hit. This provision ensures that the money is not squandered on unprofitable prospects; it is also known as a "tranched" investment.

4. Earn out agreement — A payment system consisting of a postponed payment of a part of the original acquisition price. This is done at the realization of defined performance indicators fixed a priori by a common agreement between the seller and the venture capitalist. This check is made within a year or two after acquisition of the shares. This tool reduces the financial investor's economic risk.

5. Stock options — The holder of the venture-backed company's stock has the right to buy or sell it at a pre-determined price and a specific date. These stock options can be assigned both to the management and to the entrepreneur to motivate and increase their desire to maximize the company's value. This is easily accomplished with a public company where the parameter of the objectives reached is exposed by the stock's price, while in non-public companies they can be used after specific adjustments. It is common to fix operation and managerial goals for each function, but the parameters to which they are linked are easily manipulated. The solution is to use stock options linked to the final value of the company at the exit moment, utilizing the IRR realized through the investment as the parameter.

6. Callable and putable securities — These are part of the financial agreement in which the private equity investor has the right to sell the stocks to the existing shareholders (putable) and the existing shareholders have the right to buy the stocks from the private equity investor (callable). In both cases, the option agreement can be executed with or without a specific date on which to exercise these dates. These securities can be single or combined; that is, only callable or putable or callable and putable together.

7. Tag alone right — An agreement that states when the private equity investor has a minority participation in the financed firm. If the majority shareholders sell their participations, the private equity investor has the right to join (pro quota) the deal so he can sell his minority stake in the venture-backed company at the same terms and conditions to the same buyer.

8. Drag alone rights or anti-dilution clause — If the venture capitalist wants to sell his stocks, this mechanism provides the right to ask all other shareholders to sell their stake at the same conditions and to the same buyer. This rule was created so that the venture capitalist could maximize the sell pricing by selling to all the participants included in the selling. This allows the buyer to take the entire company all at once.

9. Right of first refusal — If other shareholders want to sell their stakes, this provision allows the private equity investor to avoid including undesired new shareholders in the company. The venture capitalist has the right to

refuse the new shareholders' entrance, but he must acquire the stake of the selling shareholders at the same conditions offered by the potential buyer.

10. Exit ratchet — This is a motivation method for the entrepreneur (and manager). It provides an exit when the company's shares are re-allocated between the entrepreneur (and manager) and the venture capitalist to allow the entrepreneur to obtain a part of the capital gain realized by the private equity investor at the exit. This ratchet is based on the periodic evaluation of the increasing value reached by the ventured-back company. It is a technique frequently adopted in leveraged buyout operations (especially in case of management buyout and management buy in) combined with management objectives.

11. Asset sales covenants — Restrictions placed on selling assets above a certain value or assets representing a certain percentage of the firm's book value. This prevents the entrepreneur from increasing the risk profile of the company and changing the firm's activity from its intended focus and also from making "sweetheart"[2] deals with friends.

12. Merger or sale covenants — Limitations preventing a merger or sale of the company without the approval of the investor. Transfer of control restrictions are important because venture capitalists invest in people and, if the management team decides to remove its human capital from the deal, venture capitalists would want to approve the terms of the transfer. Controlling transfers may hurt the position of the private equity investor if the terms are unfavorable to earlier investors.

13. Asset purchase covenant — Restrictions placed on the purchase of major assets above a certain sized threshold that may also be forbidden without the approval of the venture capitalist. These restrictions may be expressed in absolute terms of value or as a percentage of the book value of the firm. These covenants may help prevent unwanted changes in strategy or wasteful expenditure by the entrepreneur.

14. New securities restrictions — Limit the issuance of senior securities without the approval of previous investors and prevent the transfer of value from current shareholders to new security holders. Approval for this must be obtained by the super majority consensus of the shareholders.

---

[2] The term sweetheart deal, or sweetheart contract, is used to describe an abnormally favorable contractual agreement.

In addition to the previously listed rules, corporate governance rules also provide a set of dispositions that discipline the structure and operation of the main company's functions. Usually the venture capitalist has his own representatives on the Board of Directors proportional to the dimension of the capital subscribed. Rules for the Board of Directors should grant veto power to the venture capitalist representatives on the most important matters.

It is a good idea to support the Board of Directors with committees that have at least one member appointed by the venture capitalist; these committees are dedicated to specific matters that can affect, directly or indirectly, the investor's interests, such as the executive committee, the remuneration committee, the nomination committee, and the audit committee. For the Board of Directors to function effectively, it is advisable to allow at least one independent member who does not have

Any type of personal relationship, such as affinity or family relationship, with the other members of the board or with the shareholders.

Directly or indirectly, any participation in the risk capital of the company.

Any power to influence the autonomy of the other members; for example, by his own economic resources.

The Board of Directors should meet at least quarterly if not monthly once the executive committee is in place. The quorum provided should be higher for all topics relevant to the company's existence such as dividends and reserves distributions, changes of the articles of association, and for all extraordinary operations; for example, a merger and acquisition or an initial public offering.

The previously mentioned veto power should cover annual budget approval, appointment and firing of the Chief Executive Officer and Chief Operations Officer, stock option plans approval, restructuring and turnaround plans, delegations of authority and remunerations of the directors, financing operations (debt issuing), capital expenditures operations, and putting up collateral.

To ensure ongoing dialog between management, the entrepreneur, and the venture capitalist, the company should produce monthly communication that allows the venture capitalist to verify the management team's skills and to exercise his deliberation power during the shareholders' assembly.

The company should communicate all information regarding

Potential risks that can affect the investment performance.

Shareholders, directors, and employees.

Financial and operation data such as balance sheet reclassified, monthly financial plan, yearly budget, and capital expenditures.

Company objectives.

Exiting

Exiting is the final step in the investment process made by the venture capitalist. This step is very important because the venture capitalist sells his stake to gain the value added created by the investment and managing and monitoring activities of the venture. When to exit an investment is planned on an individual basis and with a broad portfolio vision. At the same time the IRR of the investment has to be coordinated with the investor's specific goals.

11.1 EXITING AND TIMING

The investor maintains his participation between five and seven years. He is considered a temporary partner whose final objective is an economic return within a medium-long term. Because of the investor's objective he must agree with the entrepreneur on the best time and best way to exit. This type of investment is very risky so the venture capitalist will be never able to plan in advance with absolutely certainty the best moment to exit the participation. The investor's amount of return depends on successful fund allocations and the quality of the work done by the private equity operator. From the beginning of the investment, it is critical to have a clear idea about potential disinvestment and when participation is a minority part of the risk capital. It is fundamental to avoid any type of arbitral constraints connected with the financial partner's exit.

The following issues should be considered during the exiting strategy plan.

The specific rules and covenants of the investment — Every deal (as explained in Chapter 10) has specific agreements that regulate the relationship between the parties. This is done to prevent and mitigate any agency problem and opportunistic behavior. These agreements are meant to directly affect the reasons for exiting as well as its timing to protect the needs and the rights of the firm and the investors.

Timing opportunity driven by the company's business — The moment of exit is directly influenced by the position of the company along its life cycle, which is due to external or internal factors. For example, global recession can decrease the capacity of revenue generation or new regulatory rules changing the competition dynamics.

Timing opportunity driven by the financial and merger and acquisition markets — Economic and financial situations impact the demand or offer of money, the potential opportunity to place the shares on the market at a good price, the possible reduction of value, etc.

Capital requirement — Regulatory rules, such as "Basle 2," place specific value on capital ratios required by financial companies. Consequently, the specific needs of re-capitalization may cause an early exit in order to use the cash realized to satisfy the required ratios.

Constraints from the residual maturity of the investment vehicle and from the final IRR goal — Because the IRR is determined by the duration of the investment, the venture capitalist has to balance the duration with the IRR desired.

Exiting track record of the portfolio — Selecting the best way to exit depends on the strategy followed by each private equity fund; for example, there are some funds that prefer an initial public offering (IPO) as an exit strategy rather than a trade sale.

Investors should also consider these causes of failure connected with an exit.

A lower level of appreciation of the target company by the financial market

Lack of interest demonstrated by the public or institutional investors toward the IPO operation

Lack of interest demonstrated by the potential industrial buyer during trade sale operations

Short collaboration from the management or the co-investors

Unsatisfactory performance of the target company

Negative outcomes and feedback from due diligence

There are two exit strategies followed by venture capitalists: path sketcher and opportunistic behavior. The path sketcher strategy is realized without any exit planning. The opportunistic behavior strategy is based on management skills and the development of the company, and is usually realized through an IPO.

Finally, according to PriceWaterHouse, there are two types of investors, each with their own exit plan. The first type is defined as a proactive investor who acquires majority quotes with a stock option plan to motivate the target company management. These investors plan from the outset to target an IRR reachable by the allocated funds. The second type is the passive investor who acquires minority quotes without a clear exit strategy. This strategy is usually realized through the buy back of the participation by the management and/or original shareholder of the company with attention to IRR maximization.

11.2 EXIT ALTERNATIVES

Although equity investment has different profiles (i.e., seed, start up, expansion, replacement, vulture), theory and market trends show no correlation between the stage of investment, the holding period, and the exit strategy. Every deal has a specific strategy with rules driven by the needs of both the investor and the entrepreneur. These are typical exiting strategies relevant to today's market:

Trade sale
Buy back
Sale to other private equity investors
Write-off
IPO or sale post IPO

11.2.1 Trade sale

A trade sale exit occurs when the private equity investor sells its stake to a corporation or, for example, to an industrial shareholder. This exiting strategy is often used in European markets. It is based on industrial relationships between the private equity investor, the buyer, and the venture-backed company. The trade sale can be realized through public tender or private negotiations between the parties.

A trade sale is generally motivated by the buyer's strategic business plan and because a trade sale can be executed in different ways; it avoids specific financial market conditions and the lack of interest toward investment stakes.

Several types of trade sale can be identified:

The buyer enters the company through a minority participation to develop an alliance with the target company or to launch an offer to buy the company from the majority shareholders.
The buyer becomes a majority shareholder to consolidate this participation or merge.

The strengths of a trade sale exit consist of the chance to realize a higher premium price and the possibility for the venture capitalist to divest all of its participation through an operation cheaper and faster than an IPO. It is also easier to negotiate with fewer potential participants than with the entire financial market. This is the only exit option for investments realized in small-medium firms.

There are also disadvantages to this type of exit: lack of trade buyers in some countries, management opposition, and investors not wanting to provide the required collateral.

There are several conditions to realizing a profitable trade sale:

Private equity investors have a strong network of relationships in which to find a potential buyer.
If the existing shareholders exit at the same time as the private equity investor the buyer can acquire a majority and have total control of the company.
Existing shareholders agree to integrate with another industrial corporation.
Negotiations with potential buyers can be developed at the same level of reputation and power.

11.2.2 Buy back

A buy back exit occurs when the private equity investor sells its stake to existing shareholders in the corporation or their representatives. The buy back alternative is an opportunity to support and develop a business when shareholders do not want to leave the company.

Classic cases that lead to a buy back:

Shareholders have initiated a venture capital operation to collect funds for development of the business idea (seed financing), the business development (start-up financing), or the company's growth (development financing).
Shareholders manage a governance turnaround.
Shareholders transfer ownership to other people.

A profitable buy back can be accomplished when shareholders want to own the business, have the money to buy back the shares, and have a clear problem of turnaround or inheritance.

11.2.3 Sale to other private equity investors

This type of exit consists of selling the stakes to another private equity or venture capital fund. It is an exit strategy frequently used in the US market and is based on the strong relationships between private equity investors. In the past, this strategy was more widespread and used as a secondary buyout. The strategy was also used when the investor, who specialized in a specific stage of the target firm's life cycle, sold the participation to a partner who specialized in a different life cycle stage (i.e., from seed to start up, from start up to expansion, etc.).

Typical sales between private equity investors include:

Seed financer sells the stake to a start-up financer to "start the engine."

Start-up financer sells its stake to an expansion financer to sustain growth.

Expansion financer sells its stake to a replacement financer to develop acquisition, turnaround, or IPO.

Vulture financer (rarer) sells its stake to a replacement financer to end the work of restructuring.

Conditions that must be satisfied to develop a profitable sale to other private equity investors:

A strong network of relationships in which to find potential private equity buyers.

A market where there are vehicles dedicated to investment in the different life cycle stages.

Existing shareholders agree to a continuous presence of equity investors.

Existing shareholders have a clear plan to develop the firm from a small to medium size business.

This type of deal can be motivated also by fund duration or the status of the relationship between the investors, the entrepreneur, and the management team of the target company. This type of exit allows the ongoing development or growth of the firm. If there is a bad relationship between the shareholders and the venture capitalist is unable to realize the desired and expected return, he should accelerate the exit by accepting a lower price.

When this strategy is realized through a secondary buyout, total control of the company passes from one institutional investor to another. This type of divestment is similar to a trade sale; the only difference is that the buyer is a financial investor not an industrial partner. This strategy is utilized when there is no debt and the target company is mature.

11.2.4 Write-off

A write-off is usually included during the disinvestment as well as devaluation, partially or totally, of the participation as a consequence of money loss unrelated to a transfer of property. This is included because it is different from other exit strategies; it reduces or removes specific assets on the balance sheet. Investors decide to write off a deal when the stake and the company are unable to produce value in the future.

The write-off process is used when no economic return is generated from the stake. Bankruptcy laws are followed and sometimes an investor can get back part of the face value of his shares if the cash resources of the company's assets exceed the total amount of the debt.

The typical write-off occurs when the

Private equity investor asks the court to declare that the company is in default.
Creditor asks the court to begin bankruptcy proceedings.
Equity investor negotiates the closing of the company with shareholders and they decide to see the company's assets; this is very common in seed and start-up ventures.

Before deciding to write off an investment, the venture capitalist must make sure the following conditions are satisfied to realize a profitable disinvestment:

No possibility the company will produce profit in the future
Assets of the venture-backed company can be sold with satisfactory results through the market
Costs of write-off are insignificant with short-term management
Social impact of the write-off is irrelevant and does not generate negative consequences for the investor

11.2.5 IPO or sale post IPO

When the private equity investor sells its stake through the stock exchange, the exit strategy is called an IPO. This type of divestment is attractive in terms of reputation and economic return. The exit is complex, especially for small or medium companies, and is considered in a long-term strategy after the target firm has reached an adequate level of development and seniority.

The private equity investor is strongly involved in the IPO process, acting as a global advisor or manager. Listed next are typical categories of IPO sales.

Private equity investor drives the IPO and the selling of its stake is written into the info memorandum. This is a bad signal but it helps to control the exiting price.
Private equity investor drives the IPO and sells its stake at the start of negotiations (using the under pricing effect). This option probably maximizes the exit price through the under pricing.
Private equity investor drives the IPO and sells after, with or without lock up, a certain period of time. The lock up is an agreement between the parties

that prohibits them from exiting by selling their quotas to third parties just before the IPO. This is a good signal for the market, but the private equity investor faces the risk of floating the exiting value.

A profitable IPO can be realized during a favorable stock market if the company satisfies the required criteria for the listing. It becomes a successful solution when the venture-backed company heightens its profile in the financial community and due diligence produces satisfactory results. For an IPO to be successful it is necessary that corporate governance, management, and the company's entire organization show a positive attitude to face post-IPO life with the existing shareholders.

There are advantages and disadvantages to the IPO exit strategy. Advantages include the opportunity to sell the participation at a higher price, satisfying management, and further potential gain by the institutional investor.

In an IPO, exit strategy disadvantages to the investor include higher costs related to the exit and risk connected to the lack of liquidity in European markets. This type of exit is not feasible for the small companies because lock-up contract conditions, which prevent investors from selling the stakes before quotation, need a large number of investors to obtain a successful IPO.

11.3 QUOTATION OF PRIVATE EQUITY COMPANIES

11.3.1 Potential advantages and disadvantages

When a venture capitalist decides to go public, he selects the most appropriate market and the best possible structure in which to effectively offer his participations. Private equity operators review the stock exchange quotation and the financial market before considering an investment opportunity. Financial markets dedicated to innovative companies with an intense growth level offer venture capitalists the best opportunities.

In order to attract investors, the ability of the fund to create value must be evaluated. This is done by considering elements such as the track record of the previous investments in the portfolio, the rate of investment failure, the professional profile of the management team, the quality of the founders, the company governance, the risk profile of the specific investment activities, and the level of transparency and clarity when reporting and communicating.

Today's international banking community reflects the presence of numerous private equity companies quoted on the financial markets. There are more private equity companies in the most developed financial markets with numerous venture capital companies quoted on the NASDAQ, the London stock exchange, and the Swiss market where there is a specific segment that regulates venture capital companies in terms of admission procedures and requisites for permanence. In the past, this type of quotation was possible because financial markets trended toward riskier investments.

For private equity companies, the decision to go public represents growth, recognized by the market, and allows advantages and benefits such as

- An increase in fundraising at an international and national level due to the investor. This solves the problem of limited capital raised from other sources such as banks and debt financers.
- Access to public small investors interested in venture capital activity. This represents the opportunity to enhance visibility and increase the interaction with supplier and customer.
- International projects to view and invest in. Becoming a public company projects an image of stability.
- Easier partnerships with technological suppliers and operators connected to the high-tech sector.
- Managing a wider and more diversified portfolio of companies guaranteeing opportunities to support projects requiring large investments.
- Fulfilling private equity investors' desire to achieve liquidity.

Going public has real costs that constrain many companies from this option. Legal, accounting, and investment banking fees are heavy. As a public company there is a higher degree of disclosure and transparency, which means a decrease of privacy. Managers may be afraid that the company could be tainted by market rumors, which can affect and influence their strategies with dramatic floating of the stock price not based on the real value of the company and the global level of IPO activity.

Unlike the quotation of an industrial or service company, the quotation of a venture capital or investment company reflects a high-risk profile with high risk combined with industrial and financial risks typical of risk capital investment. The degree of risk varies according to the operator. It is higher when the investment is focused on the company's initial development phases (from start up to early stage), which operates in technological and innovative sectors with a lower degree of diversification.

In summary, it can be said that industrial or service companies invest in companies with a lower economic risk profile, while investment companies prefer to invest in funds and quoted companies that are historically found in stock markets.

Limited liquidity of the portfolio assets represents a critical element in the quotation of a company. It reflects the uncertainty of the created value as well as the ability of investors to monitor it. A company with a portfolio without quoted participations derives its value from the ability to realize capital gains only when exiting from the investment. When the exit arises through an IPO, the economic return can be dissolved over time due to lock-up conditions obliging the shareholders to maintain their shares for a specific period after the IPO (usually between 6 and 12 months). Part of the gain may be realized through the sale of the shares in an IPO at a fixed price defined at the moment of the closing; the other part can be obtained through a later trade sale or with a private arrangement at the expiry of the lock up.

Today a high-growth company has no partial exit because the presence of the institutional investor in the shareholding structure is an unconditional element when accepting a high degree of risk. The uncertainty on the value created is extended over time, as the effective time and value of the exit for the venture capitalist depend on the market conditions and the trend of the quoted security after the quotation as well as many other specific and market factors.

These factors cause many institutional investors, particularly those operating in the most advanced phases of a company's life cycle, to prefer an exit through a trade sale instead of an IPO. This exit strategy guarantees a sure and immediate value through the capital gain realized with a sale to third parties. Although a preferred solution, it is not always possible; a full sale of shares through an IPO is more feasible for companies subjected to an LBO or turnaround operation. Younger companies with a higher risk return profile and a lower level of fame and prestige normally receive new capital to finance growth so the sale of existing shares is not compatible with its quotation (at least not in the initial phase of the company life cycle).

In the absence of exiting, the value of participations in a portfolio must be periodically estimated to calculate the net asset value of the fund or the assets in the financial statements. This practice, based on techniques used by specialized operators, must deal with the uncertainty and structural difficulties in defining values for companies still immature and subject to market, technical, commercial, and operating forces.

The uncertainty and the possible lack of significance of the net asset value of a pool of investments is critical in the quotation of a venture capital company. Long-term duration of the investment and the difficulty comparing it with other similar companies should also be considered. This is reflected in two different problems: the lack of alternative diversification and the difficulty forecasting annual results for these private equity funds. It is difficult to forecast annual results of a private equity even when the quotation imposes quarterly reporting and analysis. Therefore, the quality and quantity of research available for operators in these sectors tend to be limited, particularly in smaller markets.

Considering the advantages and disadvantages of the issuer of the quotation and the market, venture capitalists must review their exit strategy for each investment. The issuer considers that the

1. Quotation increases the funds collected and reduces the time spent for fundraising, providing a channel normally used by institutional operators. In favorable market conditions such as during the high-tech boom in the United States, quotation allowed the quick raising of funds and a high diversification of the fundraising channels.

2. Moment of quotation provides liquidity to the fund's original subscriber from the buyer; however, effective liquidity depends on the negotiation of shares on the secondary market.

3. Quotation increases and enforces the reputation and visibility of the fund influencing the companies financed by the fund and taking advantage of new business opportunities.

4. The original holder of the fund is an industrial company or a diversified holding, so the quotation allows a better valuation of the total assets held by the original holder because it permits the separation of the investment activity from other businesses.

These operations can be attractive to the market because of the following reasons.

1. Private equity companies, with quotation, offer an investment opportunity that includes securities issued by several different companies. This type of investment allows retail investors to put their financial resources into shares that otherwise would be unavailable. During the high-tech boom in the United States, investors were looking for participations in new companies due to the expected high returns. They were able to realize these investments because these high-tech securities were included in venture capital quoted funds. The appeal of the investment in a fund, or in the investment company, is greater when the participated companies are closed to quotation because of the expectation that the exit value will be higher than the net asset value of the companies and the market will reflect it with a higher stake price. If the market is trending up, then investor behavior supports the investment company, but if the market is trending down, the sensibility to the risk is higher and can damage the operation. The mood of the market can lead to a higher level of expected default of the underlying portfolio penalizing the private equity companies more than the companies financed due to the greater liquidity costs and uncertainty of obtainable results.

2. Composition, size, and diversification of the portfolio strongly influence the placement of venture capital funds on the stock exchange. Industry specialization makes these investments more desirable for highly specialized institutional investors (industry related funds). Still, the preference is to quote funds with a significant amount of quoted investments due to the higher level of transparency of net asset value and the higher liquidity of assets. The size is usually related to the company's diversification (or by companies and funds), therefore representing additional criteria for market opinion.

3. The required quoted fund return is compared with its risks and other potential investments in equity to appraise its potential for increasing portfolio return.

4. The reputation and track record of the fund managers (past successful investment operations and the relative high IRR generated) should be evaluated during the investment decision. The qualities of possible co-investors, represented by strategic participations in other funds, are also important factors because funds with good reputations act as a guarantee. Co-investment with these funds provides an important message to the market about the quality of the relationship.

The previous list provides several elements that help explain the relatively recent and important phenomenon of venture capital quotation. The venture capital quotation trend, which started in the United States during the high-tech boom, moderately developed in Europe, and never took off in markets where private equity industry is historically more developed. High risk and lack of suitable European target companies (most of them based in industrial investment) made it difficult for a venture capital quotation boom to occur in European markets because industrial groups are rarely subject to spin-offs or quotations.

11.3.3 Segmentation of private equity operators

Analysis of the advantages and risks of private equity operators in the stock market cannot be performed without considering the segmentation of the specific market in terms of risk and economic return correlated to the different phases of the company life cycle. For this purpose it is useful to organize private equity operators into three macro categories: incubators, venture capitalists, and investment companies. These categories are differentiated by the financial commitment and timeliness of the investment, type of risk faced, and the support needed.

Financial commitment and timeliness of the investment depend on the growth curve of a company over time. The greatest investment made by an institutional investor occurs in the initial start-up phase with a limited financial commitment and greater correlated risks due to the high level of company mortality during this phase. The financial commitment in this phase is typically medium-long term (4 to 7 years) with limited liquidity of the participation. Investments made in a company during a more mature level of development are higher with a lower risk of company mortality. The length of these investments is shorter with greater liquidity. In summary, the rate of return requested is higher when the investment is related to the initial phases in the life cycle of a company and decreases over the time.

The type of risk faced by an investor is strictly connected with the life cycle phase of a company. During the start-up phase, the risk of failure is typically embodied in the fact that the company must still build a business model, develop a product/service, set up a business structure, source managerial expertise, acquire market share, etc. For more mature, consolidated companies the greatest risk is the financial risk related to the relationship between debt and equity and the optimization of financial leverage. Support requested by start ups consists of a series of operating services offered by the investors who not only act exclusively as the financier of the initiative, but also contribute to the company growth by providing added value services.

Incubators take part in the initial phase of a start up with a limited financial commitment and a greater risk of company mortality. This requires higher returns and offers financial and operative support such as rental of space, recruitment, accounting, consulting, etc.

Investment companies are involved during the maturity phases of a firm providing a high level of financial resources with a lower company mortality risk. During this life cycle phase economic return will be lower and the investor offers just financial support.

Venture capital companies intervene in the intermediary business life cycle arranging their portfolios to balance risks and returns. It is important to emphasize that venture capital activity is specialized in terms of a business model. Venture capital companies can be either incubators or investment companies.

Because there is no precise boundary between the different typologies of private equity operators, it is difficult to identify which type is necessary. The business model and the value creation of private equity companies change significantly depending on whether they are incubators, venture capitalists, or investment companies. The incubator's value creation is developed through five critical phases.

1. Identification of investment opportunities by analyzing the business plan and the management team

2. Investment of financial resources, typically consisting of seed capital, necessary to launch the entrepreneurial initiative
3. Supporting the company at an operations level so that business development can be realized by management
4. Sharing their network of contacts to support management activity
5. Divestment with a high level of return through the best possible exit

Investment companies create portfolios of diversified participation to realize a diversification strategy in terms of value and risk. Their business model is structured to

1. Identify investment opportunities in non-public companies in development phases, companies already quoted, or companies in need of funds
2. Invest financial resources needed for expansion
3. Divest with a higher value and exit compatible with the diversification strategy

When incubators, venture capitalists, and investment companies go public they respond to the different requirements expressed by the market: higher risk and consequently higher returns for the incubator and greater risks and diversification for investment companies.

Valuation and the "Art of Deal Making"

3

Company evaluation in private and venture capital

12.1 COMPANY VALUATION

As explained in Part Two, the private equity process can be divided into different phases. One of these is the investing phase, which includes choosing and closing the deal. Within this phase, company valuation is critical since it is fundamental to the venture capitalist's future economic return.

The types of financing available to venture capitalists are completely different; for example, an entry strategy with a majority participation and a position of control (typical in a buyout) and minority participation that supports the quotation of a firm for a short time.

It is possible to identify standard phases common to all investments.

Identification of the target company — This is executed differently in US, UK, and European markets. In the US and the UK investment opportunities offered to venture capitalists are already defined and structured by the entrepreneur. In Europe researching potential target companies is up to the institutional investor and done by direct marketing operations; therefore, European venture capitalists need a developed and efficient network or relationship to find potential and interesting deals (deal flow).

Valuation of the entrepreneur profile and/or the management team — This phase follows the identification of the target company and consists of a complete analysis of the entrepreneur and/or the management team's profile, especially when they invest risk capital together with the private equity operator. It is important to check the reliability, knowledge, expertise, and reputation between the management team and the validity or coherence of the business idea.

Deep valuation of the target company and the operation structure — This phase is critical because it focuses on researching the equilibrium between the entrepreneur's needs, the investor's goals, and the real necessity of the target company. Analysis verifies the potential and actual market of the company, its technology potential, possible increase of company value, and the likely exiting strategy. If the results are satisfactory then the venture capitalist proceeds with the deal structuring and defining the company's value.

Negotiation and setting of price — This is the direct outcome of the previous phases. It is focused on price setting as well as timing and payment execution.

Monitoring and exiting — After closing the deal the investor monitors the venture-backed company's performance to identify any problems inside the target company. On exit the venture capitalist realizes the economic return from the deal.

12.2 FIVE PHASES OF COMPANY VALUATION

Company valuation calculates the fair value of the target company as well as supports value creation among investors so they can reach their economic goals in terms of expected IRR. The process of company valuation is realized through these phases.

Business plan analysis
Financial needs assessment
Enterprise value analysis
Price setting
Exiting

It is important to accomplish the previously listed valuation steps in the right sequence. Before this can be completed, it is necessary to know and use specific techniques and methods to approach the items in the correct order. First, the venture capitalist must have focused goals that support the whole valuation process to execute appropriate investing or exiting decisions. However, the process has to be coordinated within the constraints of the investment vehicle such as global portfolio IRR, residual maturity, capital requirements, and expected IRR on the specific investment and the entire portfolio.

Before analyzing each valuation phase, it is necessary to clarify critical aspects and key issues. This chapter identifies and discusses the content of each phase, the equity investor's role, and the goals and content of each stage.

12.2.1 **Business plan analysis**

To start the valuation process the business plan must be created and analyzed. This document explains and illustrates the strategic intention of the management team, competitive strategies, and concrete actions necessary to realize company objectives, key value drivers, and financial outcomes. It shows the management team's vision and allows investors to evaluate and understand the potential returns of the business. The business plan has a large target audience including not only the investors and the management team, but other financial supporters such as banks or leasing companies and members of the Board of Directors.

A typical business plan that supports risky capital investment contains the status of past strategies (history of the firm) in terms of performance and analysis of strengths or weaknesses and opportunities or threats. Based on the analysis, the business plan describes the future of the company regarding the development of strategic goals, an action plan needed to realize the value proposition, assumptions about financial planning, and financial forecasts (see Figure 12.1).

A business plan contains these elements.

- Global view on the company — Information about the past, actual, and future organizational structure, relevant industries including the analysis of the competitive factors, and all the critical elements for an in-depth knowledge of the company such as legal entity structure, revenues, mission, and dimension.

- Global view and explanation of the entrepreneurs and shareholders — This demonstrates the importance of the human factor in a business deal. A critical element is the clear disclosure of who the controls the capital.

- Market competitive analysis — Includes the macro economics profile (definition of its global dimension). The business plan uses the Porter Model[1] to analyze the market at a lower level.

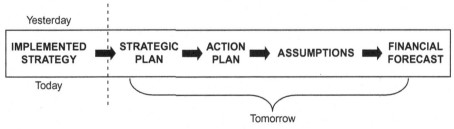

FIGURE 12.1

Business plan structure.

[1] See Chapter 9, Section 9.1, Valuation and Selection.

- Technological characteristics of the product and or services of the firms — This section describes the product and/or the service of the company in the easiest possible way emphasizing the innovative content of the offer.

- Operation plans and financial data — Contains detailed information regarding the operative actions executed in terms of production and marketing plans and timing data and costs. This part of the business plan shows a series of simulations about how the product and/or service would be realized considering different levels of bulk production.

- Financial structure — Based on the previous analysis and defined needs, this phase covers two main areas: financial requirements and the desired equity debt ratio. Financial requirements, satisfied by equity and debt, include different types of investments such as working capital investments, capital expenditures, immaterial expenditures, merger and acquisitions investments, and repayment of debts raised in the past. Equity contribution does not create any charged interest guaranteeing the company in case of default, and the investor is directly interested in the performance of the firm. This structure limits the entrepreneur's decision power as well as the profit he must split with the new shareholders. Raising debt avoids the entrance of new shareholders, but interest has to be paid regardless of positive economic results. This form of financing requires collateral issuings, which are not obviously apparent to the entrepreneurs. The key aspect of debt is the tax benefit created by a significant contribution to the global value generated by the business idea.

The business plan is usually prepared by the company with the help of a consultant and is the proposal sent to investors. It is common for the private equity investor to take part in the business planning process, even if it is risky and time-consuming. It usually happens with incubation strategies and previous venture-backed companies. Private equity investor assistance comes from the network of relationships in which the investor is involved.

Different stages of investment, from the seed to vulture financing, have specific capital requirements and assumed levels of risk. This is reflected in the business plan.

Seed financing — Three key issues: assessment of the potential entrepreneur's curriculum vitae, creative understanding of the feasibility of the business idea, and identification of the product's potential market.

Start-up financing — Verifying both the market potential of the business idea, in terms of potential demand trend and expected level of price, and plan of investments is necessary.

Expansion financing — The expansion trend of the demand and the sustainability of the required investment must be checked.

Replacement financing — Key issues include the feasibility of the acquisition and restructuring the deal.

Vulture financing — Focuses on verifying the new potential market with an accurate analysis of costs and the investment plan.

The validity of the business plan, decided by the private equity investor, depends on the financial sustainability of the industrial project. Sustainability is established based on the quality and quantity of the financial resources, coherence between the realized strategies, strategic intention, real conditions of the firm and its economic and financial hypothesis, and its reliability. The last condition is satisfied when the industrial plan is drawn based on a realistic and reasonable hypothesis and expected and acceptable results. When the business plan includes a comparison with the past performance, it also includes further analysis related to forecasting possible scenarios and statements consistent with the competitive dynamics of the relevant industry.

From the business plan the investor should trust the management about the business, the way capital will be used, the motivation of the management team, and the risk sharing.

12.2.2 Financial needs assessment

If the analysis of the business plan is favorable, the investor moves to the second step of the company valuation process: financial needs assessment. This step calculates the amount of money required to sustain company growth.

The financial assessment adds forecasting statements to the business plan, and its goal is to define external financial requirements and verify their use by the company.

This step further identifies the size of the potential demand for investment, percentage of the potential equity investment, and potential new debt to be raised in a medium term run. The financial needs assessment is typically executed in house by the private equity investor, even if interaction with the company is necessary to discuss and/or to revise the business plan.

For an accurate financial assessment it is necessary to answer a series of key questions to help decide whether or not it is convenient to launch an investment. First, the capital investor must understand the size of the financial need and then have a clear idea of how much can be financed from the investor, the correct mix of debt and equity and, at the end, if it is possible and or necessary to recruit a new equity and/or debt investor.

It is impossible to predict a financial solution. It depends on the deal's level of risk, risk profile of the project, and trust in the entrepreneur skills.

During the financial needs assessment there are key issues to be addressed.

Seed financing — Financial requirement consists of sustaining the investment to study, develop, and test the business idea or the project. It is very hard to identify the correct mix of debt and equity. The resources needed are not usually considerable, but it is necessary to have a large amount of support for a high-tech initiative.

Start-up financing — Financial needs evaluation is the key point of the deal. It is critical to verify how much of the deal is financed through equity capital. The resources required are designed to define and develop an already launched project. The outcome of start-up financing depends on the quality of the previous investment (seed financing). The investment requirement is not urgent because it is needed for the enlargement of existing corporate and business competences.

First stage financing — Represents the moment of launch for the initiative and the consolidation of previous research. This stage needs considerable financial support, because funds are necessary to hire suitable human resources and develop know-how. The level of risk is quite high, but if the business initiative is successful, remuneration is considerable.

Expansion financing — Financial resources support corporate growth. The business idea and the combination of product and market have already been tested, consequently, financial resources support commercial and marketing activities. Funds will probably be absorbed by the working capital because warehouse goods increase and payment terms are postponed to satisfy customer demand.

Bridge financing — The position acquired by the company is steady and reinforced by the introduction of new operative structures, the launch of new products or services, or an international expansion strategy. The funds required are tremendous, but risk is limited because the company has the capacity to forecast the business trend.

Replacement — Controlling how finances are used during the development of corporate finance deals is a key issue. Economic resources are provided to re-launch the company through restructuring and development operations. Since the re-launch is a new activity for the firm, an enormous amount of money and specific competences are necessary.

Vulture financing — Similar to start-up financing, the financial needs evaluation is key in the decision to turnaround a business. This type of financing includes the re-launch and renewal of a mature company, and the available resources are used to maintain market position and sustain the development process, which can be realized with either existing or non-existing technology (diversification strategy).

12.2.3 Enterprise value analysis

During the screening phase, the investor decides if the financial need, as defined and evaluated, is sustainable. In doing so he moves to the third step of this process — analysis of the company's value. This phase is based on the forecasting statements included in the business plan. The goal is to understand and quantify the real value of the company and the business plan to define the value of the investment.

The enterprise value analysis identifies the amount of money to be spent, the percentage of shares to buy, and the financial impact on the company. The private equity investor executes the enterprise value analysis in house and listens to his advisors and technical committee. The valuation of a private company, especially when it is in the early stages of the life cycle, is difficult and subjective because early stage companies usually forecast a period of negative cash flow with uncertain future economic returns.

Enterprise value analysis finds a "right value" and an "adjusted value" of a company after comparing general trends in valuation within companies operating in the same business. Usually, the output of the analysis consists of values attributed to the equity of the company. The analysis further focuses on different valuations for different stages of investment.

Seed financing — Equity valuation is impossible and can only be developed if the business plan is built on a realistic business idea.

Start-up financing — Valuation is based on forecasting, but there is a high risk of uncertainty regarding the future sales trends and the terminal value. Comparison with similar deals is useful here.

Expansion financing — Valuation analysis faces the same issues as start-up financing. At this point comparison with similar deals can be very useful. Evaluation is usually easier here than during start up because the company is considered successful and there are similar firms with which to compare.

Replacement financing — Equity valuation is connected to the profile of the deal and related to the replacement structure. Typical deals are LBOs or buy-ins and family and management deals where the counterparties involved are critical and affect the definition of the company value (inheritance).

Vulture financing — Typical target companies are mature and equity valuation is based on forecasting, but there is a high risk of uncertainty regarding sales trends. The terminal value of the deal and the amount and structure of costs carried are hardly quantifiable. It is also difficult to support the equity valuation through comparison with similar companies.

In later chapters the methods used for company evaluation will be analyzed more deeply. Next are highlights of the most widespread methods.

1. Comparables — Provide a quick and easy way to obtain a rough valuation for a firm. This method is used when a firm with similar values exists. Elements compared include risk, growth rate, capital structure, and the size and timing of cash flow. This method is quick, simple to understand, based on the market, and common in the industry. There are many potential problems when this method is used for private companies, such as the lack of public information on private companies and problems finding comparable firms. When it is used to compare public companies, it is necessary to adjust the outcomes due to the private company's lack of liquidity. Their shares are typically less marketable then public firms, so a discount for the lack of liquidity is applied (lack of marketability discount falls between 25 and 30%).

2. Net present value — Most common method for cash flow valuation. Net present value of a company is obtained by computing the expected value of one or more future cash flows discounting them at a rate reflecting the cost of capital. This method considers the potential tax benefit created by leverage. It presents a serious problem with forecasting cash flow because the terminal value is greatly affected by the interest rate used, so it is critical to identify the correct interest rate when discounting future cash flow. one solution is to use the weighted average cost of capital, which is quite easy to calculate based on the current debt equity ratio at the time. In reality this ratio is always subject to change, especially in LBO operations.

3. Adjusted present value — A variant of the NPV approach used when a company's level of indebtedness is changing or it has past operations losses that can be used offset tax obligations. This method attempts to solve the problems faced by the NPR by calculating cash flow without debt and discounting by using an unlevered (defined as the equity capital invested in the company) interest rate. It further requires the quantification of interest and the relevant tax benefits discounted at the pretax rate of return on debt. This method is appropriately used when the capital structure (highly leveraged transactions such as LBOs) and the tax rate are changing. It is more complicated then the net present value and presents

difficulties when estimating future cash flow and selecting the correct discount rate.

4. Venture capital — Values the company at the end of a defined period of time using one of the methods previously discussed. Then it discounts this terminal value by a target rate of return that is the yield assumed by venture capitalists as remuneration for the risk and efforts of this specific investment. This TRR is usually between 40 and 70% and is the biggest source of criticism of this method. Venture capitalists use such a high level of discount because of the lack of liquidity of private firms, the provision of strategic advisors to the target company, and because the entrepreneur's forecasting, included in the business plan, is usually too optimistic.

5. Asset option — The methods previously explained are not usable when managers or investors are capable of making flexible decisions. This flexibility affects the value of the company, and these changes are not accurately computed in the discounted cash flow methods. According to the venture capitalist, the value of a company depends on the value assumed by independent predictor variables. The asset option method is not well known and the real-world opportunity for simple options and the exact pricing of these options are difficult to define.

12.2.4 Price setting

Finance theory on company valuation states that value and price are two different measures, not always coincident and sometimes clashing, that depend on various factors. The theoretical concept of company value, which differs from market value, is connected with the idea of economic capital: the value of a company in normal market conditions compatible with company capital without the considerations of the parties, their contractual power, their specific interests, and potential negations. As per this definition, the economic capital, as a measure of the company value, is independent from the eventual deal between the parties, the possibility that a new buyer will interfere, the contingent demand and supply situation, and the status of the M&A market. Calculating the economic capital is necessary to have an objective value creation realized by management defined as fair value.

It is easy to understand that the market value of a firm is affected by the same external pressures as company value. These pressures are influenced by financial market efficiency and demand and supply. The price of a public company depends on the participation negotiated; should the participation allow a minority presence in the capital subscribed or a majority control of the firm.

Market and company values are also measured by cash flow forecasting and the determination of risk and other stock variables computed through specific formulas, whereas the price is defined by market dynamics.

For private equity deals, the valuation of a firm is never theoretical; it is always linked to a real and concrete price so the final value defined is the result of the counterparty's negotiations. The estimate of the target company's value is usually executed using simple and proven methods and techniques such as the comparables approach to avoid complicated financial models.

Price setting while negotiating equity value with the entrepreneur moves from the value of the company to the price (value) of the deal. During this phase the entrepreneur has specific personal goals, over self-estimation, and personal and moral involvement while the investor reduces the amount of money requested by the single deal and aligns the capital requirement and IRR targets. It is impossible to identify any standard rules within this negotiation, because it is a complex struggle to agree on a final price and, consequently, many deals fall apart over price disagreement.

Price setting is typically developed by the management team with the support of the directors and advisors during the negotiation phase. The negotiation for price setting is more relevant than valuation with mature companies and corporate governance based deals. The way negotiations are conducted is influenced by both technical and structural variables from the operations side and psychological and cultural values related to the profile and knowledge of the counterparts and their advisors. It is critical to select appropriately skilled advisors and intermediaries during negotiation.

The final step in this phase is closing the deal. Investors need to understand how price setting is used during specific stages of the investment.

Seed financing — Insignificant because it does not affect this phase.

Start-up financing — Company valuation is more relevant than price setting because money is channeled to the development of the investment.

Expansion financing — Investors balance company valuation with price setting, but firm valuation is more relevant.

Replacement financing — The main point is the price setting.

Vulture financing — Price setting is insignificant.

12.2.5 Exiting

During this phase enterprise value and price are calculated based on the investor's exit. The same enterprise value analysis and price setting activities are carried out, but the investor has to calculate the "right value" of the firm and negotiate with the potential buyer of the stake.

Price setting is critical for the investor to get the effective IRR of the investment and to sustain global portfolio IRR. For that reason, price setting becomes more relevant than enterprise value analysis when choosing an exit strategy.

12.3 VALUATION OF THE COMPANY AND MARKET DYNAMICS

Before concluding this chapter, it is important to consider the impact of the capital market on the banker's attempts to fairly valuate deals. The consequences of the current heavy losses and market volatility make it difficult for financial intermediaries to valuate companies.

Valuation of a company covers a wide range of topics starting from forecasted cash flows to the selling prices of company assets. In 2008–2009 capital markets suffered tremendous depreciation of quoted securities and a high level of volatility; this situation directly affected the validity of the old and tested methods based on historical data. The current financial world is completely distorted compared to before 2008 and, consequently, the usual metrics for valuation are no longer applicable.

This situation makes it likely that gaps between the expectations of buyers and sellers will increase until the restart of the M&A market. It also makes it hard for financial operators to analyze valuation with traditional methods.

The combined dynamics of the present credit crunch and the low level of competition in the M&A market, linked to a minor presence of private equity, affected the prices paid for acquisitions. Acquisitions are at a minimum level when compared to the previous 15 years, volume of trading activities are reduced 30 to 60%, and the premium paid for control is now around 20 to 22% compared with the historical average of 30%.

Aligned with the information in this chapter and the financial market, during the last quarter in 2008 and the first quarter of 2009, the value of acquisitions that have been cancelled is almost equal to the value of deals that have been completed. This current slowdown should be spent by relevant operators to better understand the function of the market, to protect the value of their current portfolio, and to be ready for any opportunities that may come their way.

Techniques of equity value definition

13.1 ENTERPRISE VALUE ANALYSIS

Company valuation is a critical phase of investment policies put in place by venture capitalists. It is important because the value of the company gives both the entrepreneur and the venture capitalist a place to bargain over the amount of money required by the entrepreneur and the number of shares that the shareholders can give up in favor of the venture capitalist. After agreeing about money and shares, the deal is then closed.

The importance of enterprise value analysis is evident when the object of valuation is a high-risk, high-tech company with no historical data (or a limited track record) and poor economic and financial performance. In this situation, a development fund cannot be provided by traditional financial tools, such as bank loans, so the biggest part of the financial need must be covered by equity capital supplied by investment companies. This makes the correct pricing of an equity stake one of the most important keys to success in the venture capital industry.

Company evaluation is based on the forecasted financial statement and balance sheet. An inaccurate business plan leads to an incorrect equity value. To calculate the value of equity, it is necessary to use dedicated techniques to identify the real and underlying value of a firm.

Theoretically, these techniques are used to calculate the equity value of a potential venture-backed company:

1. Comparables
2. Net present value

3. Adjusted present value
4. Venture capital method

These techniques originate from the theory of corporate finance and each one provides a different perspective of and rationale for the equity value.

Comparables — Calculates the equity value by comparing similar companies in terms of industry, dimension, and country during valuation.

Net present value — Equity value is the present value of future cash flows of the company; a defined period of time is used to calculate the terminal value.

Adjusted present value — Just like the net present value except the financial structure of the firm is analyzed too.

Venture capital method — Equity value is calculated as the present value of the terminal value of the firm taking into account the expected return of the investment and a particular expected holding period.

These four theoretical approaches have pros and cons, but in the real world and in practice it is well known that comparables are a key step in producing inputs for the net present value and the venture capital method as well as when comparing the outputs of the other approaches.

The most widely used approach is net present value or discounted cash flow (DCF), whereas the venture capital method is used primarily when price setting is more important than enterprise value analysis.

13.2 CHOOSING A VALUATION METHOD

Before company valuation begins, an appropriate method of valuation must be chosen. Factors that affect this choice include:

1. Country where the company is based
2. Industry to which it belongs
3. Quality of data needed for the valuation
4. Condition of company — public or private

13.2.1 Country where the company is based

When a company has to be appraised, the business practices of the country it is in must be considered. If a venture capitalist estimates the value of a company using a method unknown in the relevant country or unaccepted by the counterpart and its advisors, the probability of the deal closing is strongly reduced.

The differences in valuation methods among countries, especially between Continental Europe, the UK, and the US are less important today, but they still exist.

In Continental Europe academics and professionals prefer a valuation based on data captured from the balance sheets, or income statements, of a firm. Income-based methods, balance sheet-based methods, or a mix of the two are used in Italy, Germany, and France. Decidedly less used are cash flow-based and market-based (or multiple) methods, because they lack objectivity in the final estimation of value and because the stock exchanges and capital markets in Continental European countries are of little importance to a company's value.

In the UK and the US, the chosen method is based on the idea that the value of a firm is in its ability to generate positive free cash flows to debt and equity holders. If a company is going public, then the value should be close to the price that the markets are ready to pay for similar companies.

13.2.2 Company industry

Different industries have different value drivers that reveal where the value of a firm is created. In industries where tangible capital (fixed assets and working capital) is a large part of the capital invested — such as the manufacturing of metals, banking and insurance, chemistry, or the real estate business — the value of this capital should be included in the final valuation. Other industries such as fashion, consulting, biotechnology, or Internet-related firms do not report a large amount of tangible capital because their competitive strength is connected to intangible assets that are not included in the balance sheet. Brand equity, R&D, or marketing expenses are not counted as assets because it is not allowed in many countries, but these expenditures positively impact the future performance of a company. In these types of industries only cash flow-based or income-based methods can be used to correctly estimate the company's value.

13.2.3 Data availability and reliability

The choice of valuation method is strongly affected by the availability and reliability of data on the firm, its markets, the future evolution of its sectors, and its competitors. These data should be comprised of the past, present, and future value of all relevant variables regarding the firm's performance. If the conditions of availability and reliability are not satisfied, the valuation must be performed with cash flow and income based methods making it strongly subjective and inaccurate. The availability of reliable data on the firm and its competitors allows valuation to be executed with forward-looking methods.

13.2.4 **Public or Private Status of a Company**

The fourth element used to choose the correct valuation method for a company is its availability of market prices and stocks. If a firm is quoted on a public, regulated stock market, the valuation can be based, as a control method for other estimates, on the market prices over an extended period of time. The use of market prices allows the analyst to calculate multiples derived from stock quotes of comparable firms. This approach can be used to value companies without historical information or with little or no available data. The main problem with this method is finding companies sufficiently similar to the one to be valued.

13.3 **BASIC CONCEPTS OF COMPANY VALUATION**

Before analyzing the three main techniques used to calculate equity value, it is necessary to define the basic financial and economic elements of a company: the balance sheet, the profits and losses statement, the financial statement, and the cost of capital.

13.3.1 **The balance sheet**

The first element is the balance sheet as seen in Figure 13.1.

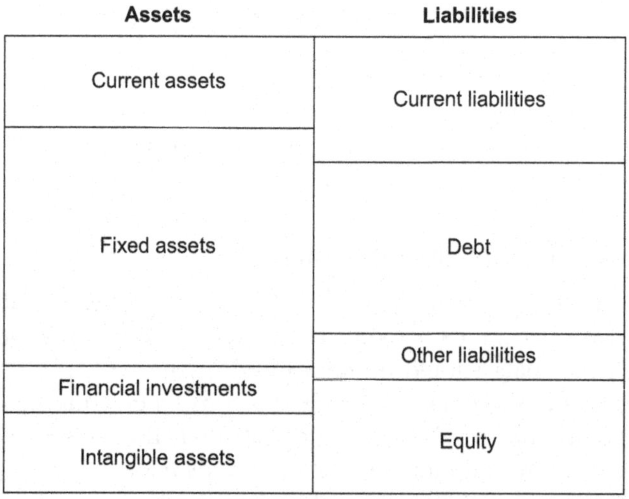

FIGURE 13.1

Balance sheet.

The left side of the balance sheet includes all of the company assets divided into:

1. **Current assets** — Account receivables, inventory, and liquid assets.
2. **Fixed assets** — Material investment realized during the life of the company used to execute operations such as plants, equipment, land, and buildings.
3. **Financial investments** — Participation in equity of other companies and marketable security.
4. **Intangible assets** — Patents, trademarks, and goodwill.

On the right side are the company's liabilities:

1. **Current liabilities** — Accounts payable due to all the products and services provided by the suppliers (trade debts).
2. **Debt** — All financial debt raised by the company, both long-term debt (bonds and loans) and short-term liabilities.
3. **Other liabilities** — Allowances for retirement plans and deferred taxes.
4. **Equity** — The company reports the original capital subscribed by the shareholders, plus or minus all the increases and decreases related to the yearly profits and losses, and plus or minus every special operation realized on the stakes; for example, an increase in the equity capital value.

13.3.2 Profits and losses statement

Figure 13.2 illustrates how the company has performed netting the incomes realized with the sustained cost starts from the revenues realized by the core activity

PROFITS AND LOSSES STATEMENT
+ Sales and other operating revenues
− Operating costs (including R&D)
= **EBITDA**
− Depreciation
= **EBIT**
+ Other income
− Interest expenses
= **EBT**
− Income taxes
= **NET INCOME OR LOSS**

FIGURE 13.2

Profits and losses statement.

of the company. Deducted first are all the costs created by the operations including research and development expenditures and obtaining the earnings before interest, tax, depreciations, and amortizations (EBITDA). This value is the gross margin realized by the company. Obtained from the EBITDA, just after deducting all company depreciation, is the operating profit (earnings before interest and taxes; EBIT). Then, netting the EBIT by the revenues not realized during operations (usually financial revenues) and by interests paid servicing the debt, we have the earnings before taxes (EBT). Netting the EBT by all taxes paid, we have the net income or loss.

13.3.3 The financial statement

The financial statements, starting from the EBIT computed through the profits and losses statement, outline whether or not the business has created or absorbed cash flow. To calculate the cash flow, the EBIT is reduced by the taxes paid, the increase in net working capital (WC), and the capital expenditure (CAPEX). These last two items are calculated comparing the value of the WC and the CAPEX with the current and previous period. The value obtained has a negative impact; if it is greater than zero then the company has absorbed cash, for example, increasing the stock of inventory between the two comparison periods. If the company has reduced the inventory, it means the cash flow has increased, so the value of inventory reducing has a positive effect on the company's cash flow. The final cash flow includes the depreciation realized during a specific period of time; it does not represent real cash movement so it has to be added to the EBIT. This method of calculating the cash flow (free cash flow unlevered) does not contain information about the capital structure. Instead it represents the cash flow available for the financer and shareholders calculated without considering raising new debt and the repayment of the old debt.

If obtaining a cash flow that includes the impact of the debt and the changes realized on the debt equity ratio is the goal, include the increase and decrease of the debt. To be more accurate, add all of the new debt raised to the free cash flow unlevered. This will show that the company has new cash to spend, and the repayments of old debt are deducted because they absorb liquidity. This value is called free cash flow levered (see Figure 13.3).

13.3.4 The cost of capital

There are three costs of capital: cost of debt capital, cost of equity capital, and weighted average cost of capital (WACC). The use of these three measures has to be perfectly in synch with the free cash flow discounted and the perspective of the valuation. The cost of equity capital has to discount cash flow for the shareholders

FINANCIAL STATEMENT
EBIT
− Income taxes
+ Depreciation
− Increase in net working capital
− CAPEX
= FREE CASH FLOW UNLEVERED
+ New debt
− Debt repayments
= FREE CASH FLOW LEVERED

FIGURE 13.3

Free cash flow statement.

(levered cash flow), whereas the WACC has to discount the cash flow for the firm (unlevered cash flow) because it contains information on capital structure.

These three costs of capital are also calculated differently. The cost of debt capital is easily computed, because it is based on information reported on the balance sheet:

$$i_d{}^* = i_d(1-t)$$

where:

i_d is the average weighted cost of debt capital obtained from the balance sheet and analytically;
t is the corporate tax ratio;
$i_d{}^*$ is the cost of debt capital netted by the benefit of debt leverage.

The cost of equity capital is difficult to calculate, because it is not reported on the balance sheet. The Capital Asset Pricing Model (CAPM)[1] suggests the following formula to compute the cost of equity capital:

$$i_e = r_f + \beta(r_m - r_f)$$

---

[1] The CAPM is a model of financial market equilibrium, proposed by William Scarpe in 1964, that establishes a relationship between the return of a security and its risk level, measured by only one risk factor, β.

where:

r_f is the risk free rate (matched in terms of maturity with the investment);

r_m is the risk premium, i.e., the return investors expect from the market (measured by historical series);

β is the degree of correlation between the investment and the market;

i_e is the cost of the equity capital.

To estimate the β coefficient of a stock, the regression of the returns of the stock against returns on a market index is used. If the stock does not have a β coefficient, it is necessary to use the β of the comparables. This requires identifying the β of a comparable, then unlever (exclude the effect of capital structure) the β with comparable data, and at the end re-lever (insert the capital structure of the firm) the β with the company's debt and equity structure.

The method to unlever the β is represented by

$$\beta_u = \beta/[1 + (1 - t)(D/E)]$$

where D and E are the market value of debt and equity of the chosen comparable firm.

The formula used to re-lever the β is

$$\beta = \beta_u[1 + (1 - t)(D/E)]$$

The third measure of capital cost is the WACC. It is calculated when both the equity and debt cost of capital are available. It represents an effective measure of the cost of all liabilities of the company weighted for the capital structure (debt equity ratio). The formula is

$$i_{WACC} = i_d{}^*(D/D + E) + i_e(E/D + E)$$

13.4 THE FUNDAMENTAL OF COMPARABLES

Comparables are ratios calculated on performances realized by firms that are similar to those of the company being evaluated. Using comparables it is possible to calculate or estimate the value of a company. Comparables are widely used, especially in private equity business, because these ratios are a good combination of risk, plans, accounts, and valuations of similar companies. At the same time, comparables use common metrics and methods used worldwide to verify the effectiveness of other valuation methods. For this reason, comparables are mostly used to fine-tune valuation, create inputs for valuation, and compare across the market valuation.

To completely understand this approach, it must be emphasized that comparables become less important when companies are evaluated in the seeding and start-up phases; firms are usually unprofitable and experiencing rapid growth at this time.

The most common comparables include:

EV/EBITDA — The ratio between the enterprise value and the EBITDA illustrates the capability of the firm to produce value through gross margin. EBITDA is a good measure of the company's ability to create cash from its operational activities and avoid distortions from accounting policies that affect the net income.

EV/EBIT — This ratio expresses the ability of the firm to produce value from operating profit. It avoids distortion connected with debt structure and tax strategy, and it can be both the actual value at the moment of evaluation and the prospective value of the firm. With this ratio, the EBIT value is a prospective figure that can be discounted to present the corresponding years considered in the estimation of future margins. The EBIT is useful to value a company because it only includes ordinary depreciations such as material depreciations, leasing fees, and immaterial depreciations including trademarks, patents, and computer software. Immaterial depreciations do not include the depreciation of goodwill and transaction costs incurred during buyout and acquisition operations.

EV/S — "How many times do I have to multiply the sales to buy the company?" is a question answered by the ratio of enterprise value/sales, which is based on the ability of the firm to produce sales. Sales are the easiest measure to determine, but the value must be computed considering only the revenues realized through the sale of goods and services offered by the firm excluding discounts and returned products.

P/E — Price/earnings is a ratio used by listed companies to investigate the relationship between the current price of the stock and the ability to produce earnings. Since earnings (profit after tax) reflect the capital structure of the company, they are calculated after interest expenses and taxes. This can be misleading. It would be better to use EBIT to further investigate this relationship.

P/BV — Price/book value of equity can be obtained from listed companies by identifying the relationship between the current price of the stock and the nominal value of equity.

Enterprise value is the sum of the equity (100%), shareholders' value, and financial debt. It represents the total value of the company divided between the shareholders by the equity subscribed, and the debt holders by the debt subscribed.

An example of valuation by comparables is provided in Appendix 13.1.

13.5 DISCOUNTED CASH FLOW APPROACH

The discounted cash flow (DCF) approach includes the determination of future cash flow generated by the company for 5 or 10 years. This is then discounted with an appropriate discount rate and summed. The final value of the company is obtained by combining the actual value of this flow and the net financial position. The net financial position will be deducted if it is negative and added if it is positive.

There are two main steps of valuation: cash flow determination and the identification of the discount rate to be used. Results from DCF are verified with comparables to check if the results can be compared with similar companies.

DCF is used because the value of a company includes the future cash flow even if the different definitions of cash flow must be coordinated with appropriated discount rates. Depending on the type of cash flow (levered or unlevered) and the discount rate used (WACC or cost of equity capital), two different methods of DCF can be identified: net present value and adjusted present value.

13.5.1 Net present value method

The most common DCF approach is the net present value (NPV) method where enterprise value is calculated using WACC and unlevered cash flow of the firm. WACC includes the effects of the capital structure in this rate and not in the cash flow. The enterprise value is equal to the present value of future unlevered cash flow added to the terminal value; however, it is necessary to reduce the enterprise value for the minorities and the net financial position and to increase the value for non-operating assets if they exist.

The formula used to calculate enterprise value for a mature investment is

$$EV = \sum\nolimits_{t=1}^{n} \frac{CF_t}{(1 + WACC)^t} + TV_n + (SA\text{-}M\text{-}NFP)$$

where:

TV is the terminal value of the firm at time n;
SA are surplus (not operating) assets;
M are minorities;
NFP is net financial position;
SA, M, and NFP refer (if they exist) to the time of valuation.

The determination of the terminal value, which is an important element used to define enterprise value, is a critical item calculated by the following formula:

$$TV_n = \frac{\dfrac{CF_n{}^*(1 + g)}{WACC - g}}{(1 + WACC)^n}$$

where g is the perpetual growth rate of the cash flow.

13.5.2 Adjusted present value method

An alternative to the net present value is the adjusted present value (APV), which is a DCF approach using the cost of equity capital and the cash flow levered for the shareholders in its calculations. APV is more appropriate to use than NPV when the firm's capital structure is unsteady or when the company has realized net operating losses that can be used to offset taxable incomes. NPV is inappropriately used when the capital structure is initially highly lever-aged but the level of debt is strongly reduced as repayments are made. Typical deals include leveraged buyouts where the target capital structure changes over time.

The APV method overcomes this drawback by dividing the analysis into two levels. First, it considers the cash flow created by the company's assets. Not taking into consideration its capital structure, these flows are discounted with a rate that expresses the capital cost of the company, including the leverage structure. (Refer to the cost of equity capital as explained in Section 13.3.4.) Using the cost of equity capital means that the capital structure effects are included in the cash flow and not in the discount rate. Secondly, APV calculates financial flow created by the capital structure of the company including the tax benefits of the deductible interest paid servicing the debt. These flows are discounted to the pre-tax rate of return on debt that is lower than the cost equity capital.

The equity value is equal to the present value of future cash flow and terminal value of both the NPV and APV. Analysis must consider the effects on the enterprise value created by the minorities, the net financial position, and the non-operating assets.

The previously described DCF methods are particularly useful for

The valuation of a private company where the shareholders are less interested in a stable and continuous flow of dividends. It is more important to know the amount of cash still available after investing in working capital and fixed assets, rather than the amount of dividends in the short run.

The valuation of a firm performed by a controlling shareholder or a financial partner because the key point is the identification of the amount of cash needed to fund new investments. If free cash flow is negative, shareholders have to decide how to fill the gap. This is often a strategic choice for the future success of the company.

For the valuation of highly leveraged firms, in the process of changing leverage over time, APV is important because high debt can affect the development strategy of a firm when cash available after the needed investments is not enough to repay the old debt.

The valuation of turnaround plans. DCF helps identify if the turnaround that depends on generating sufficient unlevered free cash flow to repay the debt is feasible.

13.6 VENTURE CAPITAL METHOD

The venture capital method focuses on the relationship between the expected IRR, the growth of the firm, and the percentage of shares to buy. Its use depends on the definition of the participation price and the return required for the single investment. This approach is typically used when the price setting is dominant and during seed or start-up deals where there are negative cash flows and earnings with high uncertainty but potentially substantial future rewards.

The venture capital method asks a very simple question: What amount of shares does the investor buy based on the amount of money needed to invest and the expected IRR? To answer this question valuation of cash flow is considered the final expected value of the investment at divestment. The value is usually defined using comparables.

In a second step, the terminal value is discounted back to the present using a very high rate between 40 and 75%. This high discount rate is a source of criticism of this method, but venture capitalists argue that a large discount rate is appropriate to compensate for the illiquidity of investments in private firms. Venture capitalists provide a very valuable service so the high discount rate compensates them for their efforts. Finally, because the entrepreneur's projections are often too optimistic, a large discount rate is used to mitigate these inflated forecasts. The discounted terminal value and the expected rate of return on the investment is necessary to calculate the desired ownership interest of an investor.

Major critics of the venture capital method feel that the venture capitalist has to presume there will be no dilution of his participation and that very often venture-backed companies go public or require other types of financing.

13.6.1 **Key steps to the venture capital method**

The key steps to the venture capital method are

Step 1: Terminal value calculation
Step 2: Future value of the investment
Step 3: Percentage of shares to subscribe
Step 4: Amount of shares to issue
Step 5: Value of newly issued shares

Step 1: Terminal value calculation — The expected holding period and the calculation of the terminal value are addressed. The terminal value is usually calculated with comparables, typically P/E and DCF approaches. **For example**: If the expected holding period is 4 years and the expected net income at $y - 4$ is €6 million, a terminal value calculated through a P/E comparable of 5 would be €30 million.

Step 2: Future value of the investment — Calculation of the future value of the investment taking into account the expected holding period and the expected IRR, which is defined from the constraints of the investor. **For example**: If the investment is €2 million, the holding period is 4 years, and the expected IRR is 55%, the future value is €11,54 million.

Step 3: Percentage of shares to subscribe — Calculation of the shares the investor has to buy to acquire the expected IRR. The number of shares is found by dividing the future value of the investment by the terminal value of the firm. **For example**: If the future value of the investment is €11,54 million and the terminal value is €30 million, the percentage of shares for the investor is 38,46%.

Step 4: Amount of shares to issue — Calculation of the number of new shares that the venture-backed company has to issue to ensure a particular percentage of capital to the investor. This calculation consists of a simple proportion:

$$\% \text{ share} = \frac{\text{new}}{\text{new} + \text{old}} \qquad \text{new shares} = \frac{\text{old} * \% \text{ share}}{1 - \% \text{ share}}$$

where new and old represent the number of new and old shares. **For example**: If the percentage of shares the investor must have is 38,46% and existing shares are 300.000, the number of new shares available to issue is 187.488.

$$187.488 = \frac{300.000 * 38,46\%}{1 - 38,46\%}$$

Step 5: Value newly issued shares — Calculation of the price of newly issued shares for the investor is executed dividing the amount of the investment by the number of new shares. **For example**: If the investment is €2 million and the number of new shares is 187.488, the price per new share is €10,67. The implied pre money valuation is 10,67 so the value of 300.000 shares equals €3,201 million and the post money value of all 487.488 shares equals €5,201 million.

It is important to point out that venture capitalists presume there will be dilution of their participations. To mitigate the effect of this dilution, the retention ratio is used to quantify the decreasing participation realized between the closing and exiting of the deal. In the previous example, if 20 to 30% more capital is subscribed, then the participation of 38,46% will become 24,36% of the final equity capital and the retention ratio equals 64%. Therefore, to ensure an equivalent participation to the first investor, the actual percentage of the participation will be 60%; that is the ratio between the percentage of 38,36% and the retention ratio.

The formula of retention ratio is

$$\text{Retention ratio} = \alpha/(1 + \beta)/(1 + \gamma)$$

where:

α is the percentage of equity capital subscribed by the investor at first issuing;

β is the percentage of equity capital subscribed at second moment;

γ is the percentage of equity capital subscribed at third moment (see Figure 13.4).

Steps	Formulas applied
1 Terminal value calculation	P/E or DCF approaches
2 Future value of the investment	Investment $(1 + \text{expected IRR})^{\wedge(\text{expected time})}$
3 Percentage of shares	Future value of the investment/terminal value
4 Number of new shares to issue	(existing shares * percentage)/(1 − percentage)
5 Value of new issued shares	Investment/number of new shares

FIGURE 13.4

Venture capital method steps.

Appendix 13.1

A business case: MAP

MAP S.p.A. is an Italian retail distributing company operating in the food sector. It has local branches in central and southern Italy with more than 650 shops with an average size of 650 m². Growth is expected to be quite strong, and the real estate policy is not to buy shops but to rent them due to their strong negotiation of rental installments. In 2002, MAP needed a private equity investor to support the expansion strategy, but the existing shareholders did not want to lose control. No acquisition of competitors was planned in the short-medium run, and the general forecast of selling food was expected to be positive in the central and southern part of Italy.

The forecasts (see Figure 13.5) were based on the following assumptions that came from the business plan realized with the supervision of the private equity investor.

The unlevered approach is adopted to calculate cash flow for the firm. The main information came from the balance sheet regarding data on assets and liabilities. The company did not have surplus assets or minorities within the equity, and the net financial position was €20 million coming from a cash position of €20 million (see Figure 13.6).

The main comparables on the market came not only from Italy (where only the company Eat&Food can be considered a comparable, even if it is not listed) but from all over Europe. See Figure 13.7 for the data.

Considering the capital structure of MAP, the book value of the debt was €30.000 and the book value of equity was €3.000. The risk free rate was 3% (calculated as 5-year 2003 Italian Government bonds) and the return on market investment was estimated at a level of 10% with an expected holding period of 5 years.

	2003	2004	2005	2006	2007
Sales	197,004.00	240,306.00	283,251.00	297,358.00	312,203.00
Operating costs	184,138.00	223,889.00	263,005.00	275,977.00	289,768.00
EBITDA	*12,866.00*	*16,417.00*	*20,246.00*	*21,381.00*	*22,435.00*
Depreciation	−5,492.00	−7,289.00	−8,583.00	−8,538.00	−7,651.00
EBIT	*7,374.00*	*9,128.00*	*11,663.00*	*12,843.00*	*14,784.00*
Other income	−	−	−	−	−
Interest expenses	−1,428.00	−1,724.00	−1,474.00	−1,184.00	−817
EBT	*5,946.00*	*7,404.00*	*10,189.00*	*11,659.00*	*13,967.00*
Taxes	−2,238.00	−2,763.00	−3,519.00	−3,891.00	−4,482.00
NET INCOME	**3,708.00**	**4,641.00**	**6,670.00**	**7,768.00**	**9,485.00**

FIGURE 13.5

Profits and losses statement (€/000).

	2003	2004	2005	2006	2007
(+) EBIT	7,374	9,128	11,663	12,843	14,784
(−) Income taxes	−2,238	−2,763	−3,519	−3,891	−4,482
(+) Depreciation	5,492	7,289	8,583	8,538	7,651
(−) Increase net working capital	−14,779	5,870	−3,121	−6,021	−6,677
(−) Capex	−15,785	−16,650	−6,800	0	0
CASH FLOW	**−19,936**	**2,874**	**6,806**	**11,469**	**11,276**

FIGURE 13.6

Cash flow unlevered statements (€/000).

	Beta	EV/sales	EV/EBITDA	D/E
Manger & Boire	0.92	1.20	16.00	6.70
The Kroeger Company	0.88	1	18	7.2
Safeway, Inc	0.72	0.9	14	4.5
Tesco	0.62	1.3	20	3.4
Mangiare & Bere	not listed	1.4	17	8.1

FIGURE 13.7

Comparables.

A13.1.1 Sample valuation using comparables

It was decided not to use the data from the comparables because there were too many differences between these business and MAP such as the average size of the shops, the geographical area covered, and the status of company (public or private). For this reason, the average value of the ratios EV/S and EV/EBITDA were calculated:

Based on the averaged values, two values were identified, as shown in Figure 13.8. The German company Essen&Trinken was used even though it was not an Italian company, because it has a market very similar to MAP in terms of population and average salary, but the average size of its shops is smaller, only 350 m² and it is quoted on the stock market. Assuming that Essen&Trinken is the most comparable competitor to MAP, its valuation is calculated by applying the EV/EBITDA equal to 18, thus obtaining €231.588.

After these calculations it was possible to define an enterprise value for MAP of €218.722 to 231.588, but considering the MAP's private status, it would be appropriate to apply a discount of 15 to 20% leading to a new value of €174.978 to 185.270.

	EV/sales	EV/EBITDA
Manger & Boire (FR)	1.2	16
Essen & Trinken (DH)	1	18
Eat & Drink (UK)	0.9	14
Food & Drink (USA)	1.3	20
Mangiare & Bere (ITA)	1.4	17
Average	**1.16**	**17**
MAP Implied Value €/000	**€ 228,525**	**€ 218,722**

FIGURE 13.8

Average of comparables and MAP's implied value (€/000).

A13.1.2 Sample valuation using the net present value method

The key point of this method is identifying the WACC by calculating the cost of debt. Based on this, the book value of the debt was €30.000 and the interest forecasted for 2003 was €1.428 and the cost of the debt equaled 4,76%, which was obtained by using the ratio between the two values.

The second step is to identify the cost of capital necessary to find the correct β. Because MAP was a private company, the only way to consider the average of the β of the comparables, excluding the effect of the capital structure and then re-levering the β according to MAP's capital structure, was to follow the formula from Section 13.3.4. The average β of the comparables equaled 0,785, the tax rate was 33%, and the average D/E ratio of the comparables equaled 5,98, so the β unlevered equaled 0,1568. The MAP's β levered was calculated applying the relevant formula as per Section 13.3.4. The D/E ratio of MAP equaled 10 and the tax rate was 33%, so a re-levered β equaled 1,207. Using this β, the desired risk premium equaled 10% and the free risk rate was 3%, so the MAP's cost of equity capital was 11,45%.

The next step was to identify the weight of the debt and equity of MAP, which were 91 and 9%, respectively. Then the averaged value of the cost of debt and equity capital was calculated obtaining a WACC equal to 3.94%.

Using the cash flow shown in Figure 13.6 we obtain:
Present value of the cash flows for the years 2003 to 2007 equal to €8.662,18.
Terminal value discounted to year 2002 equals €235.909,42.

The NPV of MAP was calculated adding the terminal value and the present value of the cash flow. This result was deducted by the net financial position, €20.000, so the NPV equaled €224.571,60. In this sample, there were no surplus assets or minorities.

Appendix 13.2

Business case Rainbow: Sample valuation using the venture capital method

Rainbow is a company active in the biotechnology industry and the two entrepreneurs, who are also the two founder engineers of the company, have developed a new product and registered the patent. They have already reached an agreement with a big European partner who is a leader in pharmaceutical product distribution for a future launch of their innovative product.

They asked Iris Partners, a private equity investor specializing in start-up financing, to finance their initiative, focused on implementing the plant needed to start the new business, with an investment of €4,5 million. Iris' strategy for this type of investment requires an IRR of 45% to be realized within 5 years, so the future value of the investment equals €28.843.803,28 as per the formula included in Section 13.6.

Based on the business plan redacted by the entrepreneurs, the terminal value of the company was €42 million, calculated by the formula in Section 13.6 using a terminal year net income of €3,5 million and a comparable P/E of 12.

Iris Partners considered the correct percentage of new share to be issued and subscribed 68,68% calculated with a total of 100.000 old shares; the total new shares to be issued is 219.241,20 with a price of €20,53.

The valuation of Rainbow before the investment was €2.052.534, after the investment it was valued at €6.552.533,94. The difference between these two values is equal to the investment of €4,5 million realized by Iris Partners.

Financing seed and start up

14.1 GENERAL OVERVIEW OF EARLY STAGE FINANCING

Each entrepreneurial project is developed through several phases according to the life cycle time of a company. It is easy to identify the development phase by the problems that occur at different points in the firm's structure. During this phase the venture capitalist is considered more than a simple supplier of risk capital and he ends up as a financial intermediary able to support and improve the growth of venture-backed companies. How and why the venture capitalist decides to invest in a business idea that has to be defined and planned before the company even exists are reviewed in this chapter.

To understand the investment activity in risk capital, it is necessary to analyze the key management process realized by the investor. This analysis focuses on critical topics related to the relationship between the entrepreneur and the venture capitalist and all the building steps necessary to organize the complex structure owned by the venture capitalist initiative. The classical approach to the venture capitalist investment, realized in the emerging entrepreneurial initiative, leads to the study of financing and managerial resources and their importance. The resources are destined to be used for highly innovative projects with good potential. These are matched with minority participation to reach capital gains because of the revaluation of the stakes and the opportunity to differentiate the risk.

It is therefore important to emphasize that venture capitalists

Operate with a pre-established and limited period of time, usually between 3 and 5 years

Acquire only minority participation because of the entrepreneurial risk and difficulty selling the control participation

Point out, from the first time with the target company, the importance of the return on the investment; his investment is in part remunerated during the holding period, by dividends and advisory fees, paid by the target company

14.1.1 Seed financing

Figure 14.1 identifies the different stages during the life cycle of a company. This chapter focuses on the first phase — early stage financing. It is possible to further subdivide this phase into two parts, risk and return profile. Each part has specific objectives.

Seed financing is defined as a participation in favor of using a special purpose vehicle (SPV) specifically meant for developing a research project. It is important to underline the difference between seed and start-up financing. In the start-up financing phase there is no company to finance, but there is a person or team of researchers who want to invest in and develop a project that hopefully will produce a successful business idea.

Industry sectors typically targeted for seed financing include information technology, pharmaceutical, chemical, telecommunication, and biomedical.

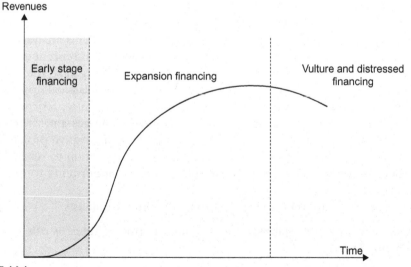

FIGURE 14.1

Life cycle of a company.

Regarding the risk profile, two things must be considered. First, entrepreneurs in need of seed financing have no existing firm, and are usually a team of researchers ready to join a capital investor to obtain funds necessary to found a company that will lead and develop their business idea. Secondly, the venture capitalist has to consider the management and its risk profile related to a good performance of the financed project.

Risks that affect investors include:

1. Sudden death — In the beginning the project is owned just by the researchers. The first thing they do is share their valuable know-how with the founders. Usually the first promoter of the business idea obtains the copyright.

2. Support structure for the researchers — To facilitate research, the private equity investor has to provide an adequate infrastructure:

    Incubator — A group of instruments and infrastructures necessary to ensure the correct development of the project.

    Joint venture between several centers of research — The return will be shared if the project becomes a successful business (bilateral agreement).

The incubator structure is very expensive when compared with the bilateral agreement. It does not allow the private equity investor to invest in different industries, but if the project is successful the investor does not have to share his earnings. Bilateral agreements permit the investor to operate in different industries at the same time, but they impose the division of the investment return if the business idea is profitable. Considering the industries involved, seed financing is similar to charity. Most researchers can collect the money they need with a fundraising campaign. As mentioned in Chapter 9, during the screening of potential projects to be financed, the private equity investor applies the famous golden rule: start with one thousand projects valuated, go through one hundred projects financed, and just ten projects will be successful.

There are two tools used to manage investment return: diversify because of the large amount of resources divided between different business initiatives and mitigate the potential risk on the capital invested by having sub-products guaranteed by the project. There can be potential ethical problems with the second tool.

14.1.2 Start-up financing

This type of participation finances an already existing company that needs private equity resources to start the business. The risk is based on launching a company built on a well-founded business idea and not on the gamble of discovering a new business idea.

At this point in the business, risk depends on two variables: the total amount of the net financial requirement and the time necessary to reach the breakeven point of the activity financed. The risk is not strongly connected with the entrepreneur or the validity of his business idea, which are preconditions for the participation. What is really important is the growth of the industry in terms of capital intensity required and the forecasted trend of the turnover. The high level of risk is due to the investment realized at the time (t_0) when it is uncertain if the business will reach the breakeven point.

The performance profile of a start-up initiative, in terms of IRR, is connected with the ability and capacity to re-sell the participation on the financial market. The track record and credibility of the private equity investor are key factors in the success of the exit strategy when obtaining the desired return from the investment realized. The main investor's goal (a good and successful exit from the investment) can be facilitated by drawing up agreements with other private equity funds regarding their availability and commitment to buy the participation after a predefined period of time. Another solution is to sign a buy back agreement with the entrepreneur or other shareholders who agree to repurchase the venture capitalist's participation in the company after a predefined period of time.

14.2 OPERATION PHASES DURING EARLY STAGE FINANCING

Different stages of a company's development need different types of capital investment. From the origination to the implementation up to the exit strategy, each phase needs different capital and know-how. During the start-up phase, the venture capitalist has an intense and complex interaction with the entrepreneur to verify the necessary financial and managerial support. During the seed financing phase the technical validity of the product or service is still unproven, so the venture capitalist offers limited financial resources to support the development of the business idea and the preparation of the commercial feasibility plan. Consequently, there is huge risk faced by the investor.

Start-up financing provides the funds needed to start production without commercial validity of the product or service offered. During this stage, the entrepreneur risk is huge, but there is also risk connected to the financial resources provided. This is usually more important than the risks invested during the seed phase.

First stage financing is linked to the improvement of production capacity after it is completed but the commercial validity of the business idea is still not totally verified. This requires a large amount of financial resources, but is less risky and managerial support is still limited.

Due to the high level of complexity that exists in the markets today, it is not easy to clearly classify these investments; it is more logical to classify them in relation to the potential emerging strategic needs of the company, industry problems, specific threats or opportunity, and final goals of the investor.

14.3 STRUCTURE OF VENTURE CAPITALISTS IN EARLY STAGE FINANCING

Financial markets are often unable to sustain projects presented by companies; most of all those with innovative initiatives. Because of this, the venture capitalist presents an interesting and important opportunity to develop entrepreneurial projects. The specific remuneration structure of the venture capitalist is different when compared with a typical bank. The professional investor who invests risk capital wants to be reimbursed, but he wants first to share the eventual success of the business. The bank is solely interested in reimbursement.

Two types of organization structures are used in venture capital operations during the seed or start-up initiative: Business Angels and corporate venture capitalists. A Business Angel is a private and informal investor who decides to bring risk capital to a small or medium firm during its start up or first development phase. Business Angels are sustained by networks that match them with companies to meet the demand and supply of financial funds. This type of financial operator is common in the United States, but faces problems in Europe. Because of this situation, which directly affects new business, the European Strategy was launched in Lisbon in 2000.[1] It defined the central role of Business Angels as concrete contributors to the improvement of European competitiveness and productivity.

Corporate venture capital is an investment in risk capital executed by very large industrial groups. The necessity to strengthen research and development to continue the high-tech evolution has created investment opportunities. Unfortunately, increasing investments is not linked with satisfactory results. Small companies have shown a high level of efficiency and competence in the innovation sector so several industrial groups have started to specialize in the development of new projects; either founding them directly or acquiring participation. These groups have also acquired minority participations in small enterprises that are technologically qualified. This form of financing allows small or medium firms to collaborate in a positive way with the big industrial groups.

The private and venture capital system is a financial tool with potential to accomplish the competitiveness, innovation, and growth objectives implemented

---

[1] The investment is ongoing.

by the Lisbon protocol. The venture capitalist is motivated by the potential quality and long-term growth of industrial leverages operating in innovative industries as well as the ability to improve management skills.

Private equity operations realized during seed and start-up financing have to focus their attention on:

Supporting the development of an entrepreneurial environment. Knowledge-based firms are still not widespread in Europe because there are no structured and uniform legal regulations. The prevalence of innovative businesses is possible due to the acquisition of financial, strategic, and corporate knowledge, which can be offered by a professional financial investor with international experience.

Implementing research and development and the ability to spread the innovation through centers of excellence by firms focused on research. A key factor toward this evolution is a structured relationship between firms and universities.

14.4 SELECTION OF THE TARGET COMPANY

The first aspect the venture capitalist has to consider, to guarantee the optimal composition of his investment portfolios, is the effectiveness of his deal flow. In American markets, where risk capital is widespread and well established, deal flow is represented by a relevant number of well-structured business proposals formalized with business plans. These are sent by firms to specific groups of venture capitalists selected based on their previous investments and their industry and/or geographical areas of interests. In financial markets where risk capital is not so widespread, the venture capitalist needs specific ways to promote this form of financing; for example, his network of relationships is an effective and useful tool to create financial business opportunities.

Important to the venture capitalist is the opportunity to analyze the largest number of business projects, which allows a better range of choices, and proposals that include the optimal and ideal requirements needed by investors. For example, in the developed and complex risk capital markets, competition between venture capitalists to finance the best projects has provoked operators to specialize their financing toward a specific stage of a firm's life cycle, the average dimension of the funds required, and the industry.

Each venture capitalist decides the minimum and maximum investment entrance. The minimum investment includes fixed costs during the screening of all business projects such as due diligence and monitoring and managerial advisory costs. The maximum investment considers the physical financial funds owned by the venture capitalist and the need to maintain an equilibrium between the portfolio of investments realized in terms of risk and return profiles. Minimum entrance level investors operate in the seed or start-up financing phase. Early growth operations, such as those in the high-tech industry, are always strongly supported by extra financial services that require special and advanced preparation to guarantee the success of the target company, especially during the screening phase.

14.5 SUPPORTING INNOVATION DEVELOPMENT

The venture capitalist is a financial intermediary whose mainstay is the financial and managerial support of firms in the start-up phase. These firms operate in markets with huge information asymmetry regarding their valuation and guarantee of financial support from traditional lenders such as banks. The first example of information asymmetry is represented by what is known by the entrepreneur or management team and what is known by the investor. To better understand this situation, high-tech industries must be identified:

1. Software applications
2. Pharmaceutical technologies
3. Biotechnology

These industries need to concentrate their resources in research and development to reach their performance potential. Because of this it is impossible to represent a valid guarantee for traditional banks.

The high level of uncertainty, typical for a firm with a high level of innovative development, makes it difficult to use traditional financing for two reasons: it is impossible to forecast, with a high degree of certainty, the success of a highly innovative business project and the very real possibility of negative economic results for a long period of time. These conditions introduce a high level of complexity into the firm's valuation. The chances to select business projects with a positive net present value and a long-term view are few. This makes it possible for the venture capitalist to invest financial resources in highly innovative projects that are very risky, but may generate high economic return if the supported firms are successful.

The venture capitalist, because of his highly specialized knowledge in multiple investment areas, is able to collect and analyze all available financial information and make the most conscious and optimal investment decision. The successful venture capitalist must be a highly specialized investor with topnotch managerial skills to successfully work with entrepreneurs and managers. He must also know the most important changes financed firms need:

Easy improvement of the organization including planning and development of the company's informative flows and processes. This allows for wider contractual power and a better company image. These improvements make it easier for the shareholders to exit without damaging or taking resources away from the company.

Introduction of advanced systems for management and budgeting to increase the rationalization of the target company due to joint ventures, acquisitions, and mergers that represent important solutions for the company's development.

14.6 **PRIVATE INVESTOR MOTIVATION AND CRITERIA**

Private investors are motivated by:

1. Return on investment — Venture capitalists have building operations that allow a minimum ROI of 30%.

2. Improved self-image, self-esteem, and recognition — Private investors desire satisfactory economic returns from their investments as well as the opportunity to increase the value of their brand to guarantee a successful investment.

3. Alleviating concerns and helping others — This is especially seen in Business Angels. Because early stage financing seems like charity, Business Angels very often decide to invest money in business ideas connected with an emotional past experience (if a relative of the investor has died due to a cancer, the investor might finance projects that can help find a cure).

4. Getting the "first crack" at the next high rise stock, prior to IPO — They realize this is the way to acquire higher economic return without dealing with public securities.

5. Having an aptitude for high risk — This is a critical element that distinguishes this type of investor from all others. Without this aptitude they would not consider such high risk business ideas.

6. Having fun and leading challenging projects to economic success.

When studying how private equity investors operate in early stage firms, it is important to understand not only their motivation, but also the criteria they apply during their investment activity. Usually, venture capitalists want to know all about the businesses in which they invest, particularly the technology and the market, to execute due diligence with higher awareness of the people and the business idea. They especially search for investments that allow proprietary advantages for unique technology and leaps in innovation leading to growth opportunities to pass the competition.

Private investors have important criteria for selecting business ideas and start-up firms. These include a solid financial forecast leading to a return of 5 to 10 times their original investment with a minimum ROI of 30%. To ensure these requirements, private investors evaluate the existence of possible future profitability, because it demonstrates the ability of the Business Angel to select a good idea and improve their image in the financial market. According to these criteria, venture capitalists decide and select the investment opportunity based on a business plan, even if they must face the difficulties of analyzing just an idea and not an operating business. This makes forecasting the future performance of an investment formidable and a wrong evaluation plausible.

During the fundraising phase, the quality of the management team and the equity investor's track record, personal financial commitment, and the desire to achieve success are important to collect financial and economic data. It is easy to understand the value of managers who work hard and collaborate constructively and enthusiastically with the investors to build a trustworthy relationship between the funds provider and the team of promoters or researchers.

The level of commitment from Business Angels changes depending on how they wish to invest. We can identify, in terms of active and direct participation in the business project, four main types of Business Angels:

1. Angels who sit on a working Board of Directors — They are passive and not looking for operating management responsibility, but usually require periodic financial reports.

2. Angels who act as informal consultants — They are investors who provide consulting help when needed and requested.

3. Angels who are full- or part-time manager investors — They are investors who create value from the support provided, market knowledge, and contacts offered to the entrepreneur or to the research team.

4. Angels who are investor-owners — They assist founders by bringing other financing after presenting and promoting the business initiative to new investors and establishing strategic alliances with other companies that represent future clients or potential providers of technologies and manufacturing enhancement.

In early stage deals, private equity investors use these criteria to choose an investment:

Possibility of entry in new markets
Cost advantages
Proprietary advantages or unique technology
Business idea easily understood by investors
Opportunity to have fun from the investment
High level of ROI linked with solid financial indicators
Business idea that is both innovative and profitable
Management teams with competences, good track records, ability to finan-
    cially commit, and the desire to succeed
Geographically close
Clear exit strategy

Appendix 14.1

A business case: TROMPI

A14.1.1 Target company

TROMPI is a retail company founded in the 1990s. It started as a concessionaire to a European retail firm. In 2001 TROMPI launched its retail shop chain with its own brand. Today, it is a leader in retail products for home, decoration, fashion accessories, and gift items; 75% of its selling proposal comes from Far East suppliers.

A14.1.2 Investment structure

Private equity investors were involved in the early stage deal in 2004 through a minority participation.

A14.1.3 Critical elements of the investment

TROMPI was evaluated by venture capitalists as an interesting company in terms of originality and high potential performance.

A14.1.4 Management phase activity

During the short holding period the number of shops doubled; the support of the private equity investor was covered not only by the marketing and distribution processes, but also by the development of the business idea, a more effective reporting system, improving the planning and control process, and hiring highly skilled managers.

A14.1.5 Exiting

After two years the private equity investor sold its minority participation of 41% to another venture capitalist who specialized in supporting companies during the next stages of their life cycle.

Appendix 14.2

A business case: INBIOT

A14.2.1 Target company

INBIOT was founded in 2002 as a spin-off from a European pharmaceutical company to develop a business idea in the research and development of medicines dedicated to the cure of urologic and chronic inflammatory diseases. INBIOT, at the close of investment, had important research and development agreements with leaders in the pharmaceutical market.

A14.2.2 Investment structure

Project financing was realized in 2006 with €11 million due to the collaboration of three private equity firms. INBIOT, before the 2006 investment, had been the target of private equity investments valuing €100 million.

A14.2.3 Critical elements of the investment

Private equity investors saw high potential for the business idea and the IPO opportunity as an exit strategy.

A14.2.4 Exiting

Private equity investors exited the investment in 2006 with an IPO in a Zurich-based public equity market specializing in biotechnological companies. The IPO was successful; the share price of INBIOT increased by 20% in only 6 months.

Appendix 14.3

A business case: COMPEURO

A14.3.1 Target company

COMPEURO, founded in 2002, researches, develops, manufactures, and markets mini and high-speed computers. Today, the company's market includes Europe, the US, and China. Activity consists of research and production plants with commercial branches. COMPEURO is the European leader in high-speed computers and one of the top 10 world manufacturers of mini computers. The company earns €65 million in revenue.

A14.3.2 Investment structure

Venture capital investment was realized through two stages since the start-up phase and focused on launching the company. The business idea was so successful that in 2001 a different private equity investor financed the firm's external and internal operations expansion. COMPEURO went public during 2005 and, with the fresh financial resources, acquired the North American company MORCA, which operates in the same industry with similar business characteristics and equal dimensions.

A14.3.3 Critical elements of the investment

Private equity invested in COMPEURO because its business idea had high potential and an IPO opportunity as an exit strategy.

14.3.4 Exiting

The private equity investor exited from the investment in 2005 with an IPO.

Appendix 14.4

A business case: NORWEN

A14.4.1 Target company

The company, founded in 1999, researches and develops medicines and was spun off by an international pharmaceutical company. NORWEN has been focused on the development of two medicines: one dedicated to the cure of neurological disease and one dedicated to the cure of neuropathic, inflammatory, and post-operative pain.

A14.4.2 Investment structure

The investment was realized in different steps and for different objectives. In 1999 the first financial resources were dedicated to the foundation of the company through the subscription of risk capital and convertible bonds by a private equity operator. After three years, an increase in the risk capital was realized with the involvement of two new private equity firms, and in 2005 two other investors financed the new issued risk capital.

A14.4.3 Exiting

Private equity investors exited in 2006 with an IPO in the Zurich based public equity market specializing in biotechnological companies.

Appendix 14.5

A business case: COSMY

A14.5.1 Target company

COSMY specializes in cosmetics and operates in different European countries through commercial branches. The proposal of COSMY consists of a commercial and distribution structure that offers highly specialized selling services to cosmetic manufacturers.

A14.5.2 Investment structure

The investment was realized at the start-up phase allowing the company to build business activity by opening commercial branches in Europe and hiring highly qualified managers.

A14.5.3 Critical elements of the investment

Private equity investors targeted this company because of its successful business idea, highly skilled founders, and existing commercial agreements that were critical financial resources for the firm.

A14.5.4 Management phase activity

Management activity has focused on two critical steps:

1. Becoming the most important European retailer of cosmetic products

2. Moving toward a global distribution and marketing company due to the expansion of the business by launching new products

Private equity investors supported COSMY during both of these steps with financial resources and strategic advice about acquiring new patents.

The success of the business idea guaranteed expansion in 10 countries covering 70% of the global market. Even if the firm had maximized its growth but not its economic performance, the big success of this initiative was reflected in the economic return gained by investor at the exit.

A14.5.5 Exiting

The private equity investor exited in 2006 with a trade sale of the participation to another private equity investor that realized a management buyout with the internal management of COSMY.

Appendix 14.6

A business case: FINSERV

A14.6.1 Target company

FINSERV, founded in the 1990s, is a financial services group operating in the domestic market as a distributor of financial products through the Internet and telephone. It is also an outsourcing provider of credit processes.

A14.6.2 Investment structure
The investment was realized at the start-up phase.

A14.6.3 Critical elements of the investment
The investment was closed in 2000 by a domestic private equity investor who was attracted by the business idea even though the domestic consumer credit market was still undeveloped and without mortgage intermediaries. This market status created big opportunities for FINSERV, not only from offering financial services as a broker, but also from improving the effectiveness and efficiency of the approval process of financial third parties.

A14.6.4 Exiting
The private equity investor exited in 2007 with an IPO.

Appendix 14.7
A business case: SPINORG
A14.7.1 Target company
SPINORG, founded in 2003, was created through a spin-off realized by scientific researchers coming from the domestic national center of research. The company operates in the spin electronic industry researching and developing innovative materials. It is financed by scientists and technologic advisory services and by selling its innovative machines.

A14.7.2 Investment structure
The investment was realized at the start-up phase.

A14.7.3 Exiting
The private equity investor exited in 2004 through a buy back.

Appendix 14.8
A business case: FLUFF
A14.8.1 Target company
FLUFF, founded in 2006, operates in the innovative and high-tech industry that processes, recovers, and disposes residual produced during motor vehicle chipping. The company was founded by a promoter who subscribed the majority of the risk capital.

A14.8.2 Investment structure
The investment was realized at the start-up phase to finance an innovative plant for the disposal of fluffs in 2008.

A14.8.3 Critical elements of the investment

This company was targeted by private equity investors because it was the only available alternative for the disposal of fluffs. Consequently, it had a high potential for success and the business idea represented a big opportunity to create an innovative fluffs treatment.

A14.8.4 Exiting

The investment is ongoing, but in 2008 an industrial partner, operating in the pollution control industry, was involved in the risk capital of FLUFF.

Financing growth

15.1 GENERAL OVERVIEW OF FINANCING GROWTH

The investment activity of venture capitalists is subdivided according to the different financing needs of the target company connected with its phase in the life cycle.

Figure 15.1 illustrates that development, consolidation, and maturity are all phases of growth that a target company goes through. The financial goal at this time is to support the growth in terms of revenues realized, products developed, and markets and customers serviced.

The demand of financial resources made by the target company at this stage depends on:

1. Its competitive capacity, measured in terms of turnover trend
2. Quantity of capital invested, which is connected with changes in the firm's industry
3. Cash flows generated, which rely on the efficient structure of the costs and revenues and the industry in which the firm competes

These three elements help define the financial resources needed to sustain the development and growth of the existing business.

Financing growth is an alternative to corporate lending with the same high-risk profile in terms of the large amount of money invested and uncertainty of future performance. However, financing growth guarantees the direct involvement of the venture capitalist in the management of the company, which means the company will be managed skillfully and competently.

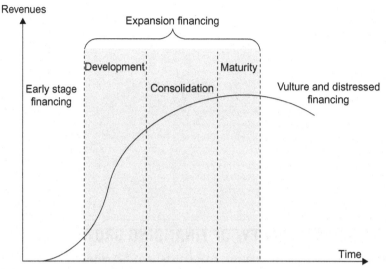

FIGURE 15.1

The second part of the company life cycle.

The investment realized during the second part of the life cycle mainly:

Covers manufacturing tool-up and marketing commitment costs
Builds or improves the necessary facilities
Supports the working capital needs

Expansion capital deals finance two types of growth:
Internal growth:

1. Entry by rights issue, subscribing minority or majority stakes of the target company

2. Increase in production capacity by building new production plants and acquiring new equipment

3. Internationalization or domestic market enlargement to cover profitable groups of customers

4. Implementation of more aggressive commercial strategies and marketing activities; usually done in a very competitive industry

5. Exit by listing or a trade sale of the target company

External growth:

1. Growth opportunity in a fragmented sector by unifying different firms

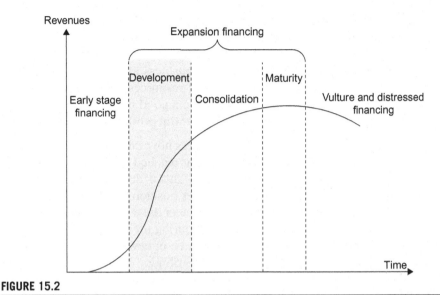

FIGURE 15.2

Life cycle of a company — development stage.

2. Concrete opportunity for acquisitions of non-exploited products and or technologies

15.2 THE CLUSTER OF FINANCING GROWTH DEALS

Expansion financing includes all risk capital invested in already existing and established companies used to incentivize development, dimensional growth, and potential quotation in a public financial market. This type of participation is less risky than those in the initial and start-up phase of a company, because there is already a tested and well-functioning company with a good base of customers. There is less difficulty valuating these investments because the venture capitalist is able to consider the company's historical data and economic information; conditions that are impossible to satisfy in seed and start-up financing operations. In Europe, investing in expansions is the most important private equity activity. They are usually realized by large closed funds and financial intermediaries with expertise and knowledge about the domestic and international financial markets. Sizable investors with expertise can better support entrepreneurs during the pre-IPO phase. Expansion can be divided into three main clusters:

1. Second stage financing — In Figure 15.2 the second stage of the company's life cycle is divided into two sub-parts, development and consolidation. Financing for this stage supports the company's development (accelerated growth). After commercial validation of the product or service offered by the target company, the venture capitalist intervenes and increases production and the selling and marketing capacity. The company is still medium or little, but the growth capacity of the business idea has improved. It is important to emphasize that the financial resources invested are reduced because the company has already acquired a good part of the market, and selling guarantees the resources needed for the production process.

2. Third stage financing —Figure 15.3 illustrates how third stage financing supports the consolidation of the development reached by the venture-backed company. At this point, it has passed the initial development phase and wants to consolidate and enlarge its market position. The venture capitalist contributes a large amount of money to protect the target company's market position and to support the management during the design of new growth plans. These types of plans involve the launch of new product, enlargement or diversification of manufacturing and distribution activities, or the acquisition of a competitor. Consequently, it becomes necessary to collect new funds dedicated to research and development, marketing, and production.

3. Fourth stage or bridge financing — Figure 15.4 illustrates the maturity stage of a company's life cycle. By this time the target company has grown considerably by enlarging the markets reached and the range of products or

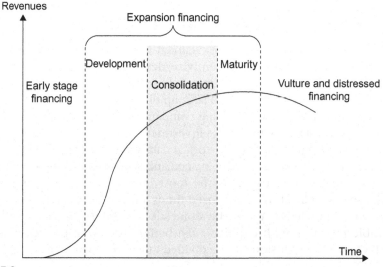

FIGURE 15.3

Life cycle time of a company — consolidation stage.

services offered. Financing is geared toward going public or for a planned trade sale with venture capitalist support to facilitate the next steps. The venture capital financing can also bridge financial difficulties and the quotation of the company. In this phase the level of risk is very low with occasional financial operations that involve large amounts of money.

Expansion deals involve not only equity capital but also debt financing when a leveraged buyout (LBO) is realized. Expansion deals only provide minority participation in the equity of the target company, whereas an LBO requires a majority participation. These deals change the property composition of the target company allowing for the differences in participation.

15.3 ADVANTAGES FOR VENTURE-BACKED COMPANIES

Venture-backed companies with private equity financed company growth have several advantages:

1. Support in building business — Experienced venture capitalists assist the target company in recruiting managers, developing relationships with customers, and fixing business strategy.

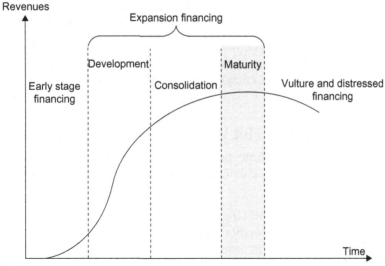

FIGURE 15.4

Life cycle of a company — maturity stage.

2. Cash feed — Private equity investors provide the funds necessary to support key business activities.

3. Higher overall return — The support of private equity firms allows the original shareholders to obtain a higher return from their investments in the target company, especially when exiting through an IPO.

4. Sponsor in going public — Experienced venture capitalists are key assets in reassuring IPO investors, so their involvement increases the possibility of success in going public. Usually, IPOs realized with private equity investors create higher returns.

5. Spin-off support — Venture capitalists with a wide range of relationships can help when the target company wants to sell its subsidiaries.

6. Venture capitalists improve the target company's ability to satisfy market demands — Today markets change quickly due to customer needs or technological revolutions, so it is critical to a company's success to be able to quickly exploit market opportunities.

7. Venture capitalists support the target company upon entry into new markets or industries because they are able to share their management skills and business know-how.

8. Private equity investment is a clear signal a business idea has potential. On the other hand, the lack of interest is a good indicator of an existing problem not easily recognized by the management team or the original shareholders.

9. Original shareholders receive critical support from the private equity investor — The bottom line of the balance sheet will be diligently watched and every possible action placed to maximize the potential return on the investment.

15.4 DISADVANTAGES FOR VENTURE-BACKED COMPANIES

To have a clear picture of how private equity investments impact the expansion of a target company, a recurring group of potential disadvantages should be considered:

1. Culture changes — The target company's managers and employees have to work with a new partner who has a high-profit-oriented culture combined with an intense pressure to continue to develop the business.

2. After investing in the target company, private equity firms have greater control of the agendas and activities of the original shareholders and managers.

3. Timing of exit strategies may not be consistent with the plan of the original shareholders and management. Many conflicts can arise while managing the right time to exit.

4. Buy back options are usually limited. This means that original shareholders may not be allowed to re-purchase the participation from the venture capitalist if the deal was unsuccessful. Private equity firms are usually reluctant to include a buy back option, because it can affect the real potential of the investment return.

5. Private equity investors require a high return from the investment. This means a high level of the value transfers from original to new shareholders. The high return expectations include the value of the money invested as well as the soft support consisting of invested time, networks, experience, and expertise. The original shareholders, before closing the deal with equity investors, have to understand that if the value of their business will be higher after the deal, then this justifies the high percentage of value that they must give to the investor.

6. Closing a transaction with private equity firms is complex and time-consuming, because this type of deal includes agreements on liabilities and obligations that can take up to a year to close.

7. A typical private equity approach comes with fast decision making. If there are bureaucratic delays, due to the timetables and procedure of the previous shareholders, the investors can decide to abandon a partnership.

8. The willingness of a private equity firm to commit additional financial resources in a specific investment already part of its portfolio is limited by the continuous focus on its expected returns. This situation can force original shareholders into adding new funds to the venture-backed company to avoid losing new business initiatives or opportunities due to lack of funds.

15.5 CHARACTERISTICS OF GROWTH

Expansion financing deals work best with middle or small size firms that want to grow quickly. Small medium firms have flexible production systems that adapt quickly to demand changes. Consequently, firms turn to expansion financing to reach another element for their success — dimension. Increasing dimension allows the small medium companies to exploit business opportunities that they otherwise would lose due to the lack or the low availability of effective and alternative tools for internationalization.

During this strategic process, soft support given by private equity investors is critical. Their ability to provide financial resources as well as a set of advisory services helps the small medium company to improve its competitive skills. The extensive support provided to these types of companies is also demonstrated in the average duration of the holding period, which is around four years or more when compared with the holding period of buyout operations.

The support given for the dimensional growth of the firm can be classified in two ways: quantitative and qualitative. Company performance can be quantitatively compared in terms of revenue and improvement of the margin and numbers of employees between venture-backed companies and companies that have never needed professional investors. Research demonstrates the high impact of the private equity operation by analyzing the increase in the employment level and turnovers. An expansion deal can lead to qualitative development facilitating the collaboration and joint venture with foreign partners that can result in export business.

15.6 EXTERNAL GROWTH

As stated previously, it is possible to realize an expansion investment through internal and external growth.

There are three main reasons for external growth:

1. Reinforcing the competitive advantages of the company to strengthen its distinctive skills in the existing activities and businesses — Acquisitions usually involve firms operating in the same markets with similar products and services.

2. Expanding competitive advantages to improve and extend the company's distinctive skills to neighboring sectors — Companies targeted for acquisition usually offer products and services with technological and marketing elements.

3. Exploring the competitive advantages of the company when entering a new sector that requires new skills — This type of target firm operates upstream or downstream or in sectors without any correlation.

External growth refers to merger and acquisition (M&A) operations with several different objectives; some need a long period of time to be reached, while others are realizable more quickly. Long-period objectives are classified in three different clusters. The first type desires to increase the company's value and satisfy the interests of the different stakeholders. The second type is connected with a manager who wants to reinforce his personal visibility, and the last type looks for opportunities to collect earnings in a capital account.

The short-term objectives, also considered strategic motivations, refer to:

Researching and exploiting the scale and scope economies — These companies want to use their experience in marketing or production to improve production capacity through the skills and technologies of the acquired firm.

Managing interdependence with stakeholders by accelerating growth in the industry where the acquired firm already successfully operates to improve their own skills.

Improving the proposal system and markets served by acquiring a higher market share and entry into new markets by using the marketing skills of the acquired company and increasing the client base.

Entering in new businesses to obtain critical resources from the acquired company or to reduce the risk related to the expansion in new industries.

Exploiting and optimizing financial resources through the leverage capacity of the acquired company, stabilization of the cash flow, or the acquisition of an underestimated company that can be sold with a good economic return.

Appendix 15.1

A business case: REM

A15.1.1 Target company

REM was founded in the 1930s and operates in the industrial machine sector. It was family controlled until 2003 when a venture capitalist acquired minority participation. After this investment, the company developed a strategy of acquisitions and a partnership, becoming a global leader of life science and testing equipment. REM operates in more than 50 countries and 70% its total revenues is made in exports. REM's markets are the electronic, automotive, aerospace, and defense sectors.

A15.1.2 Investment structure

The operation, closed in 2003, was an expansion capital deal consisting of a minority acquisition of about 14% evaluated at €6 million with €40 million as the pre-money value of the target company. Shareholders agreements provided an exit strategy of listing the company or the opportunity to realize a buy back by minority shareholders within a fixed period of time and with a predetermined method for price determination.

A15.1.3 Critical elements of the investment

The main reasons for the deal were the strong competitive market position and the international exposure of REM, their operation within several markets, and their clear strategy of external growth in a high potential industry.

A15.1.4 Management phase activity

Despite tough pressure on the operating margin provoked by the unfavorable exchange rate of the US dollar with the euro, between 2003 and 2007 REM, with the support of a venture capitalist, realized 6 acquisitions in and out of its domestic market, making it a global player. REM has since started to reorganize its production cycle.

A15.1.5 Exiting

The founder family terminated the deal in 2008 with re-acquisition of the minority participation owned by the venture capitalist.

Appendix 15.2

A business case: MAP

A15.2.1 Target company

MAP was founded in the 1950s starting with a wholesale food business. Over the years the company expanded toward oil production and fresh food trading. Today, MAP is a wholesale and retail distributor of food and consumer goods including the manufacturing and packaging of food. Its channel is a mix of hypermarket, large stores, and supermarkets with three different brands.

A15.2.2 Investment structure

The operation was realized at the end of 2003 with the acquisition of a minority stake by two venture capital firms of €12,8 million and was a typical expansion capital transaction with an evaluated enterprise value of €106 million. Agreements between the shareholders regarding exit options consisted of a buy back by the majority shareholders or the listing of MAP.

A15.2.3 Critical elements of the investment

This investment was realized because of MAP's leadership in a specific area of its market, its attractiveness to big foreign players, and high growth trend and good profit performances.

A15.2.4 Management phase activity and exit

During the investment, the external growth strategy was unsuccessful so the venture capitalist exited from MAP with a buy back.

Appendix 15.3

A business case: FMM

A15.3.1 Target company

The company was founded in the 1930s because a group of workers started providing facility services to a big transportation firm. FMM business consisted of specialized management services for buildings and equipment including maintenance of electrical and lighting services, refrigeration equipment, and catering and canteen services.

A15.3.2 Investment structure

The investment was realized by two venture capitalists for a total of €20 million, 12% of the equity capital of NewCo, which was built to realize an expansion capital transaction. NewCo involved two business units: facility management and a cleaning and environmental services unit. FMM has subscribed 75% of its equity capital; the remaining stakes were subscribed by other minor private equity operators. This deal structure allowed FMM to collect money to sustain and maintain the strategic growth and control of the two main business units of NewCo. There were two options included in the exit agreement between the shareholders: the listing of NewCo to be realized within a certain period of time or buy back by the minority shareholders.

A15.3.3 Critical elements of the investment

This deal was done because FMM was a leader in the domestic market with a wide range of diversified services. Venture capitalists were attracted by the high potential growth of the domestic market, the highly skilled management team, the attractive price, and the likelihood of realizing an IPO considering the appeal of the facility management services sector to the financial market.

A15.3.4 Management phase activity

The contribution of the venture capitalist was important because it allowed the company to follow and realize an intense growth strategy of expansion from the facility management industry to the global industrial services sector. FMM has been focused on the integration of new activities as well as the acquisition of a business unit dedicated to healthcare services.

A15.3.5 Exiting

Early in 2008 shareholders planned to list the company, but due to the negative situation of the financial market, they decided instead to seek out venture capital. They signed an agreement with a venture capitalist to sell 25% of their stake in the company.

Appendix 15.4

A business case: S&S

A15.4.1 Target company

The company was founded in the 1960s as a typical firm led by two families with equity participations equal to 60 and 40%, respectively. The core business of S&S is the production and distribution of passive security products such as locks for wooden and aluminium frames, padlocks, security locks, and master key systems. Within a few years, it became a leader in its domestic market. S&S expanded its business into the access and safety control systems industry providing both single products and global services. Their main distribution channels include wholesalers, dealers, ironmongers, retails chains, and industrial and banking groups. The revenues are divided between domestic and European markets and the rest of the world at 40, 50, and 10%, respectively.

A15.4.2 Investment structure

The deal, realized in 2004, consisted of an expansion capital transaction where the venture capitalist acquired a participation of 15% of €13 million and an S&S equity value of €84 million while the enterprise value was €106 million. The exit agreement between the shareholders and venture capitalists was to list the target company within a certain period of time or a buy back by the minority shareholders with a predefined method of price calculation.

A15.4.3 Critical elements of the investment

This company was targeted because of its strong and competitive market position. S&S was the leader in the domestic security market with huge potential value creation realizable by changing from passive security to safety and security integrated systems. This change created a higher possibility of growth and better profits. The venture capitalist was interested in exiting from the investment with an IPO. Another interest was the newly started external growth process, initiated by the acquisition of a European company, which was a source of potential manufacturing and commercial synergies.

A15.4.4 Management phase activity

The performance of S&S during 2004 and 2005 was lower than expected because of the down European and the domestic markets. Another issue faced by S&S was the inability of management to handle the increasing raw material costs during the turnaround phase. Support provided by the venture capital firm was critical in redefining and implementing the new strategy from S&S.

A15.4.5 Exiting

Following the investment in S&S, the venture capitalist had to face emerging problems in the relationship between the two founder families. There were completely opposite points of view on the strategy and its implementation. One view targeted a larger expansion while the other view wanted to keep the old strategic vision of focusing on the passive security industry. Due to these problems, the venture capitalist exited from the deal through a buy back of S&S because he did not agree with the spin-off operation decided on by the founder families.

■

Appendix 15.5

A business case: RDC

A15.5.1 Target company

This manufacturer of vegetable conserves was founded during the second half of the 1800s. The control and property of RDC was acquired by different owners over the years. In 2003 the controlling group of RDC was declared in default so the temporary receivership divided RDC into two businesses. RDC was purchased by VC, an industrial company that manufactures vegetables, with the support of a venture capitalist, making RDC the leader in the domestic market of fruit juices and one of the most important companies in vegetable products and tomatoes.

A15.5.2 Investment structure

The deal, concluded at the end of 2004, was realized to support an expansion capital transaction. The venture capitalists involved in the investment subscribed 49% of the NewCo with an enterprise value of €113 million and €45 million as debt financing. Even if the private equity firms subscribed a minority participation, the agreement between the shareholders was very effective. The exit strategy agreed upon was to list the target company within a certain period of time or a buy back by the minority shareholders with a predefined method of price calculation.

A15.5.3 Critical elements of the investment

Venture capitalists invested in this company because of its well-known brands and market leadership, despite decreasing market shares due to the default. Also attractive was the opportunity to improve RDC through product innovation strategies, extension of the brands, and the possibility of realizing an IPO at the end of the investment.

A15.5.4 Management phase activity

During the holding period, RDC tried to reorganize the company through functional distribution and completed the strategic merger between RDC and VC.

A15.5.5 Exiting

During the management period, problems arose due to a conflict of interests between the shareholders, so, early in 2006, the venture capitalists agreed with VC and placed a put call option on their RDC participation. Luckily, after a few months, they sold their shares.

■

Appendix 15.6

A business case: MED

A15.6.1 Target company

MED was founded in the 1990s as a publishing company realizing an average yearly growth of 33% until 2004. Today, MED is involved in areas such as information technology, home entertainment, and video games. It leads the market in home entertainment and information technology, while it is second in the video game industry.

A15.6.2 Investment structure

The deal was realized at the end of 2004 as an expansion capital transaction. Venture capitalists subscribed a minority participation of MED equal to 22% with an enterprise value fixed at 23 million. The agreement between the shareholders was very effective; the exit strategy provided for the listing of the target company within a certain period of time or the possibility for the venture capitalist to put 100% of MED up for a trade sale.

A15.6.3 Critical elements of the investment

MED was targeted because of its terrific growth potential and leading position in the entertainment and technology industries as well as the appeal of the domestic publishing market and the opportunity to increase the firm's advertising revenues.

A15.6.4 Management phase activity

The management phase of the MED deal had many milestones:

Launches of new magazines focused on the video game industry
Agreement with an international publishing company for the production and distribution in the MED domestic market of a foreign information technology magazine
Launch of DVD film series with the fulfillment of significant financial performances

A15.6.5 Exiting

Venture capitalists exited in 2007 by selling the owned participation to another private equity firm.

Appendix 15.7

A business case: FC

A15.7.1 Target company

The company was founded in the 1980s and manufactured clothes for the fashion industry. Over time it built a retail chain in its domestic market. In 2005, FC launched an expansion strategy to increase the international arm of its business by opening shops in prominent European cities such as Berlin, Barcelona, and Paris. FC operates through two different brands: one focused on women's clothing generating 80% of the company's revenues, and one consisting of unisex clothing. The distribution channels are composed of retailers, flagship stores, and outlets.

A15.7.2 Investment structure

The deal was closed in 2007 by two private equity firms that purchased a minority stake of 45% through the constitution of a NewCo, with the remaining shares still in the hands of the founder shareholders. This was an expansion capital investment operation. The agreement between the shareholders was good for the venture capitalists; the exit strategy, agreed upon by all shareholders, provided for listing of the target company within four years or the possibility of a trade sale of 100% of FC with a specific covenant for the EBITDA realized by the company. If the gap between the planned and actual EBITDA was above a predefined value, the two private equity firms can place a put option on 100% of the shares owned by the founder shareholders.

A15.7.3 Critical elements of the investment

This deal was realized because FC had what private equity firms want in a target company:

Strong market position
Well-known and appreciated brands
High potential growth in international and domestic markets with the opening of new shops, launching of new brands, and new clothing lines
IPO opportunity

A15.7.4 Management phase activity

The management phase of FC began by reorganizing the commercial and production structure to support the expansion of the two original brands in the international market. FC successfully closed important and high strategic brand licensing agreements with other fashion houses.

A15.7.5 Exiting

The investment is ongoing.

Appendix 15.8

A business case: BALTD

A15.8.1 Target company

BALTD is a world leader in the automotive and industrial supplier sector. It is divided into three business segments: automotive pipes and cooling technologies, industrial pipes, and die cast assemblies. Their expansion strategy was to enlarge market coverage by acquiring a foreign player, CANCO, to increase their range of products and improve and develop international growth.

A15.8.2 Investment structure

During 2008, BALTD founded a NewCo to realize the acquisition of CANCO and its equity capital was subscribed by a pool of private equity investors and a group of managers from both BALTD and CANCO. The enterprise value of BALTD was fixed at €120 million for an equity value of €55 million.

A15.8.3 Critical elements of the investment

Private equity firms targeted this company because of the consolidation of leadership at BALTD, and their acquisition strategy created an important opportunity to increase the product range of both companies. Other reasons included a very skilled management team and an IPO opportunity.

A15.8.4 Management phase activity and exit

The investment is ongoing.

Appendix 15.9

A business case: MC

A15.9.1 Target company

MC is a mobile content company spun off from TMCS. It operates a wide range of services focused on high end customer service and access to multi-channel features such as SMS and the Internet. The main services of MC are divided in several areas such as music, images, games, and infotainment (news, gossip, horoscopes). With their specific brands, MC targets both young and an older audiences.

A15.9.2 Investment structure

The deal was closed during the fourth quarter of 2008. It included one private equity firm that purchased a minority share of 17% MC, investing €11 million for an equity value of 63 million corresponding to an enterprise value of €58 million. The main goal shared between both founder shareholders and venture capitalists is the listing of the company within four years. The agreement between the shareholders regarding governance and exit strategy allows the venture capitalist material control of FC. The exit strategy agreements state that the private equity firm has the right to put 100% of FC up for sale after a predefined period of time after having valuated the listing option with the majority shareholders.

A15.9.3 Critical elements of the investment

Private equity firms invested in MC because of the opportunities connected with the target company:

Investors were attracted to the FC industry because they had not been involved in this industry before
High potential for growth and value creation
Highly skilled management team
IPO opportunity

A15.9.4 Management phase activity and exit

The investment is ongoing.

Financing buyouts

16.1 GENERAL OVERVIEW OF BUYOUTS

A buyout is a structured financial operation that, through merger, division, or acquisition of control participation, allows the transfer of the property from the old shareholders to a new entrepreneur with economic and technical support of a financial intermediary (usually a private equity fund). In a leveraged buyout (LBO) a major part of the capital is supplied by debt securities subscribed by a pool of banks and financial intermediaries. It is possible to define leveraged acquisitions as a particular type of M&A activity that leaves the acquired firm with a debt ratio higher than before the acquisition.

LBOs have a special structure, which consists of a holding company that founds a new company responsible for the collection of funds (with the financial solution of the debt) necessary for the acquisition of the assets or the shares of a target company. After the acquisition, the new company (named NewCo) is merged with the target company. This is realized with a forward merger where NewCo absorbs the target or a reverse merger where the target company absorbs NewCo. Financial and tax needs influence which option is used. The financers of NewCo are usually bankers and the purchasers. As collateral for the debt repayment, they offer assets owned by the target company and its ability to create cash flow.

The LBO was initiated and developed in the United States in the beginning of 1970. There are two main differences when compared with venture capital operations: they acquire the majority or totality of the target company's shares and the buyer completely changes the shareholder structure. In the mid-1980s LBOs were used by banks to realize acquisitions through debt financing. They began to consider the economic value and profitability of companies and analyzed the potential development of business plans shared between the company's management and the private equity fund involved in the deal.

Based on these financial operations and the groups involved, several types of buyouts can be identified:

1. Management buyout (MBO) — This type of buyout is promoted by the management of the target company who usually acquires complete control of the firm.

2. Management buy in (MBI) — External managers plan the deal and become shareholders with a considerable quota of participation to obtain control of the company.

3. Buy in management buyout (BIMBO) — External and internal managers of the company promote this type of deal.

4. Buy in growth opportunity (BINGO) — The value invested by the financial intermediaries exceeds the value of the company to finance its growth.

5. Worker buyout (WBO) — Employees enter into the shareholder structure of the target company so the property is enlarged to allow them to take part in the firm's management.

6. Family buyout (FBO) — Occurs when the company's proprietary structure is controlled by the family promoter. This type of company is the target of a buyout upon transfer of title between generations. Very often the newest generation of owners is unable to manage the company because they fight or they do not have the necessary entrepreneurial skills to make the firm profitable. The FBO is the solution to this type of situation, because it allows a family member to acquire total control of the company by paying off the other shareholders.

7. Investor buyout (IBO) — This type of operation is realized by a financial investor, such as a private equity fund, who decides to buy the entire equity of the target company. This decision is made because the company has good growth potential, a high probability of positive return from the investment, and the ability to change and select a new team of managers chosen on the basis of their capability, previous experience, track record, and reliability.

8. Public to private (PTP) — A way to conclude a buyout by delisting the target company from the public financial market. This company had probably been the focus of an earlier buyout, but it represents a small part of the total transaction. The vast majority of buyouts are acquisitions of private firms and corporate divisions.

9. Reverse buyout (RBO) — The target company has already been subjected to a PTP and the buyout is concluded with a new quotation of the firm on the public financial market.

The most important ways to realize a buyout deal are the asset sale and merge sale; the main difference between them is the object of the acquisition. The asset sale uses a large amount of debt to acquire a defined part of the assets and liabilities owned by the target company. The merge sale modality buys the entire equity of the firm. With an asset sale it is necessary to have a friendly agreement between the parties involved in the transaction, whereas a merge sale can be concluded under hostile conditions.

Significant elements in buyout deals that guarantee improvements in the economic and financial performance of the target company can be identified:

1. Professional competences and managerial efficiency provided by the private equity funds.

2. Opportunity to realize an international growth because of the contacts and relationships of the institutional investor.

3. Creation, development, and expansion of a new entrepreneurship that allows managers to become entrepreneurs to reduce the expense and value destroyed by agency costs; this condition is particularly true during a management buy in or buyout and buy in management buyout.

4. External growth supported through new financial resources provided to the target company after acquisition.

5. Increase and development of the employment level necessary to maintain a well-balanced ratio between the structure and the fast growing nature of the target company. To guarantee a successful buyout highly qualified and trained human resources must be available to realize the corporate strategy. Involving highly qualified people is reflected in the pursuit of economically important innovations measured in terms of patents obtained after private equity investments.

To execute an accurate evaluation of a buyout, the duration of the holding period — a period of time included between the conclusion of the leveraged acquisition and the participation divestment — must be considered. The possible presence of foreign and international financial resources or investors and the debt and equity ratio should also be examined before a buyout is started.

The longevity of leveraged buyouts or how long firms stay in LBO ownership can be summarized by two disparate views. Academics argue that the buyout organizational firm is a long-term superior governance structure with strong investor discipline and strict behaviors because of the propriety and heavy leverage structure. An LBO is also seen as a short-term "shock therapy" that gives inefficient, badly performing firms an intense process of corporate governance restructuring before the company goes public. Between these two extreme point of views, there is the common opinion that an LBO is a temporary governance structure specializing in the improvement of a public company. This solves the problem of unused excess free cash flow.

16.2 CHARACTERISTICS OF A BUYOUT DEAL

16.2.1 Financial structure

An acquisition can be defined as an LBO if there is a change in the property composition and a complete restructuring of the leveraged dimension of the firm acquired. The elements that compose the financial structure of an LBO are senior debt, junior debt, equity, and all operations that create cash flow such as asset stripping and securitization. The distinction between junior and senior debt is based on the time estimated for repayment of the financial obligation and the presence of rights and specific options for the fund providers such as the covenants.

There are also differences between shareholders including their involvement in daily operations of the target company, investment duration, and willingness to maintain their economic resources in the firm. To guarantee the success of an acquisition it is absolutely necessary for investors to have a deep interest in management along with an industrial vision of the deal, because it may be a long-term investment focused on improving and growing the target company. Another category of shareholder is the financial investor whose job it is to conclude the acquisition and collect the value created from their participation in a short-term investment.

The presence of these two types of investors helps realize a successful buyout, but it is important to manage their different goals without compromising the target company. The ratchet technique is one tool used to manage and monitor shareholder behavior and interest. This technique consists of a contractual agreement between the shareholders that makes the dimension of their participation variable due to a predefined and shared financial and economic performance goal.

If a target company is acquired through the debt, it is useful to undertake steps to collect the money needed for the heavy debt repayment. One step is asset stripping — selling assets owned by the target company that are not classified as an operating resource. These assets are easily liquidated and a sure source of cash. The presence of this type of asset on the firm's balance sheet is one of the reasons a company should be considered for a buyout acquisition. A second way to collect cash is the securitization of positive entries on the balance sheet unsuitable for asset stripping due to their operational nature such as unexpired commercial credits and financing inside firms controlled by the holding company.

16.2.2 **Corporate governance**

Leveraged acquisitions strongly impact shareholder structure, so it is important to understand the role, function, and characteristics of boards. Their function in a public company is to provide management supervision. In private equity acquisitions boards seem useless as the private equity partner can easily directly monitor and support the firm in an advisory capacity. Therefore, it is important to identify the real role of board directors in companies acquired by one or more private equity groups, since it seems that a successful deal concentrates the ownership of the company into the hands of a few shareholders. Private equity investors are deeply involved in running the acquired company with extensive restructuring experience, so they have a strong incentive to maximize the value of the firm.

In private equity deals tough control is exercised by the general partner over the executive managers when defining and planning the implementation of the portfolio strategy. In many cases the venture capitalist sits on the board of companies in which they have invested and their participation increases during significant decisions such as changing the CEO. What happens in an LBO when the private equity sponsors are not actively involved in the management of the company? Research that analyzes the board structure observed these findings:

Size and composition — After a buyout, the number of board members decreases significantly while external directors are drastically reduced. There is no significant difference in board size of the MBO and the LBO, but existing differences in the dimension of the company must be considered. In private equity deals outside directors are substituted by individuals appointed by the private equity sponsor, but when there is an MBO the external board member disappears because this type of deal requires heavy involvement of the managers.

Director engagement — With complex, hard, and challenging deals there is more active participation and cooperation of the private equity board members. This type of investor usually takes part when the company acquired has to realize critical investments or turnaround. Investors create a board ensuring that their power is absolute by changing the CEO and the key directors, except when there is a management buyout and buy in that excludes the external board members.

Private equity policy — Structure and composition of the target company board depend on the attitude of each investor; the venture capitalist relies less on his own partners or employees and more on outside directors. If a group of private equity investors sponsor the deal, the proportion of LBO sponsors is larger, because they want a specific delegate on the board of directors.

Permanence — Private equity investors are always present on the target company board and are active up to the exit from the investment.

Turnover — CEO and director turnover is high compared to the turnover prior to the LBO or becoming private through an MBO.

In summary, extra management support or monitoring is needed in difficult deals resulting in a larger board with the likely presence of LBO sponsors on it. This explains the central role of the board in the restructuring process and the relation between management and shareholders. It is useful to have these sponsors on the board during the restructuring process just because they bring management experience and are able to conduct successful business practices. High turnover rates of CEOs and board composition does not support the opinion that private equity deals have a long-term view that creates less sensibility to the short-term changes and a higher interest in long-term investments, growth, and return.

16.3 VALUATION AND MANAGED RISK

16.3.1 Valuation

The price of the LBO includes the funds necessary to buy the target company, which are calculated as the difference between the enterprise value (EV) and the net financial position of the firm to be acquired. The definition of the EV is very important because it represents the first step in a successful buyout. Considering the erratic state of the buyout financial structure, the calculation of the EV is very complex and creates problems when computing the rate used to discount future cash flows.

As explained in Chapter 13 (see the section Enterprise Value Analysis), to obtain a sure and precise EV, cross-validation of the results is realized through the simultaneous use of different approaches for the definitions of the deal price. This widespread practice applies both the comparables method and the discounted cash flows approach.

The use of comparables requires the availability of special economic and financial performance indicators such as the EBITDA, EBIT, and the sales or the book value of similar and listed companies, which have to be multiplied to determine the EV of the target company. The discounted cash flow (DCF) method implies that the value of the firm is defined as the sum of the future and expected cash flows then discounted at the year of the acquisition using as discount rate of a similar and comparable company operating in the same industry. The DCF approach includes both the net present value method and the adjusted present value method. This approach is perfectly suitable for the special and heavy leveraged structure used in a buyout operation.

16.3.2 Managed risk

In a buyout transaction, the main elements are the private equity investor who decides to buy a significant participation in a target firm and their key role in the management of the company in terms of control and the decision to take a private company public. Financial fundaments can predict a default of the buyout company. The deal also can be unsuccessful when it concerns a champion firm and the private equity managers have highly reputed deal expertise if the change in the debt equity ratio is as explained previously.

It is critical to understand how and if a change in the debt equity ratio can impact the value creation of a company. Discussing debt definition, the benefit and cost of the debt, tools used for assessing the leveraged level can help understand how debt equity ratio can impact a company's value.

Debt definition — There are three criteria used to classify debt.
1. Debt imposes contractual obligations that have to be respected both in good and bad times, whereas equity returns are only paid after good financial performances.
2. Contractual payment for the debt is positively affected by taxes, whereas the cash flow from equity shares does not profit from this benefit.
3. Any breach of these contractual agreements causes loss of control of the firm.

According to these criteria, debt includes all financing resources raised (long and short term) that provide interest but excludes any type of account receivable and supplier credit. Lease commitments should also be considered as debt, because interest is usually tax deductible. If the company does not meet the specific requirements it will suffer negative consequences.

The use of debt directly impacts the value of the venture-backed company in terms of costs and benefits, and the final value of the company will increase or decrease whether or not costs exceed the benefits.

Benefit and cost of debt — One benefit is that interest is tax deductible. Compared with equity, debt financing makes managers more selective about projects. Because the company has to repay the interest to investors, if a poorly performing project is selected, the firm could go into default or bankruptcy and managers could lose their jobs.

Debt has three disadvantages:

1. Increasing leverage increases the possibility of default. The direct costs of bankruptcy include legal fees and court costs as well as indirect costs. High levels of debt signal a company is in financial trouble. If this feeling is widespread among stakeholders, employees, customers, and suppliers, it can easily lead to default and bankruptcy. For example, suppliers may decide to reduce their credit or employees, worried for their jobs, leave the company looking for more reliable firms.

2. The necessity of debt limits future debt capacity, which can mean future and profitable business opportunities are out of reach for the firm.

3. Agency costs represented by the divergence of interest between equity investors and fund providers is ever present. This type of conflict causes parties to protect their respective rights by adding covenants, reducing financing, and modifying dividend policies. The natural consequence of this situation is increasing costs to monitor and service the debt.

Debt assessing tools identify a company's optimum level of debt. The first tool is the cost of a capital approach, which helps understand the debt to equity ratio that minimizes the company's cost of capital and maximizes its value. This approach is easy to use but does not include agency and bankruptcy costs. These are included when the optimal leveraged structure generates a combination between cash flow and cost of capital to maximize the firm's value.

The last tool is the adjusted present value method, which evaluates the costs and the benefits of debt separately without including any indirect costs.

16.4 CONDITIONS FOR A GOOD AND A BAD BUYOUT

To realize a successful LBO, it is absolutely necessary that the feasibility conditions are satisfied. Investors will only conclude the acquisition if they are sure the target company will satisfy all of its financial obligations. These conditions can be classified into two groups: generic conditions connected with the target company and specific conditions linked to the financial structure of both the target and the new company.

There are three generic conditions:

1. The company should mature enough to guarantee, with a high degree of certainty, the availability of abundant cash flow necessary for debt repayment.

2. Target company balance sheets should be full of assets easily used as debt collateral or as a source of cash through asset stripping or securitization operations.

3. Previous shareholders should be willing to sell their participations in the target company to reduce costs and the time needed for negotiation and transaction activities.

There are three specific conditions:

1. Annual free cash flow unlevered from the target company that is higher than the yearly reimbursement of the debt.

2. EBIT of the target company is higher than the annual financial interests.

3. Company operations should guarantee the improvement of the post buyout rating of the company as a result of reducing debt cost.

It is important to emphasize that the firms operating in markets with intense levels of growth and offering high-tech products are unsuitable for a buyout because of the huge funds needed to support the increase in commercial credits, stocks, and marketing expenses as well as the resources necessary to enlarge the production structure. There is always a risk of high-tech products becoming obsolete, which not only causes enormous costs from a research and development aspect, but it is impossible for these products to be used as collateral for fund providers.

In conclusion, the ideal target company has to operate as a leader in a mature market, offer non-sophisticated products, and have a solid balance sheet containing mostly material assets.

Appendix 16.1

A business case: STAIN & STEEL

A16.1.1 Target company

STAIN & STEEL (S&S), a firm founded in the 1960s, operates in the steel milling sector and produces laminates destined for the shipbuilding and automotive industries. The company's production capacity expanded from 3.000 to 300.000 tons becoming the second largest producer in its domestic market with a market share of 20%. Almost the half of its production is exported to European countries such as France, Austria, Germany, and Spain.

The company was acquired in 1997 when the founder family sold the firm to another industrial family. In 1999 it was acquired by a famous private equity fund with the involvement of their management team, and in 2003 it was the object of an MBO. The last acquisition was initiated by the management who bought the majority of S&S with a private equity investor.

To guarantee a successful deal, the venture capitalist assumed complete responsibility of the operation and established a strong relationship with the management team from the outset.

A16.1.2 Investment structure

The operation, closed in 2003, was a typical MBO realized using a NewCo. The private equity investor owned 49% and the remaining 51% by the management team with the goal of completely acquiring S&S. The financial resource invested by private equity was €7,8 million, and the equity value of S&S was €16 million with a corresponding EV of €65,8 million. The debt raised was €32 million leading to a debt to equity ratio of 2.

Even if the majority of the shares was in the hands of the management team, the private equity investor had complete control of the company due to a covenant and agreement between the shareholders covering the exit strategy. The strategy granted the venture capitalist the right to sell the entire stake of S&S after a predefined period of time.

A16.1.3 Critical elements of the investment

This venture capitalist sought out S&S for multiple reasons:

1. It led the domestic market with good past financial and economic performances.
2. Low intensity of growth corresponding to a limited investment dedicated to production capacity improvement. S&S presented an excellent opportunity for good cash flow.
3. High level of management commitment characterized by a 15-year long run experience and in-depth knowledge of the industry and the company.
4. Expansion opportunities in Europe and a stable, positive spread between the raw material price of the iron and the final value of the laminates.
5. The favorable situation in the steel industry and the appeal of low price and multiple ratios.

A16.1.4 Management phase activity

During the holding period, S&S increased production capacity by 25% after restructuring the production process and building a new plant. At the same time they expanded their export business to new developing countries such as North Africa, the Middle East, and China, with an increase in demand that redoubled their price in a short period of time.

A16.1.5 Exiting

The deal was terminated in 2005 when a Russian steel group acquired the entire stake of the venture capitalist and half of the management participation. The team manager has continued to run the company.

Appendix 16.2

A business case: VEGOIL

A16.2.1 Target company

VEGOIL was founded in the 1960s by two families. It refines and sells vegetable oils and fats used in the food, pharmaceutical, and cosmetics industries. The company has been traditionally run by one member of the founder families, supported by an expert management team, and has a strong market leadership position in terms of quality and market share both domestically and internationally.

The business selects and buys raw materials in the countries of origin and then sells the semi-finished goods to well-known international food companies. High quality is guaranteed because of a large investment in quality control, human resources, and research and development. VEGOIL had numerous opportunities to expand its business into Western and Eastern Europe.

A16.2.2 Investment structure

The operation, closed at the end of 2004, was an FBO realized with the support of the CEO and the acquisition of 40% of VEGOIL's shares by a venture capital fund. The new company was founded with an equity value of €5 million, €2 million subscribed by the investor and the remaining €3 million by the CEO, and raised a convertible bond with a value of €1 million. Venture capitalists had a minority participation matched with shareholder agreements regarding governance and exit that gave the major shareholder rights to acquire total control of the company after a period of four years.

A16.2.3 Critical elements of the investment

This investment was realized because of a strong CEO commitment, a great market position, an industry with strong entry barriers and high value added, existing expansion opportunities into the cosmetics and pharmaceutical sectors, a long-lasting relationship with well-known domestic and foreign food companies, and a convenient deal price.

A16.2.4 Management phase activity and exit

During the holding period VEGOIL's investment in plants and production capacity allowed further expansion. The deal was closed when the CEO purchased the venture capital stake and took complete control of the company.

Appendix 16.3

A business case: RA

A16.3.1 Target company

RA was founded in the 1970s and operates in the racing accessories industry producing and distributing fireproof cloths, racing seats, helmets, and roll bars. It is highly internationalized and services the main motorbike sport teams and drivers who take part in international championships. The majority of the sales, around 70%, is concentrated in foreign markets.

Fashion Motor, another company that operates in the same industry, wanted to launch an aggregate project with RA as the target company to become the industrial and commercial leader in the racing industry.

A16.3.2 Investment structure

The operation, closed in the beginning of 2008, was an LBO where the NewCo was completely owned by a Fashion Motor holding company with shares divided as follows:

31% owned by the venture capitalist, which invested about €2 million

51% owned by former shareholders of Fashion Motor

18% owned by a manager coming from the racing industry involved because of his skills and expertise

The global value of RA was estimated at €15,5 million and was acquired by the NewCo.

The venture capitalist only owned a minority participation, but it negotiated a shareholder agreement regarding an exit that provided three ways to divest:

1. Company going public within a predefined period of time
2. Buy back by the majority shareholders with a price defined through an agreed structure of valuation
3. Trade sale for the total control of RA

A16.3.3 Critical elements of the investment

Investors targeted RA because of the opportunity to build a leader in the racing accessories industry, potential exit through an IPO, and industry appeal.

A16.3.4 Management phase activity and exit

The investment is ongoing with plans to acquire, within a few years, other companies operating in the same sector to promote the development of RA.

Appendix 16.4

A business case: HAIR & SUN

A16.4.1 Target company

HAIR & SUN, founded around 1910, originally focused on beauty salons. It has since manufactured and marketed businesses for body and sun protection creams as well as several lotions for body care. Today it is still owned by the founder family and sells products through specific brands mainly in the domestic market with a very small international presence.

A16.4.2 Investment structure

The deal closed in the last quarter of 2008 with a typical MBI. The founder family decided to exit selling the majority stake both to private equity investors and a new management team.

The investment was realized through a NewCo owned by two venture capitalists, the founder family, and the new management team, which has acquired 100% of HAIR & SUN with an EV of €40 million and a debt raised of €19 million.

The potential exit strategy is to list the company or, if this option cannot be realized within three years, a trade sale of the total company.

A16.4.3 Critical elements of the investment

HAIR & SUN was targeted because of its brands, the realistic possibility of expansion of the foreign market share and into the global sector, and a potential IPO to be realized within a pre-defined amount of time.

A16.4.4 Management phase activity and exit

The investment is ongoing.

Appendix 16.5

A business case: BOLT

A16.5.1 Target company

BOLT was founded in the 1970s and originally focused on manufacturing fasteners and related products adding, over time, a set of value-added services including quality control and logistic and category management. It has become a leader in the domestic market. Because of this strategy, half of the revenues come from the value-added services and half from traditional trade activity.

A16.5.2 Investment structure

The deal was closed during the third quarter of 2004 and structured as an MBO with the involvement of two private equity investors. The NewCo acquired total control of BOLT with private equity subscribing 87% of the shares, leaving the remaining shares in the hands of the managers that built a longstanding relationship with former BOLT shareholders. This structure provided private equity investors full freedom of the private equity to create an exit strategy. The equity value of BOLT was valued at €22,5 million and the financing acquisition was €13,3 million with a debt to equity ratio equal to 0,60.

A16.5.3 Critical elements of the investment

BOLT was acquired because of its leadership position in the domestic market and high potential growth rate, its previous positive economic results, the strong and healthy relationship with important domestic industrial groups, the qualified and motivated management team, and the appealing multiples used for valuation.

A16.5.4 Management phase activity

BOLT's revenues during the holding period significantly increased but it needed additional investments to realize a new logistic structure to better satisfy demand.

A16.5.5 Exiting

Venture capitalists disinvested at the end of 2006 with a 100% trade sale signed with an international logistic group.

Appendix 16.6

A business case: WORKWEAR

A16.6.1 Target company

WORKWEAR, a leader in the European market of protective and work wear made of poly-cotton, was founded in the late 1960s. It has gained a strong position in the rental clothing market with more than 50% of the European market. WORKWEAR's customers are located mainly in the UK, Italy, France, Belgium, Germany, and Scandinavia.

A16.6.2 Investment structure

The LBO, launched during 2004, was built through a NewCo owned by two venture capitalists (91%) with the equity capital of the former CEO of WORKWEAR. The NewCo acquired WORKWEAR for an EV of €34 million with a debt structure of €10 million.

A16.6.3 Critical elements of the investment

This main advantages of WORKWEAR's acquisition were the appealing entry multiples, its position as the leader of the European work wear market, its technical skills, the stable relationship with important European companies, the recently completed manufacturing investment, and the realistic opportunity to enlarge the market because of strict regulations on work wear safety.

A16.6.4 Management phase activity

After the deal, WORKWEAR had unexpected increases in production costs and low sales prices due to competition from the Far East. This resulted in several years of bad performance. To deal with this negative situation, WORKWEAR executed a reorganization of the manufacturing and production process with positive financial results in 2007.

A16.6.5 Exiting

A successful exit strategy was realized in 2008 by selling 100% of WORKWEAR to a Middle Eastern textile group.

Appendix 16.7
A business case: TELSOFT

A16.7.1 Target company

TELSOFT, founded in the 1980s, develops software applications for financial and industrial use such as credit risk management and pay and cash systems. It was the target of another company, CONSULTIT (founded in 2000), which offers consulting servicing to financial and corporate institutions such as IT consulting, process and system design, package implementation, and customer development. It has also expanded its business into the travel management industry.

A16.7.2 Investment structure

The LBO launched in 2008 was sponsored by CONSULTIT management and a venture capitalist that purchased 35% of its equity capital. The value of the deal was €17 million, financed partially with debt of €11 million. The remaining investment was realized by a private equity fund and CONSULTIT's management. The shareholder agreement provides an exit strategy of listing the company within a fixed period of time or a buy back from the majority shareholders.

A16.7.3 Critical elements of the investment

This deal was realized because of the opportunity for CONSULTIT and TELSOFT to became one of the leaders in the financial services market in terms of increasing products and services offered. This deal is considered a strategic industrial project between two complementary businesses.

A16.7.4 Management phase activity and exit

The investment is ongoing.

Turnaround and distressed financing

17

INTRODUCTION

This chapter discusses two types of deals: turnaround or replacement financing representing more than 50% of the private equity market and distressed financing, which includes deals realized when the target company is in bad condition or in a crisis. These deals are discussed because they both concern companies facing management, economic, and financial problems that have a direct impact on their survival.

17.1 GENERAL OVERVIEW OF TURNAROUND FINANCING

As previously mentioned, replacement financing is 50% of the private equity market. This type of financing is given to firms that need managerial support to reorganize and restructure a mature company without financial resources. There are three main subcategories of replacement financing that are widespread with different and specific risk profiles:

1. Succession and transformation strategy — Manages a transformation or property transfer in a company. Existing shareholders involve private investors as a third party that can lead the decision process to make changes. The investor must be part of the Board of Directors to have a formal and substantial position in these decisions. To guarantee the return from this type of investment, shareholders must have contractual certainty that the venture capitalist will sell his shares at an established price within a predefined period of time on exit. This provision allows the private equity investor to obtain the desired capital gain.

2. Buyout operation — This type of deal is specifically studied and analyzed in Chapter 16. To execute the total acquisition of a target company, an LBO is realized with heavy debt financing. The private equity investor supports the deal with financial resources and the technical skills and knowledge necessary for the construction and organization of the deal.

3. Merger and acquisition strategy — This occurs when a firm decides to grow quickly through acquisitions. The management team of the company or the entrepreneur needs to be supported by a professional intermediary with financial resources and soft services such as an international network of relationships necessary to expand beyond the domestic market. Private equity investors usually subscribe risk capital to the target company so they can earn fees for their support services.

17.2 CHARACTERISTICS OF TURNAROUND OR REPLACEMENT FINANCING

Turnaround financing is risk related to target company downsizing, but the central concept that must be considered is connected leadership. During this type of deal, management skill and exceptional leadership profiles are the two most important elements for a successful outcome. Managing the replacement for a distressed company is fraught with difficulties for the turnaround practitioner. First, the turnaround executive has to persuade the key stakeholders that this type of intervention is the best solution for the recovery of their company. Then a change of management is usually necessary, but it is not always easily realized, because the financial intermediary has to negotiate with the previous chairman. Another consideration is the financial and economic condition of a firm that needs this type of financing. If it wants to avoid bankruptcy there must be a sense of urgency in the process. Usually, the turnaround practitioner decides to implement an efficient and well-organized management and financial controls to develop and communicate a new vision for the business. When this is done, he will obtain the support and collaboration of the entire group of employees.

There are two types of turnaround executives: those who specialize in crisis stabilization and those who undertake the complete turnaround process and stay and work for the target company to manage growth and organizational transformation. In general, the first group of executives stays in the company from 6 to 12 months, whereas the second group is likely to stay in a leadership role from 12 to 24 months.

17.3 THE MAIN REASON FOR TURNAROUND OR REPLACEMENT FINANCING

In the financial environment, technology, competitiveness, and the expectation of demand change quickly. This makes it necessary for companies to modify and adapt their strategies and organizational structures to survive and remain competitive. Underperforming companies have to fight to exist and deliver a service or product able to generate a return that exceeds the connected cost of capital.

These rearranged strategies include a clear sense of purpose, direction, and realistic long-term rules that are viable because companies want to perform better and maintain a competitive edge.

A company that is targeted for replacement financing has already passed its embryonic stage and is headed into the development phase. Within this next stage there are problems connected with its organizational structure (management) that make it difficult to move into a mature phase. Consequently, when a venture capitalist decides to invest in a turnaround operation, he must know that a lot of energy will be spent solving issues related to management activity. Once these are solved, successful modification of the competitive strategy and structure can begin.

Strategic changes realized by companies are meant to move toward a future desired condition such as reinforcing competitive advantages. This process is very complex and only a few successfully manage it by launching new strategies and new structures to obtain an effective and renewed value proposition. It is important to recognize the sharp difference between strategic and organizational change. Strategic change refers to the realization of new strategies that lead to a substantial modification of the normal business activity of the firm, whereas organizational change is the normal consequence of redefining the business strategy. In conclusion, a strategic change always includes an organizational change, especially when it is suddenly implemented without relevant resistance.

As previously outlined, the typical company targeted for a turnaround deal is going through its mature phase and needs a renewal of the value proposition for its economic survival. Turnaround operations are part of strategic changes that include the reengineering, reorganization, and innovation processes:

Reengineering — Sweeping change in the company's costs, production cycle, services, and quality with the implementation of different techniques and tools that consider the firm as a complex system of customer-oriented processes instead of just a cluster of organizational functions. The emergence of aggressive new competitors in the market can force the company to find new strategies to recover their loss of competitiveness. The company's management team has to focus its attention first on critical business processes such as product design, inventory, and order management and then on customer needs, constantly monitoring how to improve the quality of the value proposition with a lower price. Implementing quality methodologies such as total quality management to improve process efficiency should also be a focus of management.

Reorganization — This is the second way management can launch a change, and it is composed of two main phases. In the first phase the firm reduces, in terms of number and dimension, business units, divisions, departments, and the levels of hierarchy. The second phase begins downsizing to reduce the number of employees to decrease the operational costs. A company decides to implement a reorganization because of the external environment; for example, a technology revolution that makes their product obsolete, a recession that depresses demand, or a law deregulation that changes the rules.

A firm usually reorganizes because it has not renewed its strategies and management to align with the environmental changes. Reorganization represents the only way to survive and regain the lost competitiveness.

Innovation — A strategic change pushed by new technologies that impact the production process and lead to a new configuration of the company service and product. To anticipate competitors, a company has to introduce a new production process or technology with a redefinition of its strategy and follow the innovation wave of the industry.

17.4 VALUATION AND MANAGEMENT OF RISK

The company targeted for a turnaround deal generally suffers from cash flow problems, insufficient future funding, or the inability to service their debt. It can also have an excessive debt equity ratio and inappropriate debt structure unbalanced between short- and long-term debt, and balance sheet insolvency.

The objectives of a financial restructuring are to restore the solvency of the company, in terms of cash flow and balance sheet, align the capital structure with the planned cash flow, and ensure that enough funds will be collected to implement the turnaround plan. These objectives are reached by modifying the existing capital structure; for example, raising additional funds, renegotiating the debt, or raising new equity capital from existing shareholders or outside investors (venture capitalists).

The private equity investor has to consider four fundamental risks when structuring a turnaround deal:

1. **Social risk** — When a firm is in crisis it strongly impacts both society in general and the firm's stakeholders. During this time the firm has problems with creditors, suppliers, employees, and customers. The community is affected by the loss of taxes paid by the firm and the costs to support employees who have lost their jobs.

2. **Economic risk** — The economic crisis of a company is analyzed by their return on investment (ROI); if it is lower than the average industrial ROI, the company is underperforming. This analysis can be problematic, and a better indicator of economic problems is the decline of the entire industry. A company is in crisis when its financial performance is continually decreasing in terms of ROI and return on sales and when the net incomes are negative.

3. **Legal risk** — The bankruptcy of a company raises many legal issues.

4. **Management risk** — From a management point of view, a company is in crisis when the ROI starts to decrease. Managers are the first to understand the situation and know if the crisis can be averted.

There are five different types of turnaround strategies in terms of operation impact, operations changes, and exiting the crisis:

Management — The key factor is management change. The objective of this type of deal is to turnaround the weakness of the management and general culture of the company. This is the most frequent type of turnaround.

Economic cycle — Turnaround is provoked by the economic cycle of the sector. Management must maintain the stability of the company while exploiting the potential revival of the cycle.

Product — The company is able to exit the crisis by launching a new product because of a new technological innovation.

Competitive background — Firms come out of a crisis because general elements in the competitive background change positively, such as decreasing the costs of raw materials.

State and government — When the crisis is provoked by market conditions out of the firm's control, the government provides help to solve their financial problems; for example, the automotive industry.

17.5 MERGER AND ACQUISITION

Acquisitions represent one part of the merger and acquisition (M&A) operation. To be more precise, acquisitions are composed of all the services that support the closing of operations that produce structural and definitive modification on the corporate aspects of the involved company. M&A represent one of the technical solutions developed and supported by private equity investors during turnaround and replacement financing. M&A operations include a set of heterogeneous deals such as mergers, the acquisition of a business unit of a company, the acquisition of quotes that represent a minor participation of the capital risk of a company, and all deals that allow the transfer of the proprietary control.

In this situation, the role of the venture capitalist is not only the soft support realized through advisory services but also the direct investment in companies with turnaround needs. When they act as advisory providers, economic returns are realized in the fees charged for this soft activity. When they invest directly, the economic return is higher and consists of gains they can realize on exit of the deal through an IPO or trade sale. Advisory support from the venture capitalist is critical, because the M&A deal is composed of acquisition search and deal origination, due diligence, valuation of the company and deal design, financial advisory and funding, and post closing advisory. This type of deal has a high rate of selection so there is little relation between deals closed and the cases analyzed. This makes the presence of professionals who improve the efficiency of the information and operative processes critical.

17.5.1 M&A motivations

The main reason for M&A operation is to realize a higher total value with the merger of two or more business units or companies than can be obtained if they stand alone as single units or companies. After the merger, production costs are reduced, and there is the possibility of increasing debt capacity and reducing the cost of debt because of the company's improved rating. Finally, the company has a better market position that affects the estimated rate for the earnings growth. There are five main macro categories that determine if an M&A deal is feasible:

Strategic motivation — An M&A can impact a company's competitive position; for example, it is possible to enlarge the market share if a dangerous competitor is acquired, activity on the core business can be refocused, entry in a new market or industry, internationalization, and expansion of activity downstream or upstream. It is also an opportunity to enter networks of specific companies.

Economic motivation — One of the most important reasons for an M&A deal is the cost reduction obtained with the exploitation of the scale and scope of economies. It is widely accepted that the increase in company dimension in terms of production capacity is translated in the reduction of the average cost per unit of product. It is also well known, studied, and verified that these deals improve the scope of economies by exploiting complementary skills and resources. Mergers and acquisitions create a new composition of the corporate governance and management team of the target company, which is another way to improve economic performance.

Financial motivation — Acquisitions allow the realization of a future investment that was previously impossible to the acquisition company, because of different ways to collect financial resources.

Fiscal motivation — This type of operation creates values with newly available fiscal opportunities; for example, possible future deductions of losses realized by the target company during the period previous to the acquisition.

Speculative motivation — This trend in the M&A is related to economic and market cycles. For example, deals fall apart when the seller's expectations of future performance are vastly different from the buyer's expectations, as often happens with technologically innovative companies.

17.5.2 **M&A characteristics**

Mergers and acquisitions can be realized in different ways: merger, equity carve out, breaking down, and joint venture. The merger solution is the natural conclusion of the buy operation formalized with a union between the target company and the new company.

The merger macro category is subdivided into merger with consolidation and corporate merger. Merger with consolidation is less widespread because the entities involved do not buy each other but are consolidated into a unique entity without the desire to take over. The balance sheet of the new company is exactly the sum of the asset, liability, and equity of the original companies, and they have different net worth value but the same equity value. The corporate merger is the most common merger solution. It involves an acquiring investor who does not have any share of the target company, an acquiring investor with participation in the risk capital of the target company, and an acquiring investor who owns the total property of the target. The latter is the case of a corporate merger after a leveraged buyout or successful and total takeover bid.

These types of operations are realized with cash or shares. Cash can completely change the corporate governance of the acquired company but is really expensive. Payment by exchanging shares does not use cash funds, but it does not allow total renewal of the corporate governance structure in the target company, especially when some shareholders do not accept the agreements.

17.6 GENERAL OVERVIEW OF DISTRESSED FINANCING

A distressed financing deal is an investment realized in a company that is facing a financial and economic crisis or is close to declaring bankruptcy. When a venture capitalist decides to invest in a distressed financing deal he has to consider the pros and cons of bankruptcy, because it is negotiated with public authorities, under specific laws and rules, and without the freedom to act based on business rules in the financial market

Distressed financing is a hybrid form of investment between expansion and replacement financing. It makes one wonder why a private investor decides to acquire a distressed firm. The answer is found in the valuation and comparison between the total value of specific assets included in the balance sheet of the target company, such as licenses and patents, and the negotiated acquisition price. The only way to manage the risk and return of this type of deal is to buy a company at a very low price, and this is easily done when a private equity investor purchases a distressed company through the courts.

There are two main strategies applied by the venture capitalist after the acquisition: to immediately re-sell the company or gamble on restructuring the target company after considering the potential of its intangible assets.

17.7 CHARACTERISTICS OF DISTRESSED FINANCING

Distressed financing can be executed by reorganizing the target company on the asset or liabilities side. If asset restructuring is chosen, the venture capitalist (vulture investor) has to decide which assets are kept and which are divested to recover the target company. Asset redefinition is the starting point for the restructuring plan.

Why it is convenient to recover a distressed firm? This question can be answered after reviewing the three levels of distressed financing activity:

The opportunity to rationalize the existing structure of the target company —
    Focuses on the elements that generate economic results and reduce items

of the net working capital. Operations on the working capital improve the company's capacity to create cash flows (especially unlevered).

Asset divestment — Selling assets, such as real estate properties, that can be sold directly or through extraordinary financial operations.

Extraordinary financial operations focused on specific strategic business units — To reorganize, the decision to sell out specific divisions, controlled companies, and branches has to be made. The vulture investor decides which area has to be divested after considering the strategic business served by the company and the valuation of the linkages and synergies (productive, commercial, and technological) existing between the business units. These areas are classified as no core business; core, no strategic business; and core strategic business. The first divisions to be sold are in the no core area. It can be difficult to sell the core and no strategic businesses because they should be maintained if possible.

Asset reorganization can be typically realized through:

1. Breaking down operations, which consist of an asset exchange between the operating and the financial management. External growth strategies without investing cash resources can be realized with this option.

2. Tracking stocks are special shares issued by a company and directly linked to the performance of a specific branch or division.

3. Carve outs and spin-offs are realized by dividing two or more branches or divisions to allow shareholders to reorganize the composition of their investments portfolio and, at the same time, to take out divisions of the company still profitable.

Restructuring deals can also be identified on the liability side. The main difference between this option and the asset side restructuring is that the group of financial creditors of the target company must agree on the deal. The agreement is usually composed of these elements:

1. Debt restructuring — Debt can be redefined in different ways: consolidation that reschedules for a longer term and debt maturities as well as reduction of the debt cost.
   Debt settlement that closes the debt with the payment of only a part of the total debt.
   Debt to equity swap is an accountability movement that converts all the existing debt, or a part of it, into risk capital.

Convertible bonds or with warrant — The financial creditor receives bonds with options to convert them into shares. This is a common tool that makes it possible to realize capital gain or take over the company.

2. Cost of financial resources.

3. Guarantees and covenants — Agreements that include rules protecting the creditors' interests. Guarantees usually concern real estate properties of the company, while covenants constrain the management of the firm such as limiting the investments or prohibiting asset dispositions.

Appendix 17.1

A business case: FORFREI

A17.1.1 Target company

FORFREI is a logistics company founded in the 1920s. It started out focusing on freight forwarding until the 1970s when the firm, led by the founder family, sold it to a private entrepreneur. In 1979 the property passed to a group of internal managers. In 1996, FORFREI went public on the domestic stock exchange and was quoted until 2003. It was then delisted following a takeover organized by two top managers and a venture capitalist, who, during 2006, subscribed a minority participation of the risk capital.

A17.1.2 Investment structure

In 2006 a private equity investor was involved in a replacement capital transaction with a minority participation. The deal was developed through a NewCo founded by the venture capitalist with an investment of €8 million. The NewCo acquired 24% of the FORFREI capital. Following that a reverse merger between FORFREI and the NewCo was executed reducing the private equity participation to 7% of the risk capital.

Even if the venture capitalist owns a minority participation, the shareholders agreement is very effective in terms of governance and exit. The exit strategy was listing of the company or, if it is not realized within a defined period of time, the managers and shareholders of the company can buy back the participation according to a pre-established mechanism of price setting.

A17.1.3 Critical elements of the investment

The main reasons for this investment are because FORFREI is a leader in freight forwarding in Europe, it has a high historical growth trend in the international transportation market, the valuation of the firm was appealing, and there was an IPO opportunity.

A17.1.4 Management phase activity

During the holding period of the investment, FORFREI developed its business further by becoming a worldwide corporate network in the logistics and supply chain management.

The company is the leader in its domestic market, in particular in the North American market. It has also expanded its activity to the Far East and South America, improving business by offering diversified services.

A17.1.5 Exiting

The investment is ongoing, an IPO is planned in the first half of 2009. The private equity participation, estimated by the shareholders, is €25 million.

Appendix 17.2

A business case: NDS

17.2.1 Target company

NDS is a nuclear medicine diagnostic institution founded in the 1970s. The company is a leader in nuclear medicine and is also active in developing software that automates the diagnostic process. This software provides patients with appropriate answers with particular focus on personal comfort and privacy. NDS is particularly concentrated on medical, technical, and administrative staff selection and training, while the equipment is continuously updated to ensure cutting edge services. NDS' diagnostic services cover nuclear medicine, radiology, ultrasounds, cardiology, physiopathology, and specialized clinic consultations.

A17.2.2 Investment structure

During 2006, a private equity investor was involved in a replacement capital transaction through a minority participation of 15% of the risk capital. Two other venture capitalists who subscribed a minority participation of 15% were also involved.

The investment was realized through a NewCo with the participation of the three venture capitalists in its risk capital. The NewCo acquired 30% of NDS. The resources invested by the three private equity firms totaled €14 million with an equity value of €47 million and an enterprise value of €81 million. The transaction used acquisition financing for €22 million and a vendor loan for €11 million.

Even though the venture capitalists' participations represent a minority of the risk capital, the shareholders agreement is very effective in terms of governance and exit strategy. Exiting has been defined as a listing of the company or, if it is not realized within a defined period of time, the managers and shareholders of the company will buy back the participations according to a pre-established mechanism of price setting.

A17.2.3 Critical elements of the investment

The main reasons for this investment are

Favorable market conditions with high growth potential realized both through internal and external ways

Favorable competitive environment with many small laboratories unable to offer high quality and technologically advanced services

A17.2.4 Exiting

The investment is ongoing but, as per the criteria fixed in the shareholders agreement, private equity investor's participations are estimated at €20 million.

Appendix 17.3

A business case: STUFFED

A17.3.1 Target company

STUFFED is a company operating in the high-quality staffed animal industry and is a leader in its domestic market and in the wood toys industry. It was founded in the 1950s and its business is based on a completely externalized production, executed by Far East supplier, and on distribution of the products through sales agents in the domestic market. In the European market it operates with two owned companies, a joint venture and an agent network.

A17.3.2 Investment structure

In 2002 a private equity investor realized a replacement capital transaction to evaluate the potential exit of the entrepreneur from STUFFED through minority participation of 27% of the risk capital. The investment is a recapitalization of the company executed by the entrepreneur and the venture capitalist.

A17.3.3 Critical elements of the investment

The main reasons for this investment were the high potentiality of the brand and the possibility of developing a successful reorganization plan.

A17.3.4 Management phase activity

The management of the company was delegated to a new CEO who followed strategies defined by the venture capitalist and the entrepreneur formalized in a business plan focusing on the reorganization of STUFFED and on the maximization of the brand through:

New products
Expansion in international markets with direct investments
New licensing and franchising programs
Renewal and improvement of the wood toys brand and products

In three years, the reorganization process produced satisfactory performances with international turnover that reached 46% of total revenue, 18% of the operating margin compared with revenues (a ratio that was negative before the investment), and a net financial position reduced by 45%.

A17.3.5 Exiting

The venture capitalist exited from this investment in 2005 through a management buyout deal realized by a different private equity firm and by the CEO who executed the reorganization plan during the holding period of the investment.

Listing a private company

18

18.1 GENERAL OVERVIEW OF AN IPO

The listing of a private company can be considered from two different perspectives. First, it can be hidden inside a complex financial restructuring of the company. The IPO is a tool that allows the rebalancing of the passive side of the balance sheet because it infuses new financial resources (risk capital) into a company. Secondly, the listing process of a company is key to supporting the firm's growth; since the raised funds on the public market can be used to realize new development opportunities.

The IPO is used to exploit a stable financial source, reach specific development entrepreneurial goals and, during the succession processes of family firms, protect the financial stability of the company and the improvement of its economic performance.

The reasons to take a company public have changed over the years. In the 1990s the entrepreneurs exploited an upward trending market and placed their shares in advantageous positions. Listing a company also became an opportunity to rebalance the ratio between equity and debt, especially after a period of large investments. Until the mid-1990s the quotation decision was led by entrepreneurs wanting to divest or diversify their portfolios. During the second half of 1990, the reasons to list a company completely changed. Many family-run small to medium firms decided to go public to exploit the tax benefit and the positive economic situation. Placing shares in a regulated stakes market represented a desirable exit strategy for institutional investors and private equity funds because it allows:

> The placement of minority shares of the risk capital, obtaining a capital gain and continuing to hold the control of the company

A return higher than other exit solutions

The satisfaction of management's preferences

Potential capital gain to be obtained through the increase in the price or value of the shares over time

In this chapter, the characteristics of a target company that goes public will be addressed as will the disadvantages connected with this strategy and the relevant advantages analyzed from a management, company, and shareholder perspective. The main steps of the IPO process will be reviewed at the end of the chapter.

18.2 CHARACTERISTICS OF A COMPANY GOING PUBLIC

There are several studies focused on the characteristics of companies eligible for a successful IPO strategy. The first group of studies shows the tendency of these firms to analyze their financial structure to determine if this strategy is applicable; for example, considering the optimal level of the debt leverage connected with the cost of the risk and debt capital. The second group of studies measures the tendency to list a company based on the position of the company in its life cycle and the related potential sources of financing. Finally, it was found that the main reason and motivation to list a company are the problems raised between the majority and minority shareholders. These studies discovered changes in target companies before and after going public market.

There are several different potential types of companies interested in quotation. We can identify four main groups related to the firm's life cycle:

1. Development companies — Firms that want to leave the status of a family company and move toward a business structure that is more complex and articulated.

2. Replacement financing companies — Entities facing changes in the composition of the property related to a family succession. This category includes companies with private equity participation who want to use the quotation as an exit from their investment.

3. Financially stressed companies — Companies developed from an internal or external growth strategy that need to rebalance their financial position by addressing the new funds to cover their previous investment plan. An IPO is a way to sustain development, rebalance the debt equity ratio, and diversify financial sources.

4. Growing companies — Firms that have reached the critical dimensional threshold and intend to continue growing by using a merger and acquisition strategy (external growth strategy) or to enlarge and reinforce their

production capacity. The quotation decision is motivated by the intention to build and exploit a network of relationships that can help the company to grow its domestic dimensions by improving its position in the industry and collaborating with other firms that have complementary knowledge, skills, and resources.

18.3 ADVANTAGES OF AN IPO FOR THE COMPANY

The advantages that an IPO offers to target companies has been the center of many economic studies. One approach, based on the paradigm of the relationship between principal and agent, solves the agency cost problem by using the financial market. One benefit of quotation is higher visibility for the target company, which imposes more control by the investors and reduces agency costs in favor of improving performances from the target firm. Another approach focuses on the relationship between the development level of the financial system and the growth of the company in a particular country. The stock exchange market solves several specific problems such as facilitating a match between demand and supply of capitals, simplifying the collection of the funds needed by the firm for its development, and control transfer.

Based on these approaches, the advantages created by the quotation in favor of the target company can be classified into two clusters:

1. Economic and financial advantages — All positive effects from reinforcing the financial structure are made possible by collecting new funds (risk capital resources). Direct access to new financial sources at a low price is done without the involvement of professional intermediaries. This should be considered both from a quantity and quality point of view, since the funds collected, as risk capital, do not include a contractual agreement for the periodic remuneration and repayment, while improving the debt raising capacity. Several and specific strengths of the quotation can be identified:
   Moving from financial problem solving actions to a medium-long term financial strategy
   Ability to decide how and when the investors are remunerated
   Expansion of available financing sources due to the improvement of the contractual power and transparency that IPOs offer to listed firms
   Improvement of the company's rating translated into the reduction of funding costs
   Diversification of collected funds in quantitative terms, which means less dependence on the bank system and the possibility of reducing the cost of funding supplied by the banks
   Different and specific structured categories of financial tools

Reduction of collateral and other quantitative constraints

Improved investment capacity, due to fresh financial resources that reduce the debt servicing impact on the cash flows

2. Extra economic advantages include the positive effects caused by the quotation; being public generates a good reputation and increases visibility in the economic and financial community. These effects can be used as leverage in marketing and corporate strategies because they can attract more qualified managerial resources. Public companies are more attractive than private ones, because they have highly skilled managers with a better prospective for growth. Reputation capital, which is gained by strengthening and the qualification of the company image, is very useful in the marketing strategy because it increases the firm's visibility if there is an internationalization campaign planned.

Very often, when a company goes public, the connection and the personality of the founder tend to disappear from the operative and strategic decision processes.

18.4 ADVANTAGES OF AN IPO FOR SHAREHOLDERS

If the IPO is a way to produce positive effects on the target company, then these advantages are reflected by the shareholders. In particular, it is possible to create liquidity from an investment realized in shares of a quoted company. Monetization of a firm's value allows the entrepreneur to diversify his portfolio, and guarantees a successful way out for the private equity investments realized in private companies.

The main advantages of an IPO for shareholders are

1. A solution to succession problems
2. Increased share value
3. Exploitation of tax benefits
4. Share liquidity that allows the realization of financial operations
5. Cancellation of personal and real guarantees offered by the entrepreneur in favor of the company
6. Recapitalization of the firm without using the founders' personal resources who maintain control because shares are now are issued with voting rights

18.5 ADVANTAGES OF AN IPO FOR MANAGEMENT

There are also benefits realized by managers when a company goes public including improved personal image, international visibility, and recognized expertise.

These positive aspects are balanced by an increased monitoring of their daily performance because their work is constantly subjected to the judgement of the financial market expressed in terms of share price. The listing allows diversification of managers' salary so it can be divided into flat and variable remuneration linked to long-term incentives. The quotation for the employees is an opportunity to be involved in a stock options plan or subscribe to the increase of risk capital for free.

18.6 DISADVANTAGES OF AN IPO

An IPO for a target company also has its disadvantages. Every company going public suffers from one major disadvantage — the huge costs caused by this operation.

Ensuring an appropriate economic return to the new shareholders can be a problem particularly for the family-run company. If the net income of the firm before the IPO can be reinvested, after the listing it is important to define and follow a good dividend strategy. Going public leads to big changes for management. The global trend of the market directly affects management's decision process. A negative trend in the industry can push the company to move up investment opportunities because the risk capital operations would be unprofitable.

Once a private company is listed, it has to make several critical changes in the internal organization to work in the external financial and economic world. These changes are related to different aspects of the life of the firm such as:

1. The need for transparency pushes the company to make its activities and processes more visible. The increase of decision constraints and the potential interference of third external parties decreases the control power of the entrepreneur. These problems are solved by the establishment of a shareholder agreement.

2. Implementing reporting and control requirements that usually imply investment and changes in the information and informatics system.

3. Huge costs; the IPO process imposes costs related to the fulfillments that target companies have to execute. After listing, public firms face several costs to adjust their organizational structure. The main sources of costs include:
   Advisory services supplied by the sponsor and the quotation syndicate
   Costs related to the certification and audit of the company's balance sheet
   Marketing costs related to the promotional activities of the IPO

Fees for the public stock market manager
Print and circulation of informative prospects
Legal advice
Printing shares certificates

4. The need to split the estates of the firm and the entrepreneur apart; this is solved with a special purpose vehicle and the estate that remains with the entrepreneur is concentrated.

18.7 THE IPO PROCESS

The process for publicly listing a company can be divided into two main subphases: the organization and the execution of the quotation.

18.7.1 The organization phase

This phase consists mainly of a feasibility study of the quotation project, which analyzes all the elements that must be evaluated before going public such as the real will and desire of the majority shareholders, the market where the shares will be listed, the definition process for the price of the share, and checking the quotation requirements. The organization activities are usually executed with the involvement of one or more specialized financial intermediaries (named advisors who also participate in the quotation syndicate).

The main responsibility of the advisor is to check and verify the existence of both the formal and substantial requirements needed for the quotation. Formal requirements include all of the qualifications established by the law defined by the regulatory entities. Each country and public trade market has its own laws and regulatory rules. Substantial quotation requirements impose big changes in the structure of the company and, consequently, are more onerous than the formal ones. They can be classified into two categories:

1. Organizational requirements:
    Clear settlement of the relationship between the shareholders and the firm and, consequently, between the estate of the company and the estate of the entrepreneur.
    Check the skill level of the management team and the real delegation of power and authorities assigned to people irrelevant to the entrepreneur.
    Effectiveness of the organizational structure of the company is critical because it affects the ability of the firm to offer the necessary complete and accurate information to the financial market. The importance of the

structure depends on the appreciation of the investors, which is directly linked to the company performances and the trust existing between it and the investors. An effective structure, which works with accurate control systems, ensures better control of the company performance so faster changes can be made to the strategy in case of unsatisfactory results.

The involvement of a reliable and prestigious leader can guarantee optimal business execution of company activity.

2. Economic and financial requirements — The first aspect to be evaluated and verified is the placement of the firm in its industry to define its potential in terms of future growth. Analysis focuses on the valuation of the firm's capacity to grow not only in terms of revenue increase, but also in terms of net income to be realized with a well-balanced financial strategy. The last critical aspect is the future ability of the company to generate dividends for the shareholders. This potential attracts investments from the market and improves the company's share value.

The organization phase is closed, after analyzing the formal and substantial requirements, with the selection of the market where the IPO will be realized. This implies the valuation of three elements: the country, the type, and the structure of the market. The market country is not only the place where the shares will be negotiated, but there is the problem of dual listing. Empirical evidence demonstrates a high correlation between the domestic country of the firm and the location of the market chosen for the launch of the IPO. Choosing the market where your firm is located is justified by many reasons such as the cost, cultural similarity, and the ability to manage the relevant financial community. Selecting a foreign market increases costs and imposes a cultural gap while representing a powerful marketing opportunity for the company. During the selection of the appropriate market, the company has to consider a dual listing strategy (simultaneous quotation in two public financial markets, domestic and international). A firm considers dual listing for the marketing potential and the opportunity to launch an acquisition campaign across foreign markets. Another critical factor is the importance of the country selected in terms of its position in the company's business.

The second main aspect to be evaluated is identifying the segment and type of market. In all countries, several different markets can be identified according to specific substantial and formal factors defined by the public authority as well as the dimensions of the listed companies. These specific characteristics have a direct impact on the visibility and the reputation of the company and the volatility of the share price.

The last element considered is the structure of the market, and the choice is made based on three aspects: market making, specialist, and stand alone. Market making is when financial intermediaries guarantee their assistance to the company after the quotation. They continue to offer the bid and ask price quotation without assuming direct position in the share trading. A specialist market implies a market maker that takes a position in the negotiations related to the shares quoted with specific obligations. When the market maker and specialist are absent, there is a stand-alone market.

18.7.2 The execution phase

The organization phase ends with the validation of the substantial requirement of the company. Once the quotation is validated, a critical and complex process starts to complete the listing of the company.

The are several activities to be executed with necessary steps to be followed:

1. Board of Directors resolution — States the decision to quote the company and defines the high level guidelines of the process and appoints the financial intermediaries that will act as sponsors of the listing.
2. Due diligence — Check the legal, economic, and financial valuation of the company.
3. Meeting with market authorities to plan the activities required by the law.
4. Meeting and agreement with quotation syndicates (a group of financial intermediaries appointed to arrange the shares).
5. Company evaluation.
6. Compilation of the comfort letters that are certifications, signed by external audit companies, guaranteeing the existence of correct and effective planning and control systems in the target company.
7. Shareholder assembly resolution that allows the company to go public.
8. Preparation of the documentations for the financial analyst.
9. Pre-marketing, book building, and road show; these activities are critical to the success of the quotation because they prepare the financial market for the operation.
10. Shares price fixing and beginning of the negotiations.

Shares price definition is critical because the price assigned to the company's shares depends mainly on the financial needs of the company, the costs for collection, and the timing of the operation. In reality, the definition of the pricing is the result of the combination of five different forces. The first one is the desire of the old shareholders of the target company to maximize their economic return from the IPO. The second force is the need of the target company to get the highest possible price, even if it has a more long-term view compared with the old shareholders. The arrangement syndicate expects a price lower than the old shareholders and the company's price, because it wants to minimize the risks of the arrangement. The two forces that push for the reduction of the shares price are the sponsor market maker and all the investors; the first one is moved by the desire to minimize the speculation activities on the company's shares price, while investors want to pay the lowest possible price.

The interaction of these five forces is critical in how the shares are arranged. Two types of arrangements can be identified:

1. Initial Selling Public Offer — This quotation happens through the selling offer launched by the old shareholders. This solution is not appreciated by the market because, even if it maximizes the economic return for the old shareholders, it does not create new financial resources for the company. It is simply a handing over of the property.

2. Initial Subscription Public Offer — The sold stakes to the investors are issued ex novo through an increase of the company's risk capital. This solution is preferred by the investors because it allows the company to collect new financial resources that can be used to ensure the growth plan of the firm. This is not the best solution for the shareholders, because they do not receive the economic return from the IPO.

Usually, the interactions of the previously defined five forces lead to a mixed solution between the initial selling public offer and the initial subscription public offer.

During the execution phase of the quotation, the syndicate of financial intermediaries assumes a critical role in the process in terms of costs that the target company has to face and the final success of the operation. Depending on the specific roles attributed to the arrangement syndicate, the costs are related to the management fees, paid to the syndicate leader (global coordinator) to remunerate his advisory and organization activity, the selling fees, recognition of the intermediaries that sell the shares to the single investors, and the underwriting fees that occur on the funds supplied in advance and the back clauses.

The characteristics and the roles of the arrangement syndicate depend on the type of risk it takes. There are four types of arrangement syndicates:

1. Selling group — Distributes shares to the public investors. Residual shares not sold are returned to the company. Receives selling and management fees.

2. Purchase group — Financial intermediaries involved in purchasing the shares quoted. Sells directly to the investors. The economic return for

these intermediaries consists of the difference realized between the purchase price and the selling price of the shares.

3. Underwriting group — Purchases the shares not arranged to public investors. They require underwriting fees.

4. Arrangement and guarantee syndicate — Financial intermediaries involved in distributing shares to investors. They are obliged to purchase the unsold shares. Fees paid to this group include management, underwriting, and selling fees.

The job of financial intermediaries does not end with the quotation. There are three main post-IPO jobs they perform:

Stabilization — Moral, or contractual, commitment of the global coordinator to support the price of the listed company

Investor relation activity — Managing the periodical information flow to the market, quarterly or monthly

Market maker or specialist

Appendix 18.1

A business case: VINTAP

A18.1.1 Target company

VINTAP is a company founded during the 1950s. It started by manufacturing and selling plugs for alcoholic beverages. Today, it is a leader in the closures of alcoholic and non-alcoholic beverages and vegetable oils. VINTAP's proposal consists of a wide range of aluminum closures and security closures with international and domestic customers. The company operates in all four continents due to an international network of production structures.

A18.1.2 Investment structure

A private equity investor was involved in an expansion growth deal during 2000 through a majority participation of 55,5% of VINTAP's risk capital. The company was listed in 2006 and the venture capitalist sold, during an IPO, 60% of his participation.

A18.1.3 Critical elements of the investment

The main reason for this investment was that VINTAP was valued by venture capitalists as an interesting company in terms of future successful performance.

A18.1.4 Management phase activity

During the investment, the company realized an effective growth plan achieving important results:

Increase of international activity from 7 to 16 plants outside the domestic boundaries
Opening of new commercial branches in North and South America
Realization of four acquisitions
A large investment in the research and development division produces two patents and 15 quality certifications

Appendix 18.2

A business case: LEAGOO

A18.2.1 Target company

LEAGOO is a company active in the leather industry founded by its CEO in the 1980s. Until the end of the 1990s, the company worked on behalf of big leather firms. Then LEAGOO started to produce leather goods sold with its own brand.

The firm's proposal is focused on professional goods and goods dedicated to travel, targeting high-level customers. It has developed a strategy differentiation from its competitors. In 2000 LEAGOO started a plan of retail shops and it opened 30 points of sales with the 50% of them in the domestic market. During 2007, revenues were €46 million with 100 employees.

A18.2.2 Investment structure

Private equity investors were involved in an expansion growth deal during 2005 through a minority participation equal to 35,5% of the LEAGOO risk capital. The company was listed in 2008, and the venture capitalist exited from the investment after a successful IPO.

A18.2.3 Critical elements of the investment

The main reasons for this investment were the innovative proposal and the high potential of future successful performance.

A18.2.4 Management phase activity

During the investment, the company has realized an effective growth plan achieving important results:

Increase of international activity through new shops opened outside the domestic market
Brands registered in all the markets serviced

Strategies, business models, and perspectives of private equity and venture capital

19.1 GENERAL OVERVIEW: A WORLD BETWEEN THE GOLDEN AGE AND UNCERTAINTY

After a five-year period of economic growth and a buyout boom, for many countries the last quarter of 2007–2008 marked a turning point in the global private equity environment. The golden age has passed and a new age of uncertainty is starting, but for some it has the sweet smell of opportunity. With an estimated €200 to 300 billion in unsyndicated leverage loans on their books in 2008, it appears that banks were the first buyout players to suffer. As the attention of bankers moved from credit risk analysis to debt syndication, many say they are reaping what they sowed. The credit crunch may have been triggered by the sub-prime mortgage problems, but the consequences run deeper. In five to seven years, the leading role of banks in the corporate banking and corporate finance market evolved dramatically: from principal lenders they became debt producers and brokers on a completely different scale. Financial structuring complexity has driven debt market participants to lose the sense of risk and driven the great renaissance of the high-yield market. Private equity opponents blame big buyout partners and it is true that increased leverage multiples and loosened covenants can sound like a good thing for financial sponsors, i.e., more risk and less discipline.

Apparently, the big buyout sector seems to be the most exposed to risk, and investors tend to oscillate between optimism and pessimism when asked about the effects of the credit crunch. Some argue it is the end of the large buyout era or the end of the golden age of private equity. A large number of investors also fear the United States will be affected by a private equity downturn more than other countries: in terms of capital deployment, fund investors hesitate between the worry of not having their money put to work fast enough and the fear of being too quickly deployed in less attractive and smaller deals. Most agree that if the economic downturn affected operating companies, things would be worse. While default rates still remain at historical lows, this may be simply the result of particularly weaker terms (i.e., few covenants, new repayment scheduling, etc.). Despite the big turmoil it is causing, the change in leverage loan market conditions is welcomed as a healthy and necessary correction by many market players and investors. It might be the end of the golden age but certainly not of the adventure of private equity. The players are simply being reminded that discipline and fair management are not old fashioned European words, but pillars of a competitive advantage for private equity and the financial system.

Private equity investors focus on the long term, and it is hard to find supporters of this market timing approach. However, as this new cycle starts, investors in Europe and the United States have clearly expressed concern about the future IRR leading to an increased focus on investment strategies able to produce higher returns in a less than favorable economic environment. This means the 2009–2010 asset allocation will be both defensive and offensive at the same time; looking for a high standard of quality, a well-suited pattern of investment, and emerging potential targets of considerable interest.

Today investors agree that relevant performance will come from middle market and lower middle market players. Investors (and limited partners) are increasing their focus on teams capable of showing and demonstrating their value creation system. Europe and North America also offer significantly attractive and challenging opportunities with teams that have proven experience in building strong private equity firms to invest through a buy and hold approach adding a true "industrial touch" to their venture-backed companies. In the higher middle-market cluster, a number of teams target both privately held companies and listed companies; more and more listed companies appear as attractive targets for those larger middle-market buyout teams looking for undervalued companies to take private. Great opportunities are available for private equity firms with experience dealing with public companies both in Europe and the United States.

With Europe and the United States in turmoil, investors are turning more and more to emerging markets as the next stop for favorable performance. The growth rate of these markets has little reliance on bank debt making them even more appealing. Choosing the right private equity firms is a key challenge in that area. A rising number of investors are starting to wonder whether the next bubble lies in China, India, or Korea. The Middle East is another region where a number of family-owned investment teams have grown to become strong and experienced investors. However, some important challenges remain in these emerging markets. They include the need for regulatory framework, and a wider capital market, human resources, and political risks. For these reasons, Europe and the United States still remain a preferable market in which to invest because of the very strong private equity firms, teams who live (and to survive) both in good and bad times (the 1998 Russian debt crises, the 2000 tech-Internet bubble, and 9/11).

The newest entry in the private equity market for 2007–2008 are sovereign funds. But while the visibility of this phenomenon is quite new for the fundraising market, the actual sovereign funds investment activity is not. Some of these players have been investing for many years and have become very skilled and professional asset managing teams. But 2007–2008 proved another strong year for the secondary market too. During this time (and 2009 is following this trend) the large majority of sellers accessed the market as part of natural portfolio management activities — even the power stays in the hands of buyers.

19.2 EUROPEAN BACKGROUND

European Union GDP was quite strong in 2007, but 2008 results and 2009 expectation are not positive. In this context and despite global financial crises, European private equity remained strong as reflected by the new record investment amount (even in 2007) and attractive to investors as reflected by the fundraising flows in 2008. Today, the key figures of European private equity are

1. Three countries generated more than the 70% of the deals in 2007 and 2008 (i.e., the UK, France, and Germany)

2. The UK covered more than the 50% of the fundraising amount in 2007 and 2008

3. Thirteen general partners raised more than €1 billion in new fund closings in 2007 alone, thus hosting 50% of the 2007 fundraising

4. One-fifth of the buyout activity was represented by mega deals in 23 European companies

The dynamism of the private equity sector was driven by both organic growth and first time funds established in the last three years in both the venture and the buyout markets mainly by investment professionals with track records built in established private equity firms. In 2007, there were approximately 1,900 active private equity firms making direct investments in Europe alone.

Investments in European companies in 2007–2008 as a percentage of GDP was 0,5% on average. Even the weight of the private equity value in the overall economy varied across countries: between 0,1 and 1,2% in Sweden, the UK, and the Netherlands at the upper end and Greece, the Czech Republic, and Portugal at the lower end.

After an exceptional 2006, fundraising scaled back by approximately 30% to €79 billion in 2007 and €65 billion in 2008. Nevertheless, this was close to 10% above the total funds raised in 2005, and substantially higher than the €20 to €48 billion collected yearly between 1997 and 2004. The UK hosted more than half of the 2007 fundraising while France and Germany were next with 8,3 and 7,2%, respectively. For the first time Greece was in the top five countries in terms of fundraising, which was primarily due to the structuring of the Marfin Investment Group (a Greek buyout private equity firm). As in the past (even for 2007), the fundraising amount was driven by buyouts and 13 funds raised more than €1 billion in 2007.[1] However, by the number of independent funds raised the picture was more balanced between two segments of the market: 58 buyout funds versus 46 venture funds reaching final closing. Altogether 141 private equity funds reached final closing in Europe in 2007.

The type of investors behind the 2007–2008 fundraising — for example, the traditional British LP type — continued to lead the ranking: pension funds, banks, and insurance companies. Similar to 2000–2006 as well as in 2007 and 2008, pension funds were the number one source of funding, mainly due to the UK pension funds activism across the world.

In 2007–2008, the average fund size for private equity funds that reached final closing in Europe was €112,8 million, whereas for the buyout cluster it was only €928,7 million. Data are not so different without the UK sample. While most funds did not have a specific sector focus, there were eleven ICT-focused funds reaching final closing in 2007 with an average fund size of €140,2 million, six life sciences-focused funds with an average fund size of €132,1 million, and five energy and environment focused funds with an average fund size of €111,18 million. The ICT-focused funds were managed primarily from Poland, the UK, and France, with the life sciences funds raised mainly by the UK and the Netherlands, and the energy and environment funds mainly managed in the UK and France.

If we consider the stage distribution by percentage of amount in 2003–2007, 60% was made by turnaround and buyouts, 30% by expansion, and 10% by seed (1%) and start up (9%). Percentages change dramatically if we consider the distribution by percentage of number of investments, whereas 33% is covered by expansion, 30% by start up, and 24% only by turnaround and buyouts.

The companies targeted for investments were predominantly, as in 2006, in the 1,000–4,999 employee bracket by amount invested. Regarding the number of employees for the European companies that had access to private equity financing in 2007–2008, 32,1% of the companies employed below 19 staff members, while 31,2% employed 20–99.

On the divestment side, exits decreased by the amount divested at cost and by number, and the emphasis was put on sales to other private equity firms, which accounted for nearly one-third of the total amount divested. This is the first time divestment methods exceeded trade sales even if by a small margin. Divestment by European private equity firms decreased by 18,3% at €27,1 billion in 2007. Trade sales have increased in the €7,5 billion to 7,6 billion range, but ranked only second as an exit channel in 2007. Sales to other private equity investors took the lead, doubling their share to 30,4% at €8,2 billion. Divestments by public offering were below the five-year European average in 2007, and they moved closer to zero in 2008.

Similar to investments, the UK remained the main platform for private equity exits even when aggregating figures by country of location of the private equity firms in charge of the divestment or by country of location of the portfolio company. Similar to the ranking of countries by investment amounts, the most targeted divestment markets after the UK were France and Germany with more than €4 billion divested at cost in 2007 for each of the two countries.

When looking at exits per market segments, trade sales led the way for venture capital exits with a 30,1% share of the €5,1 billion venture divestments, while secondary sales led the way for buyout exits with a 34,6% share of the €20,4 billion buyout divestment in 2007.

19.3 STRATEGIES AND BUSINESS MODELS OF PRIVATE EQUITY FIRMS

To analyze strategy within private equity firms it is useful to identify business models that are common in Europe. A focus–ownership–positioning (FOP) approach is helpful to distinguish the

  Focus of investment made by the private equity firm, related to the country/countries area of investment

  Ownership of private equity firms, which conditions the style of investment and the long-term profit goals

  Positioning of the private equity firm on the market, related to the competitive strategy to select investment

Focus, ownership, and positioning are the three dimensions of a business model in the private equity industry and every private equity firm has a different combination of them that affects the competitive strategy and profit results for investors.

19.3.1 **The focus of investment**

The focus of investment has a relevant impact on the scale, on the team, and on the network the private equity firm has to manage and defend. The geographic area focus is the first step in identifying a strategy and building an organization; in comparison with other (even financial) services, the private equity industry is totally "human and human network based." This means a process of diversification through geographic areas is quite difficult and slow as skills are not easy to find in markets such as equipment, factories, and other tangible assets.

It is possible to distinguish three different ways to use this focus:

1. Domestically
2. Internationally (i.e., pan-European, pan-American or pan-Asiatic)
3. Globally

The most common strategy is domestic focus — if the size of the country is large enough and makes it possible and rational — because of the natural linkage between the background of the management team and its expertise and presence in the social and economic network. On the contrary, private equity firms following international or global focus are structured as a network similarly to big consulting companies. Private equity firms following international or global focus can manage the multi-country dimension in two different ways:

1. Many funds investing in many countries (i.e., like Permira, Apax partners, etc.)
2. One fund (or more) for every country (i.e., 3i, Blackstone, IFC, etc.)

Private equity firms following a global focus can act through direct investment with many funds (the so called "mega fund" strategy, like KKR) and direct investment in other funds (the so-called "fund of funds" strategy). Only the first strategy can be mentioned as a "pure" private equity strategy because of the ability to invest and stay in venture-backed companies, whereas the second strategy can be considered a financial strategy and not a "pure" private equity strategy.

The focus generates a sort of symmetry between the investment policy and the size of investment. Private equity firms can be divided into three categories based on their size/average investment ticket:

1. Small-size players invest between €1 and 5 million in each deal, typically small buyouts and expansion capital transactions. These players are mostly local, i.e., based in the country of the management team.

2. Medium-sized players invest between €5 and 20 million in each deal. Some of these players are sponsored by industrial companies or are

connected to foreign financial institutions, again the majority of these vehicles are local.

3. Large private equity players invest in equity tickets in excess of €20 million. Many of these are international or global private equity firms with widely available resources to invest, but most are branches of global funds with an established presence in a relevantly sized country.

19.3.2 Ownership of private equity firms

Owning a private equity firm is not neutral to strategy because there are both profit goals and styles of management within the investment. Using the owner-ship concept, it is possible to distinguish five different categories/strategic mod-els of private equity firms owned by:

1. Banks (or financial institutions)
2. Corporations
3. Professionals (i.e., the so-called "independent" private equity firms)
4. Governments
5. Private investors

Private equity firms owned by banks or financial institutions promote funds from financial institutions willing to operate in the private equity market through a dedicated vehicle. It is quite common in Europe because of the concept of the Universal Bank, which creates specific legal entities when the business is risky or relevant in terms of capital expenditure, like the private equity case. As a natural consequence, the activity of the bank-owned private equity firm is strictly related to the strategy of the financial group. The pros of this model are the brand name usage and leverage, the reputation effect, support coming from the network of the financial group, synergies with corporate lending, and the very high potential of fundraising. The cons of this model are the potential divergence from a "pure" profit goal (i.e., private equity sustains and subsides the corporate lending) and the potential lack of an independent strategic view. Typically, bank-owned private equity firms are quite strong in private equity where their financial know-how and expertise are required and relevant for the competitive advantage rather than the necessary industrial knowledge and hands-on approach for buyouts and pure expansion financing.

Corporate owned private equity firms promote funds from a corporation aiming to operate in the private equity market or for profit and for sustaining the core industrial business. The nature of such private equity firms is strictly related to the strategy of the corporate group. The pros of this model are again the brand name usage and leverage (similar to bank-owned private equity firms), the reputation, the network of the corporate group, deep industrial knowledge, and the potential ability to manage venture-backed companies. The cons are the potential low level of financial skills and the financial constraints coming from the corporate reputation; for example, a downgrade of the corporation can generate a negative effect both on the fundraising and on the ability to raise money for each deal. Typically, corporate-owned private equity firms are better suited for private equity investment requiring industrial know-how and presence through a strong hands-on approach like seed financing, and start-up, early stage, and restructuring financing.

Professional-owned private equity firms promote funds from a group of managers or professionals coming from industrial or consulting backgrounds. Consequently, the investment made by the firm is generally related to the previous sector of activity of professionals and the leverage and strong know-how of the managers. The pros of this strategic model are the personal reputation of the managers, the strong network of the professionals, in-depth industrial knowledge, the potentially high ability to manage venture-backed companies, and a great sense of independence. The cons are the absence of a strong organization behind the managers and the lack of resources due to the absence of a banking or industrial group creating synergies. Typically, professional-owned private equity firms excel through a pure hands-on approach into private equity deals, whereas using leverage and financial abilities are not so relevant. Medium- and small-size equity tickets are quite common for this strategic model.

Government-owned private equity firms promote funds by a governmental entity also in joint venture with other private investors and sometimes using a dedicated country law (i.e., SBIC in the US). The investment process is generally driven by the goals of the governmental entity, whereas the mix of profit and social return can have a different balance and results. The pros of this strategic model are the possibility of reducing the expectation of IRR and to increase risk, the possibility of reducing the size of each equity investment, and the easiest entrance in very risky sectors such as seed and start-up financing. The cons of the model are the potential lack of top human resources, the divergence from a pure and explicit profit goal, increasing write-offs and defaults, and the exposure to political cycle risk. Typically, government-owned private equity firms excel at a geographic focus dedicated to emerging or developing countries and at a policy of joint ventures with private investors to make the intervention into small-size equity tickets easier.

Private equity firms owned by private investors promote funds from family businesses or from a group of families to manage their wealth. The nature of this last strategic model is related to investments generally driven by the goals of the family with the support of external managers in charge of the "family office." Consequently, by definition, the pros of the model include the ability to efficiently manage private wealth, the independence from the financial system, and the use of a family network. The cons are the potential lack of top human resources, the divergence of opinion between family members, and the absence of a strong organization structure as seen in professional-owned private equity firms. Even the size and the reputation of the family owning the private equity firm could be relevant to the scope of the investment; a family office vocation generally leads the private equity firm to invest in small and medium-sized equity tickets, whereas the importance of the family network is an advantage in deals such as turnaround and family buyouts.

19.3.3 Positioning of the market

The positioning of the private equity firm in the market is a crucial decision for every fund regardless of focus or ownership. Positioning is defined as identifying the cluster(s) in which to invest money and allocate resources in the portfolio. Asset allocation and identification of market positioning generate consequences in terms of dedicated human resources and knowledge required. Positioning is a medium-long term choice of asset allocation that is difficult to change in terms of high costs to sustain the position to change the managerial team. The positioning issue can be placed into different groups (i.e., "strategies" involving the positioning itself) that highlight different solutions for managing the asset allocation by specializing:

1. Within stages
2. Within sectors
3. Within areas
4. Through an incubator approach
5. Through an alternative approach

Specialization within stages is the most common strategy followed and implemented by any focused or owned private equity firm. This specialization means the private equity firm chooses to allocate the portfolio in one of the stages of development of the firm, and the private equity firm recruits human resources and creates knowledge only on this cluster. The potential benefit of diversification is reduced, but the fund benefits from strong control of the business. Specialization within stages is also driven from different "business communities" and job profiles inside every stage that make the combination of management–business–investment simpler.

Specialization within sectors is not as common as a private equity firm strategy. In this strategic model the private equity firm chooses one industrial sector and recruits human resources and creates knowledge. Typical examples are biotech, telecoms, fashion, etc. The potential for diversification is strongly reduced, but the fund benefits from the strong control of the sector. Specialization within sectors is typically driven from the background of the managers and their relationship in the sector but, compared to the specialization within stages, the risk is higher because the fund allocates the whole amount of money only in one sector implying a bigger risk during economic downturn or changes in the sector's competitive pattern.

Specialization within areas is not a strategy typical of global funds aiming to enter and stay in new markets. In this model, the private equity firm chooses one area and invests in whatever sector and stage belongs to the area. The potential of diversification is extremely high — even linked to the size of the geographic area chosen by the private equity firm — but the fund takes great risk because of the very limited knowledge about the firms and the evolution of the country in case of entry strategy. The specialization within areas model is typically driven by gambling on the development of a country for profit goals, and it is commonly used by government-owned private equity firms operating at international or global levels.

Specialization through an incubator approach is a strategy related to seed and start-up investments. It tries to reduce the trade-off between risk and return, which is dramatically high in seed and start-up stages and is sometimes unsustainable for a profit-oriented investor. An incubator strategy is offered by the private equity firm with an infrastructure (i.e., plants, machinery, real estate, technology, etc.) and knowledge about developing ideas and research projects that a single entrepreneur/inventor would not be able to manage without strong enhancement and support. That means the private equity firm reduces the costs for the new ventures and has a stronger control on the results and on the potential return. The infrastructure (the incubator) is an investment for the fund, but it is has positive results and a more sustainable risk–return profile.

Specialization through an alternative approach is an emerging strategy of investing in alternative businesses. An alternative strategy is not driven simply from a profit goal but from the desire of the private equity firm to develop a "new vision" related to social and mutual goals. For these reasons the target of alternative funds are social services, employment opportunities for underprivileged groups of people, arts, social-health services, social housing, protection of nature, etc. The common rationale of this investment is to take an activity not (or badly) managed from the government and produce both a profit and a social return. This new concept is called "venture philanthropy" and it is sustained by a greater number of investors — mostly high net worth individuals — looking for new frontiers of investment and for a sustainable and socially performing use of money.

Box 19-1 What is venture philanthropy? (EVPA working definition, 2006)

Venture philanthropy is an approach to charitable giving that applies venture capital principles, such as long-term investment and hands-on support, to the social economy. Venture philanthropists work in partnership with a wide range of organizations that have a clear social objective. These organizations may be charities, social enterprises, or socially driven commercial businesses with the precise organizational form subject to country-specific legal and cultural norms. As venture philanthropy spreads globally, specific practices may be adapted to local conditions, yet it maintains a set of widely accepted key characteristics. These include:

1. High engagement — Venture philanthropists have a close hands-on relationship with the social entrepreneurs and ventures they support, driving innovative and scalable models of social change. Some become board members in these organizations, and all are far more intimately involved at strategic and operational levels than traditional non-profit founders.

2. Tailored financing — Similar to venture capital, venture philanthropists take an investment approach to determine the most appropriate financing for each organization. Depending on their own missions and the ventures they choose to support, venture philanthropists operate across the spectrum of investment returns. Some offer non-returnable grants (and thus accept a purely social return), while others use loans and mezzanine or quasi-equity finance (thus blending risk-adjusted financial and social returns).

3. Multi-year support — Venture philanthropists provide substantial and sustained financial support to a limited number of organizations. Support typically lasts at least three to five years, with an objective of helping the organization to become financially self-sustaining by the end of the funding period.

4. Non-financial support — In addition to financial support, venture philanthropists provide value-added services such as strategic planning, marketing and communications, executive coaching, human resource advice, and access to other networks and potential founders.

5. Organizational capacity-building — Venture philanthropists focus on building the operational capacity and long-term viability of the organizations in their portfolios, rather than funding individual projects or programs. They recognize the importance

---

(*Continued*)

of funding core operating costs to help these organizations achieve greater social impact and operational efficiency.

6. Performance measurement — Venture philanthropy investment is performance-based, placing emphasis on good business planning, measurable outcomes, achievement of milestones, and high levels of financial accountability and management competence.

Source: European Venture Philanthropy Association (EVPA)

19.3.4 Managing the value chain of private equity firms

The combination of the three sides of the FOP model generates multiple options and choices to implement strategy for private equity firms. The future and perspectives of private equity and venture capital will be examined in this chapter (i.e., an exam of possible winning and losing strategies for the future), but the focus now is to find how private equity firms can match an efficient business model with the different choices available from focus, positioning, and ownership.

To analyze the spectrum of private equity firms, it is useful to apply the traditional value chain model designed by Michael Porter in 1985 because of the great coherence within the equity investment business. The value chain scheme distinguishes primary activities and support activities inside the organization of a specific firm. The primary activities are essential to produce and deliver the product, whereas the support activities enhance the process empowering through firm infrastructure, human resource management, technology development, and procurement. Both primary and support activities, variously combined together, help create value for the firm and generate the competitive advantage by following a certain coherent strategy.

The same approach can be used to understand the private equity firm and to measure the consistency of the chosen FOP. In this case, the primary activities are identified by the phases of the managerial process, as identified in Chapter 7: fundraising, investing, managing and monitoring, and exiting. Support activities can be identified by tax and legal know-how, network management, industrial know-how, and corporate finance delivery (see Figure 19.1).

Tax and legal know-how is a fundamental competence for deal making to execute transactions and for corporate governance consulting support. Tax and legal moves from a pure add-on and peripheral around the core of equity investment to a relevant skill used to dominate a high-quality delivery process. Network management has a broad significance because there are multiple tools

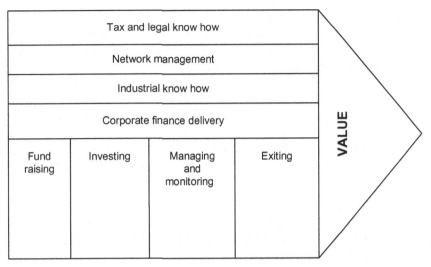

FIGURE 19.1

Value chain of private equity firms.

to manage the links and connections within the economic system. Network management is defined as the ability to interact with potential customers and suppliers of the venture-backed company to gain concrete advantages on the cost and revenue side. Network management also means to be the leader of a certain community (i.e., chemical sector, IT sector, medical sector, etc.), relevant to recruit management, and run investment and drive the proper lobbying activities. Industrial know-how becomes relevant not only to play a leading role within the venture-backed strategy, but also to advise and mentor entrepreneurs to assume the right choices. Furthermore, industrial know-how is crucial to identifying better potential acquirers to manage the exiting phase. Lastly, corporate finance delivery surrounds many private equity deals because both of them involve leverage and merger and acquisition (M&A) techniques to promote acquisitions to expand the venture-backed company.

The use of the value chain must be done as a fundamental assessment of the robustness of the private equity investment company profile and organization to follow a certain strategy and face competition in the market with a sustainable return. For example, bank- and corporate-owned private equity firms benefit from belonging to big groups in terms of strong management of support activities like networking and tax and legal as well as for primary activities like investing and exiting. But while bank-owned private equity firms are quite strong in corporate finance delivery and fundraising arenas, they do not have industrial know-how. This means they cannot follow a hands-on strategy or, if they do, they have to insert reputable managers to fill this gap. Corporate-owned private equity firms, on the other hand, have an advantage in the support activities of network and industrial know-how, but they are quite weak in corporate finance delivery. That means positioning in a finance-intensive deal could be very dangerous if they do not assess a well-suited organizational solution to fill the gap. Private equity firms internationally or globally focused multiply the option to master most (even all) of the primary and support activities by enlarging the potential of competitive advantage. In doing so they face the risk of losing the link with local network and communities if the scale of investment were local and/or small and medium sized.

19.4 PERSPECTIVES AND DESTINY OF PRIVATE EQUITY AND VENTURE CAPITAL

The great success of private equity and venture capital is to be able to change and transform itself to find new and efficient (even creative) solutions to sustain company liabilities. The 2007–2009 financial crisis marks a significant downturn in equity investment (big buyouts, stock exchange, and profit driven) and it launches global brainstorming about the future and new destiny of private equity and venture capital.

The story (and perhaps, the future too) of private equity and venture capital suggests that both strategies and business models are driven by a different combination of the three fundamental tools to create value in equity investment: multiples, leverage, and industrial growth.

Multiples are stock exchange driven and represent the explicit benchmark for entry and exit price for all equity transactions leading to sublime opportunities (1999–2000 and 2005–2006) and to dramatic pitfalls (2001–2002 and 2007–2008). Leverage is the oldest and simplest tool to multiply the value the venture-backed company creates and to place power combined with the certification effect coming from the private equity investor to introduce huge amounts of debt sustainable only at a certain level of interest rate. Industrial growth (i.e., the EBITDA growth) is the core variable of the venture-backed company's value creation, and is the most time-consuming and energy-absorbing activity to be managed and piloted by the managers and the private equity firm. The use and combination of the three variables depends on the cluster of private equity investment. In seed financing and, many times, in start-up EBITDA growth is the key variable to manage because of the impossibility (in the seed case) and the strong constraints (in the start-up case) to raise debt and the very difficult usage of IPO for the exit. In big buyouts both leverage and multiples can be successfully used to create value for the equity investment. However, the combination of the three variables is related to the strategy of private equity firms, their style of management, and investor expectation of IRR. For private equity and venture capital, the lesson learned from the 2007–2009 financial crises is to come back to a strong use of industrial growth because of the great drop in multiples and use of leverage at a very cheap price.

If coming back to fundamentals, coming back to companies, and coming back to an enhanced hands-on approach is a sign for the future, it is relevant to identify and forecast the options private equity firms have to succeed in the economic system as whole. These options can be classified into five groups:

Big buyouts and mega deals — Even though the end of those transactions has been declared definitely, they will come back in the future. The economic turmoil leading to a credit crunch and a strong de-leveraging of many structures and vehicles in which to invest makes it impossible today to deliver big equity tickets to the market. But, very big transactions are a fundamental engine for the economic system when privatization, financing of infrastructure, and financing of large corporations becomes urgent and relevant. In the past big buyouts were used to restructure and acquire big corporations, but they later were mindlessly used for the self-interest of investors. The wise use of private equity will come back when new campaigns of privatization are launched or when infrastructures governments will be unable to finance are financed again by private investors. This new perspective has the same equity ticket size, but the aims and the approach are mostly finance based and hands-off driven. Returns will also be different, and the time horizon of investment will be longer.

Mid-cap transactions — They financially fuel Europe, because of the great number of them in many leading countries. If the temptation (and the explicit strategy many times) for private equity firms in the past was to use the same pattern for big deals to finance mid-cap transactions, it will be necessary to come back to focus on EBITDA growth combined with a cautious and wise use of leverage and multiples when it makes sense in the company's perspective. The needs of mid-cap companies are growing in variety ranging from corporate governance restructuring, developing internationalization, and developing R&D and restructuring. The private equity firms will match a greater number of profiles and apply different formats to solve companies' problems and needs. Private equity firms with an international focus could be a great support if they give and share their international network to sustain international development of venture-backed companies, and they enhance technological transfer for a sustainable R&D process. Private equity firms with a domestic focus will cooperate and integrate their offers with the corporate banking and corporate finance sectors to contribute to venture-backed companies.

Small cap transactions — The financing of SMEs is the unsolved issue in private equity world. Many SMEs really need private equity intervention to grow, but their size makes the equity investment unprofitable. This occurs because the time and costs required for due diligence and the entire process of investment (i.e., scouting, investing, managing and monitoring, exiting) are more or less the same regardless of the company's size but there is a minimum threshold in terms of sales that private equity firms need to reach to break even. Variables relevant to calculate an exit price are lower than for bigger companies, but it is more difficult to find a buyer for SMEs than for bigger companies because of the very specific activity of smaller companies. Consequently, it is not profitable for private equity firms to invest in SMEs, which leaves many small because they cannot afford to grow without equity. The solution to break this very dangerous loop is smart government intervention consisting of a wise participation in joint ventures with private investors in which the government fixes the guidelines and activates controls and the private investors do their job carefully. To make these deals successful, the government must fix the expected performance and there must be an upside for the private investors. This multiplies the return for the private investor and small equity tickets can afford to grow.

Seed and start up — These businesses are risky with very high risk–return profiles combined with a need for tremendous amounts of money to launch research projects in the seed cluster. They avoid private investor finance to keep from losing growth and innovation opportunities. Only medium-long term perspectives, a non-aggressive expectation of return, and a disposal of relevant amounts of money are key variables private equity firms want. Until now, only sovereign funds had those variables because of the very specific nature in which investors and managers are the same and they are funded by the government. But the track record of investment in sovereign funds in Europe is not long enough to clearly judge the outcome. Governmental intervention again and the design of ad hoc rules seem to be the right solutions to enhance private equity firm intervention in these sectors.

Venture philanthropy — These private equity firms decide to use capital investment to satisfy the intermediate needs of social fragility. They also support the idea that different needs require different solutions. Some solutions need (above all the extreme) public operations and/or donations, whereas others (related to the social fragility) require market forms that match the economics to the social interest. It is important to match the specific need to the most adequate instrument. This type of intervention appeals to the so-called gray area of social fragility, part of which is an ever increasing range of population characterized by profound (yet not extreme) hardship. Hardship is defined as needing housing, an occupation, health as well as inter-personal relations specific to work prospects, crises and family problems, loneliness and lack of social contact, and an increasing uncertainty about the future. Not able to qualify for government welfare programs, and similarly unable to access the free market, this segment of population does not meet its needs. Venture philanthropy promotes new and more efficient models of social services to satisfy this new increasing population segment. These models provide market-like solutions and, for this reason, they should be sustained by customer contributions as well, matching social impact with the economic sustainability. The supported social enterprises are positioned in the intermediate market segment, in between public and private, offering good quality products and services at controlled prices. The promotion of these social enterprises needs two main factors: the presence of social entrepreneurs and the availability of private capital. Social entrepreneurs must be able to develop the idea/project and to supervise with efficient criteria the necessary financial resources for its implementation. The availability of private capital, that is "patient" and responsible, or rather the availability of investors who believe in the concept of social responsibility of the wealth and are willing to promote it by putting their capital at the disposal of innovative projects and accepting the concept of simple capital preservation at a high social return is important.

The future we see is not just related to the options players in and out of the market will use to implement private equity useful for the economic system, it is also be based on actions and decisions policy makers take. In the first part of this book it was shown how policy makers intervene differently in many countries and how it was successful for the growth of private equity and venture capital. Today is not the time for spending but for wisdom and the smart use of power and well-written rules. In an environment of regulation, the destiny of private equity and venture capital is related to taxation rules and smart solutions/schemes to sustain the open options previously highlighted. A durable and stable policy of taxation incentive to promote equity raising among SMEs, to sustain

R&D, and to invest abroad are the basic pillars for growth. But it must be combined with a more incisive action that promotes tax transparency (American limited partnerships and small business investment companies) for private equity vehicles subject to their investment in sectors considered relevant/critical for a specific country. A more aggressive policy of incentive for investors could be used to attract off-shore resources (produced in-shore) that could be used for private equity and venture capital to promote development and growth. The quest of efficient joint ventures between public and private partners to balance risk and return will accelerate intervention in small and medium transactions. And last, the challenge in Europe is related to the creation of efficient synergies between non-profit and profit investors to grasp growth options that otherwise will die into a gray area that runs from the universities and research centers to small and potentially very big entrepreneurs.

Glossary

Accrued Interest: Interest due securities or bonds since the last interest payment date.

Acquisition: Process of taking control, possession, or ownership of a company, or a branch or part of it, by an operating company or conglomerate.

Advisory Board: Group of advisors external to a private equity group or company supplying different types of advices, from overall strategy to portfolio valuation.

Allocation: Amount of securities assigned to an investor, broker, or underwriter during the offering process. The value of the allocation, due to the market demand, can be equal to or less than the amount indicated by the investor during the subscription process.

Alternative Assets: Non-traditional asset classes, which include private equity, venture capital, hedge funds, and real estate. Alternative assets usually have a higher risk profile than traditional assets but, at the same time, generate higher returns for investors.

Amortization: Accounting procedure that gradually reduces the book value of an asset periodically charging costs to the income.

Angel Financing: Capital for a private company from independent investors used as seed financing.

Angel Investor: Person (typically successful entrepreneurs often in technology-related industries) who provides backing to early-stage businesses or business concepts.

Anti-dilution Provisions: Contractual agreements that allow investors to maintain a flat share of a firm's equity despite subsequent equity issues. These provisions may give investors pre-emptive rights to purchase new stock at the offering price.

Asset-backed Loan: Typically supplied by a commercial bank, which is covered by asset collaterals, often consisting of guarantees supplied by the entrepreneurial firm or by the entrepreneur.

Asset Management Company (AMC): Financial institution regulated by EU laws (i.e., Financial Services Directive) and devoted to manage funds, both open- and closed-end.

Automatic Conversion: Immediate conversion of an investor's privileged shares to ordinary shares at the moment of a company's underwriting, before an offering of its stock on an exchange.

Average IRR: Arithmetic average of the internal rate of return.

Balance Sheet: Formal financial statement that shows the nature and amount of a company's assets, liabilities, and capital on a given date.

Bankruptcy: When debts incapacitate a company into discontinuing its business.

BATNA (best alternative to a negotiated agreement): No-agreement alternative that indicates the course of action that parties, during a negotiation, will follow if the proposed deal is not possible.

Best Efforts: An offering in which the investment banker agrees to distribute as much of the offering as possible and return back to the issuer any no placed shares.

Board Rights: Allowing an investor to be part of the Board of Directors of a company.

Book Value: Stock value is defined based on the company balance sheet. The calculation consists of adding all current and fixed assets then deducting its debts, other liabilities, and the liquidation price of any preferred share. The result of this calculation is divided by the number of common shares outstanding obtaining the book value per each common share.

Bootstrapping: The activity of financing a small firm by employing highly creative ways of using and acquiring resources without raising equity from traditional sources or borrowing money from banks.

Bridge Financing: Limited amount of equity or short-term debt financing that is usually raised within 6–18 months of an anticipated public offering or private placement. This financing offers a "bridge" to a company until the next round of financing.

Business Judgment Rule: Legal principle that the Board of Directors has to respect during its activity. It consists of acting in the best interests of the shareholders. If the Board ignores this rule, it would be in violation of its fiduciary duties to the shareholders.

Business Plan: A document that explains the entrepreneur's idea and the market issues as well as business and revenue models, marketing strategy, technology, company profile, and the competitive landscape. It also describes future financial data.

CAGR (compound annual growth rate): Year over year growth rate calculated on an investment using a base amount.

Call Option: Owner's right to buy a security at a given price by a specific time period.

Capital (or Assets) Under Management: Amount of capital available to a fund manager to invest.

Capital Call: Approach to investors executed by venture capital firms when it has decided where to invest. The money usually has already been promised to the fund, but the capital call is the formal act of transferring the money.

Capital Gains: Difference between an asset's purchase price and its selling price when the selling price is greater than the purchase price.

Capitalization Table: Recaps the total amount of the different securities issued by a firm; it usually includes the amount of the financial resources raised from each source and the securities distributed.

Capitalize: Booking expenditures as assets rather than expenses.

Captive Funds: Venture capital firm owned by a bigger financial institution.

Carried Interest: Portion of any gains realized by the fund without contribution to capital. Carried interest payments are widespread in the venture capital industry as an important economic incentive for venture capital fund managers.

Cash Position: Amount of cash available to a company at any given moment.

Claw Back: Obligation consisting of a promise made by the general partners that they will not receive a share greater than the fund's distributions. When the partners violate this rule, they have to return excess amount to the fund's limited partners.

Closed-end Fund: Fund whose risk capital includes a fixed number of outstanding shares that are offered during an initial subscription period. After closing the subscription period, the shares are exchanged between investors in a regulated market.

Closing: Investment event occurring after the required legal documents are signed between the parties.

Co-investment: Syndication of a private equity financing operation or an investment realized by individuals next to a private equity fund in a financing round.

Collar Agreement: Consists of conventional adjustments of the number of shares offered during a stock-for-stock exchange to account for price fluctuations before the completion of the deal.

Committed Capital: Total amount of capital committed to a private equity fund.

Committed Funds or Raised Funds: Capital pledged by investors equal to the maximum cash that may be requested or drawn down by the private equity managers. The difference between this amount and the invested funds: most partnerships will initially invest only between 80 and 95% of committed funds, it may be necessary early in the investment to deduct the annual management fee used to cover the operation costs of a fund, and payback to investors usually begins before the final draw down of commitments has taken place.

Common Stock: Security representing the base unit ownership of a company. In a public company, the stock is traded between investors on various public markets. The stocks entitle their owners to vote on the appointment of directors and other important events. Common stock owners receive dividends and an increase of the stock price creating capital gains. Common stocks do not include any performance guarantee and, in the event that a corporation is liquidated, their owners will be satisfied only after the repayment of secured and unsecured debts and of bonds and preferred stock, and only when the financial resources are available.

Company Buyback: Repurchasing company shares by the original owners of the company from the venture capital firm.

Consolidation (leveraged rollup): Investment strategy in which a leveraged buyout firm acquires companies in the same or complementary sectors to become the dominant player in the relative industry.

Conversion Ratio: Number of shares of stock into which a convertible security may be converted.

Convertible Security: Bond, debenture, or preferred stock that can be exchanged with another type of security, usually common stock, at a predefined price.

Corporate Charter: Document outlining when a corporation is founded in order to set objectives and the goals of the corporation; it also includes the complete statement of what the corporation can and cannot do during its activity.

Corporate Resolution: Official document reporting specific decisions taken by the corporation's Board of Directors.

Corporate Venturing: Venture capital provided by in-house investment funds of large corporations to further their own strategic interests.

Corporation: Legal, taxable entity acknowledged by a state law; owners of the corporation are named stockholders or shareholders.

Covenant: Protective clause included in an agreement.

Cumulative Dividends: Accrued at a fixed rate until a predefined moment. Venture-backed companies use cumulative dividends because it allows them to conserve cash when the cash availability of the corporate is increased.

Cumulative Preferred Stock: Stock that contains the provision that if one or more dividend payments are omitted, the omitted dividends must be paid before the company pays dividends to the holders of common stocks.

Deal Flow: Number of potential investments that a fund analyzes during a given period of time.

Depreciation: Expense booked to reduce the value of a tangible or intangible asset; if there is no cash expense, the free cash flow increases but reduces the value of the company income.

Dilution: Reduction in the shareholders' percentage ownership of a company caused by the issuance of new shares.

Dilution Protection: Provision that changes the conversion ratio when there is a stock dividend or extraordinary distribution to avoid the dilution effect; it is usually applied to convertible securities.

Director: Person appointed by shareholders to the Board of Directors. Directors select the president, vice president, and all other operating officers and have authority in the most important decisions regarding the corporate activity.

Disbursement: Investments realized by funds in the companies included in their investment portfolio.

Disclosure Document: Describes the risk factors associated with an investment.

Distressed Debt: Corporate bonds of companies that have declared bankruptcy or will in the near future.

Distribution: Disbursement of realized cash or stock to the limited partners of a venture capital fund at the moment of fund termination.

Diversification: Dividing investments among different types of securities and companies operating in different industries and sectors.

Dividend: Payments defined by the Board of Directors to be distributed among the shares outstanding. If there are preferred shares, it is usually a fixed amount; if there are common shares the dividend depends on the performances and the cash situation of the company and can be omitted in case of bad performance or when the directors determine to withhold earnings to invest in the development of the business.

Down Round: Issuance of shares at a later date and a lower price than previous investment rounds.

Drag-along Rights: Majority shareholder, right that obligate the minority shareholders to sell their shares when the majority wishes to execute the selling of the participation.

Dual Income Taxation (DIT): Taxation mechanism used to enhance equity issuing through a tax rate reduction in proportion to the amount of equity.

Due Diligence: Process executed by potential investors to analyze and valuate the desirability, value, and potential of an investment opportunity.

Early Stage: Life cycle phase of a company that has completed its seed stage and reports minimal revenues with no positive earnings or cash flows.

EBITDA (earnings before interest, taxes, depreciation, and amortization): Measure of cash flow calculated as revenue — expenses without considering tax, interest, depreciation, and amortization. EBITDA indicates the cash flow of a company because the exclusion of interest, taxes, depreciation, and amortization allows the analysis of the amount of money that a company creates.

Economies of Scale: Economic principle that states as the volume of production increases, the unit cost of producing decreases.

Elevator Pitch: Presentation of an entrepreneur's idea, business model, company solution, marketing strategy, and competition delivered to potential investors. This presentation should not take more than a few minutes or the duration of an elevator ride.

Employee Stock Option Plan (ESOP): Plan organized by a company reserving a certain number of shares for purchase and issuance to key employees. Such shares serve as an incentive for employees to build a long-term value for the company.

Employee Stock Ownership Plan: Trust established by a company to purchase stock on behalf of its employees.

Equity Kicker: Option assigned to a private equity company allowing it to purchase shares at a discounted price.

Evergreen Promise: Made by a company that agrees to pay an employee's salary for a number of years the day after he is employed or 10 years after.

Exercise Price: Price at which an option or a warrant can be exercised.

Exit Strategy: Method available to private equity funds to liquidate their investments and achieve the maximum possible return. The method chosen depends on exit climates such as market conditions and industry trends and specific characteristics of the deal and the investor.

Exiting Climates: Conditions that influence the viability and attractiveness of various exit strategies.

Exits: Way in which private equity firms obtain a return on their investment. Private equity returns generally consist of capital gain realized with the sale or flotation of investments. Exit methods include a trade sale, flotation on a stock exchange, a share repurchase by the company or its management or a refinancing of the business, and a secondary purchase of the company to another private equity.

Factoring: Procedure in which a firm can sell its accounts receivable invoices to a factoring firm, which pays a percentage of the invoices immediately, and the remainder (minus a service fee) when the accounts receivable are actually paid off by the firm's customers.

Finder: Person who specializes in arranging transactions.

Flipping: Strategy of buying shares during an IPO and selling them immediately to gain a profit.

Flotation: When a firm's shares start trading on a formal stock exchange its price is subject to flotation as per the dynamics between offer and demand of the market.

Follow-on Funding: Investment realized by a private equity firm that has already invested in a particular company in the past and then provides additional funding at a later stage.

Founders' Shares: Shares owned by company founders.

Free Cash Flow: Cash flow of a company available to service the activity of the firm.

Fully Diluted Earnings Per Share: Earnings per share calculated as if all outstanding convertible securities and warrants have been exercised.

Fully Diluted Outstanding Shares: Number of shares representing the total company ownership including common shares and current conversion, exercised value of preferred shares, options, warrants, and other convertible securities.

Fund Age: Age of a fund (expressed in years) from its first takedown to the time an IRR is calculated.

Fund Focus: Area in which a venture capital fund is specialized.

Fund of Funds: Fund that specializes in distributing its investments among a selection of private equity funds. These types of funds are specialized investors and have existing relationships with firms.

Fund Size: Total amount of capital committed by the investors of a venture capital fund.

GAAP (generally accepted accounting principles): Common group of accounting principles, standards, and procedures accumulated from the combination of standards set by public authorities and accepted accounting standards.

Gatekeeper: Specialists advising institutional investors in their private equity allocation decisions.

GDRs (global depositary receipts): Receipts for shares from a foreign company; these shares are traded in capital markets around the world.

General Partner (GP): Partner in a limited partnership that is responsible for all management decisions of the partnership.

General Partner Contribution: Amount of capital that the fund manager contributes to its own fund similar to a limited partner. This is the way that limited partners choose to ensure that their interests are aligned with those of the general partner.

Golden Handcuffs: Provisions that incentivize employees to stay with a company. One type of golden handcuffs includes employee stock options that are assigned several years after that the employee has worked for the company.

Golden Parachute: Provides employees, usually upper management, a large payout upon the occurrence of certain control transactions such as a certain percentage share purchase by an outside entity or when there is a tender offer for a certain percentage of a company's shares.

Hedge of Hedging: Reducing the fluctuation of the price by taking a position in futures equal and opposite to an existing or anticipated cash position. This practice can also include shorting a security similar to one in which investor has a long position.

Holding Company: Corporation that owns the control of other companies through the participation (usually majority participation) to their risk capital.

Holding Period: Duration of the investment realized by an investor. It begins on the date of the deal closing and ends on the date of exit from the investment.

Hurdle Rate: Internal rate of return that a fund must achieve before its general partners, or managers, can receive an increased interest in the management of the fund. If the expected rate of return of an investment is below the hurdle rate, the investment is not closed.

Incubator: Investor specializing in business concepts or new technology financing and development. An incubator usually provides physical space, legal services, managerial advice, and/or technical needs.

Initial Public Offering (IPO): Process of sale or distribution of a corporate stock to the public for the first time. IPOs are often an opportunity for the existing investors as well as for venture capitalists to realize important economic returns on their original investment.

Institutional Investors: Organizations specializing in professional investments: insurance companies, depository institutions, pension funds, investment companies, mutual funds, and endowment funds.

Intellectual Property: Intangible assets such as patents, copyrights, trademarks, and brand name.

Investment Firm: Financial institution regulated by EU laws (i.e., Banking Directive) and committed to giving money through loans, by investing in equity, and selling payment services. The investment firm cannot collect money from deposits (i.e., like a bank), and it is supervised at different levels.

IRA Rollover: Reinvestment of money received as a lump sum distribution from a retirement plan. Reinvestment may consist of the entire lump sum or a portion.

IRR (internal rate of return): How venture capital funds measure their performance. Technically, an IRR is a discount rate that is the rate at which the present value of a series of investments is equal to the present value of the returns on those investments.

Issue Price: Price per share paid for a series of stocks at the issuing date. This value is used for cumulative dividends, liquidation preference, and conversion ratios.

Issued Shares: Amount of shares that a corporation has sold.

Issuer: Organization issuing or proposing to issue a security.

J-Curve Effect: Represents the returns generated by a private equity fund during the holding period of the investment. Following the usual dynamics of this type of investment, the private equity fund will initially receive a negative return and, when the first liquidations are realized, the fund returns start to rise.

Key Employees: Professional managers hired by the founder to run the company.

Later Stage: Fund investment phase that involves investors in the financing of the expansion of a growing company.

Lead Investor: Member of a pool of private equity investors with the biggest participation in the deal. Usually in charge of the operation and in the management and control of the overall deal.

Leveraged Buyout (LBO): Occurs when an investor acquires the controlling interest in a corporate equity through a complex investment operation financed with a combination of equity and borrowed funds. The acquiring group uses the target company's assets as collateral for the loans subscribed. Repayment of the loans is realized using the cash flow generated by the acquired company.

Limited Partner: Investor participating in a limited partnership without taking part in the management of the partnership. A limited partner has limited liability and, usually, has priority over the general partners during liquidation of the partnership.

Limited Partner Claw Back: Clause usually inserted in private equity partnership agreements that protects the general partner against future claims if he becomes the subject of a lawsuit. A fund's limited partners pay for any legal judgment imposed upon the limited partnership or the general partner.

Limited Partnerships (LPs): Organization established between a general partner, who manages a fund, and limited partners, who invest money but with limited liability and without being involved in the day-to-day management activity of the fund. Usually, the general partner receives a management fee and a percentage of the profits or of the carried interest. The limited partners receive income, capital gains, and tax benefits.

Limited Partnership Agreement (LPA): Agreement, written and signed in a contract, between the limited partners and the general partners to regulate both duties and rights and the private equity activity managed by the general partners.

Liquidation: Activity of converting securities into cash or the sale of the company assets to pay off debts. In a corporation liquidation, investors holding common shares are satisfied only after repayment of the claims raised by secured and unsecured creditors, bonds owners, and preferred shares holders.

Liquidation Preference: In a corporate liquidation it represents the amount per share that a preferred stockholder receives prior to the distribution of the amount per share to holders of common stock. It is usually defined as a multiple of the issue price, and there may be multiple types of liquidation preferences as different groups of investors buy shares in different series.

Liquidity Event: Occurs when venture capitalists realize a gain or loss by exiting their investment. The most common exits are IPOs, buy backs, trade sales, and secondary buyouts.

Lock-up Period: Period of time stockholders agree to waive their right to sell their shares. This clause is used when investment banks underwrite IPOs to ensure their support during market negotiation. Shareholders usually involved in lock-up are management teams, and directors of the company as well as strategic partners and large investors.

Lump Sum: One-time payment of money as opposed to a series of payments made over time.

Management Buyout (MBO): Financing from private equity companies to enable current operating management to acquire or buy the majority of the company they manage.

Management Fee: Compensation paid by the fund to the general partner or the investment advisor based on the management activity of a venture fund.

Management Team: Group of people who manage the activities of a venture capital fund.

Mandatory Redemption: An agreement between the investor and the company financed that gives the investor the right to require the corporation to repurchase some or all of his shares at a defined price and at a certain future time. It can occur automatically or may require a vote of the preferred stockholders with redemption rights.

Market Capitalization: Total value of all outstanding shares. It is computed by multiplying the number of shares by the price per share current in the public market.

Merchant Banking: Focuses on giving advice about financing, merger and acquisition, and equity investments in corporations.

Merger: Combining two or more companies into one larger corporate.

Mezzanine Financing: Corporate financing immediately prior to a company's IPO. Investors taking part in this financing activity have lower risk of loss than the investors who invested in an earlier round.

Mutual Fund (also open-end fund): Allows investors to subscribe as many shares as they require. As money flows in, the fund grows. Open-end funds sometimes exclude new investors but, at the same time, the existing investors continue to increase their investment in the fund. When an investor wants to sell his participation, he usually sells his shares back to the fund

Narrow-Based Weighted Average Ratchet: Prevents the anti-dilution of the participations in a corporation. It reduces the price per share of the preferred stock of investor 1 if the issuance of new preferred shares to investor 2 are priced lower than the price investor 1 originally paid.

NASDAQ: Market provides participating brokers and dealers with price quotations on securities traded over the counter by the automatic process of information management.

NAV (net asset value): Value of all investments in the fund divided by the number of outstanding shares of the fund.

NDA (non-disclosure agreement): Agreement signed by two or more parties to protect the privacy of their activities and ideas when disclosing them to each other.

Net Financing Cost (also cost of carry): Difference between the cost of financing the purchase of an asset and the asset's cash yield. With positive net financing cost the yield earned is greater than the financing cost; negative carry happens when the financing cost exceeds the yield earned.

Net Income: Net earnings of a corporation after deducting all costs faced by the company during the execution of its business such as production costs, employees' salaries, depreciation, interest expense, and taxes.

Net Present Value (NPV): Method of valuation that uses the actual value of future cash inflows subtracting future cash outflows.

New Issue: Stock or bond that is offered to the public for the first time.

NewCo: Newly organized company used in LBOs.

Non-Compete Clause: Agreement signed by employees and management that states they will not work for competitors or establish a new competitor company for a defined period of time after termination of employment.

NYSE (New York Stock Exchange): Founded in 1792, it is the largest organized public securities market in the United States.

Open-end Fund (also mutual fund): Allows investors to subscribe as many shares as they require. As money flows in, the fund grows. Open-end funds can exclude new investors but, at the same time, the existing investors can continue to raise their investment in the fund. When an investor wants to sell his participation, he usually sells his shares back to the fund.

Original Issue Discount (OID): Bond or debt-like instrument discounted from the par value. This tool generates unfavorable tax effects because the IRS considers this cash flow as a zero coupon bond upon which tax payments are due annually.

OTC (over-the-counter): Securities market in which dealers who may or may not be members of a formal securities exchange operate. The over-the-counter market is conducted through telephone contacts.

Outstanding Stock: Amount of shares of a company owned by the investors equal to the amount of issued shares deducted by treasury stock.

Over-subscription: During a public offering of shares, this happens when the demand for shares exceeds the offer. In private equity deals, this occurs when a deal has a great demand due to the company's growth opportunities.

Over-subscription Privilege: Occurs when shareholders have the right to subscribe any shares that have not been purchased.

Paid-in Capital (also cumulative takedown amount): Committed capital transferred by a partner to a venture fund.

Participating Preferred: Occurs when a preferred stock entitles the holder to the stated dividend and to additional dividends on a specified basis over the payment of dividends to the common shareholders. Preferred stock gives the owner the right to receive a predefined sum of cash, which is usually the original investment plus accrued dividends, if the company is sold or the subject of an IPO.

Participation: Sharing rights and duties of ownership of company securities with other investors.

Partnership: Legal entity in which each partner shares the profits, losses, and liabilities. Each member is responsible for the applicable taxes to its share of profits and losses.

Partnership Agreement: Contract agreed and signed between investors and a private equity company for the duration of the private equity investment.

Pay to Play: An existing investor's right to participate in the next investment stage.

PIV (pooled investment vehicle): Legal entity that collects different investor capital and manages it following a specific investment strategy.

Placement Agent: Company specializing in locating investors that want to invest in a private equity fund or company securities. Using a placement agent allows the fund partners to focus on management activities.

Poison Pill: Allows an owner to purchase shares in his company at a discounted price. This security is issued to make external takeover difficult.

Pooled IRR: Calculated as an aggregate of different IRRs based on a pool of cash flows.

Portfolio Companies: Firms included in the investment portfolio of a private equity fund.

Post-Money Valuation: Valuation of a company realized just after a round of financing.

Pre-Money Valuation: Valuation of a company realized before a phase of the investment. This amount is defined by using different valuation models.

Pre-emptive Right: Allows a shareholder to acquire an amount of shares in a future offering at current prices to maintain her percentage of ownership at the same level before the offering.

Preference Shares: Shares of a firm that assigns the owner special rights over ordinary shares, such as the first right to receive dividends and/or capital payments.

Preferred Dividend: Dividend paid to the owners of preferred shares.

Preferred Return: Minimum return that has to be realized before a carry is permitted. A hurdle rate of 15% means that the private equity fund must achieve a return of at least 15% per annum before it can share the profits realized.

Preferred Stock: Class of preferred shares. These securities can pay dividends at a specified rate and have priority in the payment of dividends and the liquidation of assets. Usually, venture capitalists invest in companies through preferred stock.

Private Equity: Equity shares of companies that are not listed on a public exchange. Exchange of the participation in private equity is realized between buyers and sellers outside of the marketplace.

Private Investment in Public Equities (PIPES): Investment realized in a public company by a private equity fund.

Private Placement: Sale of a security directly to a limited number of investors.

Private Placement Memorandum (also offering memorandum): Official document explaining the terms and characteristics of securities offered through private placement.

Private Securities: Not traded on a public exchange market and their price is fixed through negotiations realized between seller or issuer and buyer.

Prospectus: Written document containing information needed by an investor to make an informed decision. A prospectus must report any material risks and information according to the relevant laws and rules defined by regulatory agencies or authorities.

Put Option: Gives its owner the right to sell a security at a predefined price during a certain period of time.

Re-capitalization: Reorganization of the risk capital of a corporation to improve the total value of the capital. It can be an exit strategy for private equity investors.

Redemption: Right or obligation that pushes the company into repurchasing its own shares.

Reorganization: Consists of critical changes in the equity structure of a company; for example, all shares converted to common stock or reducing the number of shares.

Right of First Refusal: The owner has the right to refuse the closing of a proposed contract.

Rights Offering: Offering the right to purchase additional shares, usually at a discount price, to existing shareholders. These rights can be transferable so the owner can monetize their value on the trade market.

Risk: Possibility of suffering losses on an investment; the sources of risk include inflation, default, politics, etc.

Secondary Funds: Used to purchase investment portfolios from other private equity funds providing liquidity to the original investors.

Secondary Market: Market where participations are traded to private equity funds.

Secondary Sale: Selling participations held by private equity funds to other investors.

Securities and Exchange Commission (SEC): Independent, non-partisan, US market agency responsible for protecting investors; maintaining fair, orderly, and efficient markets; and facilitating capital information. The SEC checks up on participants in the securities market and it is concerned primarily with promoting the disclosure of important market-related information, maintaining fair dealing, and protecting against fraud.

Seed Money: First capital investment in a start-up company. It is usually realized through loan or preferred stocks or convertible bonds or common stocks. Investors providing seed money are Angel Investors and early stage venture capital funds.

Seed Stage Financing: Funding the initial state of a company's growth. (See also Seed Money.)

Senior Securities: Preferred stocks and bonds that entitle their owner with preferential claim over other investors on a firm's earnings and also during liquidation or bankruptcy.

Shell Corporation (also specified purpose acquisition companies; SPACs): A corporation without any assets or business. It is usually organized to go public and then acquire existing businesses.

Small Business Investment Company (SBIC): Special vehicle used to invest in private equity and regulated by a special US law (Small Business Investment Act, 1958). SBIC is a perfect joint venture between private and public investors with fiscal advantages.

Special Purpose Vehicle (SPV): Special corporation founded by a company to realize special financial deals; for example, LBO or M&A operations.

Spin Out: Company established by becoming independent of an already existing division or subsidiary of a firm. Private equity investors finance this activity by providing the necessary corporate financial funds.

Statutory Voting: Process of selecting members of the Board of Directors that gives shareholders one vote per each share owned and the ability to cast these votes for each of the candidates.

Stock Options: Owner ability to purchase or sell, at a defined price, the underlying securities during a pre-fixed period of time. It is also used as incentive for employees and managers.

Strategic Investors: Investors that add value to the deals they realize due to industry and personal skills and services that assist companies in raising additional capital. They also support the business activity of the company in which they have invested.

Subscription Agreement: Investor request to join a limited partnership that has to be approved by the general partner.

Sweat Equity: Ownership of shares in a company that is assigned in front of supplying work rather than investment of capital.

Syndicate: Group of underwriters, brokers, or dealers selling securities.

Syndication: Group of investors that offers funds for a particular deal; led by a lead investor who coordinates the deal and represents the group's members.

Tag-along Rights/Co-sale Rights: Protection for minority shareholders that gives them the right to include their participation in any sale of the controlling shares at the same price offered to majority shareholders.

Takedown Schedule: Plan, in terms of timing and size, of the contributions in the risk capital that has been agreed upon by the limited partners of a venture fund.

Tender Offer: Offer made to the shareholders to purchase their shares.

Term Sheet: List of terms that investors have to accept when taking part in an investment.

Thin Capitalization (Thin Cap): Taxation mechanism that creates incentive to reduce the use of leverage through the reduction of deductible interest rate costs in proportion to the leverage.

Time Value of Money: Economic principle that assumes a different value of money during different times, looking both forward and backward.

Trade Sale: Sale of the participation in risk capital of a firm to another company.

Venture Capital Trust (VCT): Special vehicle used to invest in private equity and regulated by a special British law (Venture Capital Trust Act, 1997). The VCT is a vehicle listed on the London Stock Exchange where the investors are mostly retail.

Voluntary Redemption: Allows a company to repurchase a part or all of the investor's shares at a predefined time. The purchase price is the issue price plus cumulative dividends.

Voting Right: Assigned to stockholders allowing them to vote on company affairs.

Warrant: Security entitling the holder to buy an amount of common stock or preferred stock at a defined price for a period of time. Warrants are usually linked to a loan, bond, or preferred stock.

Write-off: Used to reduce or cancel the value of an asset. It reduces profits by changing the value of an asset to expense or loss.

Yield: Expressed as percentage calculated by dividing the gross dividend by the share price. It represents the annual return on an investment from interest and dividends, excluding capital gains.

References

Abbot, S., & Hay, M. (1995). *Investing for the future*. London: FT Pitman Publishing.

Achleitner, A.-K., & Kloeckner, O. (2005). Employment contribution of private equity and venture capital in Europe, EVCA Research Paper.

Aghion, P., & Bolton, P. (1992). An incomplete contract approach to financial contracting. *The Journal of Finance, 1*.

AIFI. - Associazione Italiana degli Investitori Istituzionali nel Capitale di Rischio. (2000). Guide to Venture Capital, Milan.

AIFI. - Associazione Italiana degli Investitori Istituzionali nel Capitale di Rischio (various years). Development capital. Guerini & Associati, Milan.

AIFI. - Associazione Italiana degli Investitori Istituzionali nel Capitale di Rischio (various years). The Italian venture capital and private equity market. Periodic reports, Milan.

Altman, E. I., & Hotchkiss, E. (2005). *Corporate Financial Distress and Bankruptcy*. John Wiley and Sons.

Anonymous. (1983). SBIC's after 25 years: Pioneers and builders of organized venture capital, October. *Venture Capital Journal*.

Anonymous. (2001). Financial snapshot for May 2001: Stocks starts to blossom, September (www.signalsmag.com). *Signalsmag, 5*.

Arnott, R., & Stiglitz, J. (1991). Moral hazard and nonmarket institutions: Dysfunctional crowding out or peer monitoring?. *The American Economic Review, 81*(1), 179–190.

Assogestioni. (1999). Mutual investment trusts. Data and statistical guide, Milan.

Axelson, U., Jenkinson, T., Strömberg, P., & Weisbach, M. S. (2008). Leverage and pricing in buyouts: An empirical analysis. Working paper, SIFR.

Bank of England. (1999). Practical issues arising from the Euro. June, London.

Bank of England. (2000). Finance for small firms: a seventh report. London.

Bank of Italy. (1999). Guidelines for banking supervision — Circolare n. 229 - 21.4.99.

Bank of Italy. (from 2000, various years). Annual Report, Rome.

Bank of Italy. (from 2000, various years). Statistical Bulletin, Rome.

Barney, J. B., Busenitz, L. W., Fiet, J. O., & Mosel, D. D. (2001). New venture teams' assessment of learning assistance from venture capital firms. *Journal of Business Venturing, 18.*

Barry, C. B., Muscarella, C. J., Peavy, J. W., III., & Vetsuypens, M. R. (1990). The role of venture capital in the creation of public companies. *Journal of Financial Economics, 27.*

Bascha, A., & Walz, U. (2001). Convertible securities and optimal exit decisions in venture capital finance. *Journal of Corporate Finance, 7,* 285–306.

Bassi, I., & Grant, J. (2006). *Structuring European Private Equity.* London: Euromoney Books.

Beatty, R. P., & Ritter, J. R. (1986). Investment banking, reputation, and the underpricing of initial public offerings. *Journal of Financial Economics, 15.*

Benjamin, G. A., & Margulis, J. B. (2005). *Angel capital: How to raise early-stage private equity financing.* John Wiley and Sons.

Benveniste, L. M., Erdal, S. M., & Wilhelm, W. J. (1998). Who benefits from secondary price stabilization of IPOs? *Journal of Banking and Finance, 22.*

Berger, A. N., & Hannan, T. H. (1997). Using measures of firm efficiency to distinguish among alternative explanations of structure-performance relationship. *Managerial Finance, 23.*

Berger, A. N., & Udell, G. F. (1998). The economics of small business finance: the roles of private equity and debt markets in the financial growth cycle. *Journal of Banking and Finance, 22.*

Berglöf, E. (1994). A control theory of venture capital finance. *Journal of Law, Economics, and Organization, 10,* 247–267.

Bester, H. (1987). The role of collateral in credit markets with imperfect information. *European Economic Review, 83.*

Bhave, M. P. (1999). A process model of entrepreneurial venture creation. *Journal of Business Venturing, 9.*

Bhidè, A. (1999). Developing start-up strategies. In W. Sahlman, H. H. Stevenson, M. Robberts, & A. Bhidè (Eds.), *The entrepreneurial venture.* Boston: Harvard Business School Press.

Billingsley, S. (1996). *Merck & company: A comprehensive equity valuation analysis.* Working Paper. Charlottesville, VA: AIMR.

Black, B. S., & Gilson, R. J. (1998). Venture capital and the structure of capital markets: Banks versus stock markets. *Journal of Financial Economics, 47,* 243–277.

Block, Z., & MacMillan, I. (1993). *Corporate venturing.* Boston: Harvard Business School Press.

Bond & Pecaro Inc. (2000). Cyber Valuation, Internet Business Trends, Analysis and Valuation, New York.

Brav, A., & Gompers, P. A. (2003). The role of lock-ups in initial public offerings. *Review of Financial Studies, 16,* 1–29.

Brealey, R. A., & Myers, S. C. (2000). *Principles of corporate finance.* New York: McGraw-Hill.

Bruyat, C., & Julien, P. A. (2000). Defining the field of research in entrepreneurship. *Journal of Business Venturing, 14.*

BVCA. (1996). Guide to venture capital.

Bygrave, W. D. (1999). The venture capital handbook.

Bygrave, W. D., & Timmons, J. A. (1992). *Venture capital at the crossroad.* Boston: Harvard Business school Press.

Cairns, J. C., Davidson, J. A., & Kisicevitz, M. L. (2002). The limits of bank convergence. *The McKinsey Quarterly Journal, 2.*

Campioni, E., & Attar, A. (2003). Costly state verification and debt contracts: A critical resume. *Research in Economics, 57.*

Canals, J. (1997). *Universal banking. International comparison and theoretical perspectives.* Oxford: Clarendon Press.

Casamatta, C. (2003). Financing and advising: Optimal financial contracts with venture capitalists. *Journal of Finance, 58*(5).

Caselli, S. (2005). The competitive models of corporate banking and the relationship towards SMEs. *Small Business, 1.*

Caselli, S. (2006). Dependent or independent? The performance contribution of board members in Italian venture-backed firms. *Journal of Corporate Ownership & Control, 4*(3).

Caselli, S., & Gatti, S. (2005). *Structured finance. Techniques, products and market.* Berlin, London: Springer-Verlag.

Caselli, S., & Gatti, S. (2006). Long-run venture-backed IPO performance analysis of Italian family-owned firms: What role do closed-end funds play? In G. N. Gregoriou, M. Kooli, & M. Kraussl (Eds.), *Venture capital: A European perspective*. Elsevier.

Caselli, S., Gatti, S., & Perrini, F. (2009). Are venture capitalist a catalysts for innovation or do they simply exploit it? *European Financial Management Journal, 1*.

Caselli, S., & Gatti, S. (2004). *Venture capital. A euro-system approach*. Berlin, London: Springer-Verlag.

Chapman, S. (1992). *The Rise of Merchant Banking*. Happshire, London: Gregg Revivals.

Chevalier, J., & Ellison, G. (1995). Risk taking by mutual funds as a response to incentives, Working paper Chicago, IL: University of Chicago; Cambridge, MA: Massachusetts Institute of Technology.

Christiansen, C. M. (1991). *The innovator's dilemma*. Boston: Harvard Business School Press.

Christofidis, C., & Debande, O. (2001). Financing innovative firms through venture capital. European Investment Bank Sector Paper.

Cochrane, J. H. (2005). The risk and return of venture capital. *Journal of Financial Economics, 75*(1).

Coopers & Lybrand. (1999). Corporate Finance.

Copeland, T., Koller, T., & Murrin, J. (2000). *Valuation — measuring and managing the value of companies*. New York: Wiley.

Credit Suisse First Boston. (2001). European technology — a game of two halves. Internal report, January, London.

Cressy, R., Malipiero, A., & Munari, F. (2007). Playing to their strengths? Evidence that specialization in the private equity industry confers competitive advantage. *Journal of Corporate Finance, 13*.

Csikszentmihalyi, M. (1991). *Creativity: Flow and the psychology of discovery and invention*. New York: HarperCollins.

Cumming, D. (2008). Contracts and exits in venture capital finance. *Review of Financial Studies, 21*(5), 1947–1982.

Cumming, D., Siegel, D., & Wright, M. (2007). Private equity, leveraged buyouts and governance. *Journal of Corporate Finance, 13*.

Cumming, D. (2002). Contracts and exits in venture capital finance. University of Alberta School of Business working paper.

Cumming, D. (2004). The determinants of venture capital portfolio size: Empirical evidence. *Journal of Business, 35*.

Cumming, D., & Walz, U. (2004). Private equity returns and disclosure around the world, Mimeo Available at SSRN: http://ssrn.com/abstract=514105.

Damodaran, A. (1994). *On valuation — security analysis for investment and corporate finance*. New York: Wiley.

Damodaran, A. (1999). *Applied corporate finance — a user's manual*. New York: Wiley.

Damodaran, A. (2000). *Investment valuation: Tools and techniques for determining the value of any asset*. New York: Wiley.

Damodaran, A. (2000). *The dark side of valuation: Firms with no earnings, no history and no comparables*. Working Paper. New York: Stern School of Business.

Degeorge, F., & Zeckhauser, R. (1993). The reverse LBO decision and firm performances, theory and evidence. *Journal of Finance* (48).

Demiroglu, C., & James, C. (2008). Lender control and the role of private equity group reputation in buyout financing, Working Paper.

Desmet, D., Francis, T., Hu, A., Koller, T., & Riedel, G. (2000). Valuing dot coms. Spring. *McKinsey Quarterly, 1*.

Diamond, D. (1989). Reputation acquisition in debt markets. *Journal of Political Economy, 97*.

DRI-WEFA, NVCA. (2001). Economic Impact of venture capital. Washington DC, October.

Drucker, P. F. (1989). *The practice of management*. London: Heinemann Business Paperbacks.

Eiglier, P., & Langeard, E. (1991). *Servuction. Le marketing des services*. Paris: McGraw-Hill.

Engel, D., & Keilbach, M. (2005). Firm level implications of early stage venture capital investments. An empirical investigation. ZEW Discussion paper 22-05.

Ernst & Young. (2000). Convergence. The Biotechnology Industry Report. Millennium Edition, New York.

Ernst & Young. (2007). *Guide to Financing for Growth*. John Wiley & Sons.

European Commission. (2002). Enterprises in Europe. 8th Report, Bruxelles.

European Information Technology Observatory. (2000). The Millennium Edition.

EVCA – Coopers & Lybrand. (1997). The economic impact of venture capital in Europe. Zaventem.

EVCA – Coopers & Lybrand Corporate Finance. (1996). The economic impact of venture capital in Europe. September.

EVCA – European Venture Capital Association. (various issues). Yearbook.

EVCA. (1999). *Private equity fund structures in europe*. Zaventem: Internal publication.

EVCA. (2001). EVCA Mid Year Survey of Pan-European private equity and venture capital. Press release, Helsinki, 17th October.

EVCA. (2001). Guide Lines. www.evca.com, March.

EVCA. (2005). Employment contribution of private equity and venture capital in Europe.

EVCA. (2008). Annual Survey of Pan-European Private Equity & Venture Capital Activity 2007, EVCA Yearbook.

EVCA. (2008). Pan-European Private Equity & Venture Capital Activity Report, EVCA Yearbook 2008, Bruxelles.

Fama, E. F. (1991). Efficient capital markets. *Journal of Finance, 46*.

Fama, E. F. (1980). Agency problems and the theory of the firm. *The Journal of Political Economy, 88*.

Fama, E. F., & Jensen, M. C. (1983). Separation of ownership and control. *Journal of Law and Economics, 26*.

Fenn, G. W., Liang, N., & Prowse, S. (1995). The economics of private equity market. Board of Governors of the Federal Reserve System Staff Studies, 168.

Financial Times. (1999). The venture capital handbook. London.

Foster, R., & Kaplan, S. (2001). *Creative destruction: Why companies are built to last underperform the market and how to successfully transform them*. New York: Currency/Doubleday.

Fried, V. H., & Hisrich, R. D. (1994). Toward a model of venture capital investment decision making. *Financial Management, 23*.

Fruhan, W. E. (1979). *Financial strategy — Studies in the creation, transfer and destruction of shareholder value.* Homewood: Irwin.

Gardella, L. A. (2000). *Selecting and structuring investments: The venture capitalist's perspective.* Charlottesville, VA: Reading in Venture Capital, Association for Investment Management and Research (AIMR).

Gartner, W. B., Starr, J. A., & Bhat, S. (2000). Predicting new venture survival: An analysis of anatomy of a start-up cases from Inc. Magazine. *Journal of Business Venturing, 14.*

Geisst, R. C. (1995). *Investment banking in the financial system.* Prentice Hall, London: Englewood Cliffs.

German Association of Biotechnology Industries. (1998). Valuation of Biotech Companies, Berlin.

Gervasoni, A., & Sattin, F. L. (2000). *Private equity and venture capital.* Guerrini e Associati.

Gilder, G. (2000). *Telecosm.* New York: The Free Press.

Goldsmith, R. W. (1969). *Financial structure and development.* New Haven: Yale University Press.

Gompers, P. A. (1995). Optimal investment, monitoring and the staging of venture capital. *The Journal of Finance, 50.*

Gompers, P. A., & Lerner, J. (1996). The use of covenants: An empirical analysis of venture partnership agreements. *Journal of Law and Economics, 39.*

Gompers, P. A., & Lerner, J. (1998). What drives venture fundraising? Brookings Papers on Economic Activity: Microeconomics, July.

Gompers, P. A., & Lerner, J. (1999). What drives venture capital fundraising? W.P. 6906, NBER Series, Cambridge, MA.

Gompers, P. A., & Lerner, J. (2000). *The venture capital circle.* MIT Press.

Gompers, P. (1996). Grandstanding in the venture capital industry. *Journal of Financial Economics, 42.*

Gompers, P., & Lerner, J. (1996). The use of covenants: An empirical analysis of venture partnership agreements. *Journal of Law and Economics, 39.*

Gordon Smith, D. (2005). Control and exit in venture capital relationships. Law and Economics workshop – University of California at Berkeley.

Gorman, M., & Sahlman, W. A. (1989). What do venture capitalist do? *Journal of Business Venturing, 4*.

Grabenwarter, U., & Weidig, T. (2005). *Exposed to the J-curve, understanding and managing private equity fund investments*. Euromoney Books.

Harvey, C., Lerner, J., Schoar, A., Fung, B., & Irwin, S. (Eds.), (2008). *Encyclopedia of alternative investment*. London, UK: Chapman Hall.

Groh, A., & Gottschalg, O. (2006). The risk-adjusted performance of US buyouts. Working Paper.

Gupta, A. K., & Sapienza, H. J. (1992). Determinants of venture capital firms' preferences regarding the industry diversity and geographic scope of their investments. *Journal of Business venturing, 7*.

Hackbarth, D., Hennessy, C., & Leland, H. (2007). Can the trade off theory explain debt structure? *Review of Financial Studies, 20*.

Hambrick, D., & Schecter, S. (1983). Turnaround strategies for mature industrial-product business units. *Academy of Management Journal, 26*, 231–248.

Hamel, G. (2000). *Leading the revolution*. Boston: Harvard Business School Press.

Hannan, T. H. (1991). Bank commercial loan markets and the role of market structure: evidence from surveys of commercial lending. *Journal of Banking and Finance, 15*.

Harris, M., & Raviv, A. (1991). The theory of capital structure. *Journal of Finance, 46*(1), 297–355.

Haspeslagh, P. C., & Jemison, D. B. (1991). *Managing acquisition. Creating value trough corporate renewal*. The Free Press.

Hayes, S., & Hubbard, P. (1990). *Investment banking*. Boston: Harvard Business School Press.

Heifetz, R. (1994). *Leadership without easy answers*. Cambridge, Massachusetts: Belknap Press.

Hellmann, T., & Puri, M. (1999). The interaction between product marketing and financing strategy: The role of venture capital. Research Paper 1561, Research Paper Series, Stanford University, May, Stanford.

Hellmann, T., & Puri, M. (2000). Venture capital and the professionalization of start-up firms: Empirical evidence. Research Paper 1661, Research Paper Series, Stanford University, Stanford.

Hellmann, T. (2006). IPOs, acquisitions, and the use of convertible securities in venture capital. *Journal of Financial Economics, 81,* 649–679.

Hellmann, T. F., Lindsey, L., & Puri, M. (2007). Building relationships early: Banks in venture capital. Sauder School of Business Working Paper.

Hellwig, M. (1991). Banking financial intermediation and corporate finance. In A. Giovannini & C. Mayer (Eds.), *European financial integration.* Cambridge, UK: Cambridge University Press.

Holthausen, R. W., & Larcker, D. (1996). The financial performance of reverse leveraged buyouts. *Journal of Financial Economics, 42*(3), 293–332.

Hunt, D. (1995). What future for Europe's investment banks? *Mc-Kinsey Quarterly Review, 1.*

Ibbotson, R. G., & Ritter, J. R. (1995). Initial public offerings. In R. Jarrow, V. Maksimovic, W. Ziemba (Eds.), *Handbooks of operations research and management science: Vol. 9: Finance* (pp. 993–1016).

Inderst, R., & Mueller, H. (2004). The effect of capital market characteristics on the value of start-up firms. *Journal of Financial Economics, 72.*

Jain, B., & Kini, O. (1995). Venture capitalist participation and the post-issue operating performance of IPO firms. *Managerial and Decision Economics, 5.*

Jeng, L., & Wells, P. (2000). The determinants of venture capital funding: evidence across countries. *Journal of Corporate Finance, 6.*

Jensen, M. C. (1986). Agency costs of free cash flow, corporate finance, and takeovers. *American Economic Review, 76.*

Jensen, M. C., & Meckling, W. H. (1976). Theory of the firm: Managerial behavior, agency costs and ownership structure. *Journal of Financial Economics, 3.*

Kanniainen, V., & Keuschingg, C. (2004). Start-up investment with scarce venture capital support. *Journal of Banking and Finance, 28.*

Kaplan, S., & Strömberg, P. (2000). How do venture capitalists choose and manage their investments? Working Paper, University of Chicago.

Kaplan, S. (1989). The effects of management buyouts on operating performance and value. *Journal of Financial Economics, 24*(2), 217–254.

Kaplan, S. (1989). Campeau's acquisition of federated — value destroyed or value added. *Journal of Financial Economics, 25*(2), 191–212.

Kaplan, S., & Schoar, A. (2005). Private equity performance: Returns, persistence and capital flows. *Journal of Finance, 60*(4), 1791–1823.

Kaplan, S. N., & Strömberg, P. (2002). Financial contracting theory meets the real world: An empirical analysis of venture capital contracts. *Review of Economic Studies, 70*(2), 281–315.

Kaplan, S. N., & Strömberg, P. (2004). Characteristics, contracts, and actions: Evidence from venture capitalist analyses. *Journal of Finance, 59*(5), 2173–2206.

Keeton, W. R. (1996). Do banks mergers reduce lending to business and farmers? New evidence from tenth district states. Federal Reserve Bank of Kansas City. *Economic Review, 81*.

Kellogg, D., & Charnes, J. M. (2000). Real options valuation for a biotechnology company. *Financial Analysts Journal, 3*.

Koller, T. (2001). Valuing dot coms after the fall. *McKinsey Quarterly, 2*.

Kortum, S., & Lerner, J. (1998). Does venture capital spur innovation? NBER Working Paper, December.

Kraus, A., & Litzenberger, R. H. (1973). A state-preference model of optimal financial leverage. *Journal of Finance, 28*.

Kuhn, R. L. (1990). *Investment banking, the art and science of high-stakes deal making*. New York: Harper & Row.

Leithner & Co. PTY. (1999). The internet and value investing. Internal report, Brisbane.

Lerner, J. (1994). The syndication of venture capital investments. Autumn. *Financial Management, 23*(3).

Lerner, J. (1995). Venture capitalists and the oversight of private firms. *Journal of Finance, 50*.

Lerner, J. (2000). *Private equity and venture capital — a casebook*. New York: Wiley.

Lerner, J. (1999). The government as a venture capitalist: The long-run effects of the SBIR program. *Journal of Business, 72*(3), 285–297.

Lerner, J., Schoar, A., & Wong, W. (2005). Smart Institutions, Foolish Choices? The limited partner performance puzzle, MIT Sloan Research Paper, No. 4523-05.

Levin, J. S. (1994). *Structuring venture capital, private equity and entrepreneurial transaction*. Chicago, IL: CCH Inc.

Lewis, M. (1999). *The new thing*. New York: Norton & Company.

Liaw, K. T. (1999). *The business of investment banking*. New York: John Wiley & Sons.

Ljungqvist, A., & Richardson, M. (2003a). The cash flow, return and risk characteristics of private equity. NYU, Finance Working Paper (No. 03-001).

Ljungqvist, A., & Richardson, M. (2003b). The investment behavior of private equity fund managers, NYU Stern Working Paper.

Llewellyn, D. T. (1992). Financial Innovation: A basic analysis. In H. Cavanna (Ed.), *Financial innovation*. London: Routledge.

Llewellyn, D. T. (1999). *The new economics of banking*. Amsterdam: Société Universitaire Européenne de Recherches Financières.

London Stock Exchange. (1999). TECHMARK, The technology market. London.

Lorenz, T. (1985). *Venture capital today*. Cambridge: Woodhead- Faulkner.

MacMillan, I. C., Kulow, D. M., & Khoylian, R. (1988). Venture capitalists' involvement in their investments: Extent and performance. *Journal of Business Venturing, 4*.

MacMillan, I. C., Siegel, R., & Subbanarasimha, P. N. S. (1985). Criteria used by venture capitalists to evaluate new venture proposals. *Journal of Business Venturing, 1*.

Manigart, S., Vanacker, T., & Baeyens, K. (2005). Venture capitalists' selection process: the case of biotechnology proposals. Vlerick Leuven Gent Management School working paper n. 17.

Marti, J., & Balboa, M. (2003). An integrative approach to the determinants of private equity fundraising. University of Madrid working paper.

Mason, C. M., & Harrison, R. T. (2000). The size of the informal venture capital market in the United Kingdom. September. *Small Business Economics, 15*.

Mauboussin, M. J., & Hiler, B. (1999). Cash Flow.com — Cash Economics in the New Economy. Credit Suisse First Boston Corporation, Internal Report, March, New York.

Mauboussin, M. J., Regan, M. T., Schay, A., & Fisher, A. M. (2000). Wanna Be GE? Credit Suisse First Boston Corporation, Internal Report, February, New York.

McBride, A. S., & McBride, R. G. (2001). The vital role of investor relations. Strategic Investor Relations, www.iijournals.com, Summer.

Mccue, J. (2000). Telecommunications and the New Economy. Lucent Client Success and Partner Conference, Doral, 30th October–2nd November, Florida.

McNamee, M. (2001). America's future — Investment Plays 27th August. *Business Week*.

Megginson, W. L., & Weiss, K. A. (1991). Venture capitalist certification in initial public offerings. *The Journal of Finance, 46*(3).

Meyers, S. C., & Miluf, N. S. (1984). Corporate financing and investment decisions when firms have information investors do not have. *Journal of Financial Economics, 13*.

Michaelson, J. C. (2002). *Restructuring for growth: alternative financial strategies to increase shareholder value*. McGraw-Hill Professional.

Millan, I. C., & Zeman, L. (1987). Criteria distinguishing successful ventures in the venture screening process. *Journal of Business Venturing, 2*.

Miller, M., & Modigliani, F. (1963). Corporate income taxes and the cost of capital: A correction. *American Economic Review, 3*.

Modigliani, F., & Miller, M. (1958). The cost of capital, corporate finance, and the theory of investment. *American Economic Review, 3*.

MSDW. (1999). Entrepreneur Workshop — Exit Strategies. www.ms.com, Proceeding of the Conference, 31 May, London.

Murray, G., & Marriott, R. (1998). Why has the investment performance of technology-specialist European venture capital funds been so poor? *Research Policy, 27*.

Myers, S. C., & Howe, C. D. (1997). A life cycle financial model of pharmaceutical R&D. Working Paper POPI 41-97, MIT Sloan School of Management.

Myers, S. (1984). The capital structure puzzle. *Journal of Finance, 39*.

Myers, S., & Majluf, N. (1984). Corporate financing and investment decisions when firms have information that investors do not have. *Journal of Financial Economics, 13*.

Nikoskelainen, E., & Wright, M. (2007). The impact of corporate governance mechanisms on value increase in leveraged buyouts. *Journal of Corporate Finance, 13*, 511-537.

Norman, R. (1984). *Service management: Strategy and leadership in service business*. Chicago: Wiley & Sons.

NVCA — National Venture Capital Association (various issues). Yearbook, Annual Economic Impact of Venture Capital Study, USA.

Ooghe, H., Manigart, S., & Fassin, Y. (1991). Growth patterns of the European venture capital industry. *Journal of Business Venturing, 6*.

Peek, J., & Rosengren, E. S. (1996). Small business credit availability: How important is the side of lender? In A. Saunders & I. Walter (Eds.), *Financial system design: The case for universal banking*. Burr Ridge: Irwin Publishing.

Phalippou, L., & Gottschlag, O. (2007). The performance of private equity funds, Working Paper.

Porter, M. (1985). *Competitive advantage*. New York: The Free Press.

Porter, M. E. (1980). *Competitive strategy. Technique for analysing industries and competitors*. New York: The Free Press.

Poterba, J. (1989). Venture capital and capital gain taxation. In L. Summers (Ed.), *Tax policy and the economy*. MIT Press.

Povaly, S. (2007). *Private equity exits: Divestment process management for leveraged buyouts*. Berlin, Heidelberg: Springer-Verlag.

Rappaport, A. (1997). *La strategia del valore. Le nuove regole di creazione della performance aziendale*. Milan: Franco Angeli.

Ravid, S. A. (1988). On Interactions of production and financial decisions. *Financial Management, 3*.

Reid, G. C. (1992). *Venture capital investment*. London: Routledge.

Reid, G. C., & Smith, J. A. (2003). Venture capital and risk in high-technology enterprises. *International Journal of Business and Economics, 2*.

Reston, J., Jr. (1998). *The last apocalypse: Europe at the year 1000 A.D.* New York: Doubleday.

Robbie, J., Wright, S., & Chiplin, M. (1999). Funds providers' role in venture capital firm monitoring. In: *Management buy-outs and venture capital*. Edward Elgar Ltd.

Robbie, K., & Wright, M. (1997). *Venture capital*. New York: Dartmouth Publishing.

Rock, K. (1986). Why new issues are underpriced. *Journal of Financial Economics, 15*.

Ross, S. A. (1977). The determination of financial structure: the incentive signalling approach Spring. *Bell Journal of Economics*.

Rybczynsky, T. M. (1996). Investment banking: Its evolution and place in the system. In E. Gardner & P. Molineux (Eds.), *Investment banking. Theory and practice*. London: Euromoney Books.

Sahlman, W. A. (1990). The structure and governance of venture-capital organizations. *The Journal of Financial Economics, 27*.

Sahlman, W. A. (1999). *The entrepreneurial venture*. Boston: Harvard Business School Press.

Santomero, A. M., & Babbel, D. F. (1997). *Financial markets, instruments and institutions*. Chicago: Irwin Publisher.

Sapienza, H. J., Amason, A. C., & Manigart, S. (1994). The level and nature of venture capitalist involvement in their portfolio companies: A study of three European countries. *Managerial Finance, 20*.

Saunders, A., & Walter, I. (1994). *Universal banking in the United States. What could we gain? What could we lose?* Oxford University Press.

Schefczyk, M., & Gerpott, J. T. (2000). Qualifications and turnover of managers and venture capital financed firm performance: an empirical study of German venture capital investments. *Journal of business venturing, 16*.

Schumacher, E. F. (1973). *Small is beautiful*. London: Blond & Brigger.

Schwartz, E. S., & Moon, M. (2000). Rational pricing of internet companies. *Financial Analysts Journal, 3*.

Schwienbacher, A., Hege, U., & Palomino, F. (2003). Determinants of venture capital performance: Europe and United States. RICAFE working paper n. 1.

Schwienbacher, A. (2002). An empirical analysis of venture capital exits in Europe and in the United States. University of California at Berkeley working paper.

Shleifer, A., & Summers, L. (1988). Breach of trust in hostile takeovers. In A. Auerbach (Ed.), *Corporate takeovers: Causes & consequences*. University of Chicago Press.

Silver, A. D. (1994). *The venture capital sourcebook*. Chicago: Probus.

Simon, H. (1989). *Price marketing*. Amsterdam: North Holland.

Simpson, I. (2000). *Fundraising and investor relations*. EVCA Association.

Sirri, E., & Tufano, P. (1993). The demand for mutual fund services by individual investors, Working paper, Cambridge, MA: Harvard University.

Slatter, S. (1984). *Corporate recovery: Successful turnaround strategies and their implementation*. Penguin.

Slatter, S., Lovett, D., & Barlow, L. (2006). *Leading corporate turnaround*. San Francisco: Jossey-Bass.

Smith, A. J. (1990). Corporate ownership structure and performance, the case of management buyouts. *Journal of Financial Economics, 27*.

Smith, R. C., & Walter, I. (1997). *Global banking*. Oxford: Oxford University Press.

Stein, J. C. (1989). Efficient capital markets, inefficient firms: A model of myopic corporate behavior. *Quarterly Journal of Economics, 104*, 655-669.

Stewart, G. B. (1991). *The quest for value — The EVA management guide*. New York: Harper Business.

Storey, D. J. (1991). The birth of new firms — does unemployment matter? A review of the evidence. *Small Business Economics, 3*.

Strahan, P. E., & Weston, J. P. (1998). Small business lending and the changing structure of the banking industry. *Journal of Banking and Finance, 22*.

Titman, S., & Wessel, R. (1988). The determinants of capital structure choice. *Journal of Finance, 43*(1), 1-19.

Tobin, J. (1984). On the efficiency of the financial system. July. *Lloyds Bank Review*.

Townsend, R. M. (1979). Optimal contracts and competitive markets with costly state verification. *Journal of Economic Theory, 21*.

Tyebjee, T., & Bruno, A. (1984). A model of venture capitalist investment activity. *Management Science, 30*.

Van Osnabrugge, M., & Robinson, R. (1999). Financing entrepreneurship: Business angels and venture capitalists compared. Harvard Business School working paper.

Van Osnabrugge, M., & Robinson, R. J. (2000). *Angel investing.* Boston: Harvard Business School.

Venture Capital Report. (1998). *Guide to private equity & venture capital in the UK & Europe.* London: Pitman Publishing.

Venture Economics. (1988). *Exiting venture capital investments.* Wellesley, MA.

Venture Economics. (1996). *Pratt's guide to venture capital sources.* New York: SDC Publishing.

Venture Economics. (2001). *Venture edge.* Spring.

Venture One Corporation, PricewaterhouseCoopers. (2001). *The pricewaterhousecoopers money tree survey in partnership with venture one.* August, San Francisco.

Venzin, M. (2009). *Building an international financial services firm.* London: Oxford Press.

Vesper, K. H. (1989). A taxonomy of new business ventures. *Journal of Business Venturing, 4.*

Walker, D. (2007). Disclosure and transparency in private equity London. *Consultation Document, BVCA.*

Wall, J., & Smith, J. Better Exits. Price Waterhouse Corporate Finance–EVCA. www.evca.com.

Walraven, N. (1997). Small Business Lending by Banks Involved in Mergers. Board of Governors of the Federal Reserve, Finance and Economics Discussion Series, n. 25.

Walter, I. (1998). *Global competition in financial services.* Cambridge: Harper & Row Ballinger.

Ward, J. (1987). *Keeping the family firm healthy. How to plan for continuing growth, profitability and the family leadership.* San Francisco: Jossey-Bass.

Wetzel, W. E. (1981). Informal risk capital in New England. In K. H. Vesper (Ed.), *Frontiers in entrepreneurship research.* Wellesley, MA: Babson College.

Wilson, J. W. (1986). *The new venturers. Inside the high-stakes world of venture capital.* Addison–Wesley.

Winborg, H., & Landstrom, J. (2000). Financial bootstrapping in small businesses: examining small business managers' resource acquisition behaviors. *Journal of Business Venturing, 16.*

World Economic Forum. (2008). The globalization of alternative investments, the global economic impact of private equity report 2008, Working Paper Volume 1.

Zingales, L. (2000). In search of new foundations. *Journal of Finance, 55.*

Index